WARHAMMER ONLINE
AGE OF RECKONING

PRIMA Official Game Guide

Mike Searle

Product Manager: Jason Wigle
Associate Product Manager: Rebecca Chastain
Copyeditor: Asha Johnson
Design & Layout: Calibre Grafix
Map Design: In Color Design
Manufacturing: Suzanne Goodwin

Special Thanks:
Julie Asbury, Andrew Littell, Andy Rolleri, Veronika Monell, Sean Scheuble, Lex Scheuble, John Browning, Paul Giacomotto, Erik Alfstad

ISBN: 978-0-7615-6007-4
Library of Congress Catalog Card Number: 2008927751
Printed in the United States of America
08 09 10 11 GG 10 9 8 7 6 5 4 3 2 1

Prima would like to thank the following people at Mythic for their contributions:

Juli Cummins, Chrissy Zeeman, Gary Astleford, Brian Wheeler, Destin Bales, Christian Bales, Mike Donatelli, Gabe Amatangelo, George Smith, Chris Lynch, Martin Smith, Kate Flack, Jeff Skalski, Mike Stone, Craig Nelson, Adam Gershowitz, Greg Grimsby, Brian Audette, Mike Wyatt, Jason Mohr, DJ Larkin, Mike Finnigan, Mike Barr, Mark James, Ahmad Zabarah, Jerry Spencer, Michelle Mulrooney, Matt Witter, Sean Bosshardt, Tom Lipschultz, Tom Schwarzenhorn, Chris Behrens, and Ellisa Barr.

Mike Searle

Mike Searle remembers playing the simple yet addictive *Missile Command*, and the days of Atari *Adventure*, where your square hero could end up in a hollow dragon stomach. His desire to play computer games into the wee hours of the morning really took hold when his parents made him play outside, instead of on the console, so the first chance he got, he bought a PC to play the *Ultima* series, *Doom*, and countless others. Mike started working with Prima Games in 2002 and has written more than 30 strategy guides, including *Lord of the Rings Online: Shadows of Angmar*, *Jurassic Park: Operation Genesis*, *Dark Messiah: Might and Magic*, *Pirates of the Burning Sea*, and several guides in the Tom Clancy's *Ghost Recon* and *Splinter Cell* series. He can't wait for thought technology, so game controls can catch up with his brain and stop all that needless in-game dying. At least, that's what he keeps telling himself about his FPS kill ratio.

We want to hear from you! E-mail comments and feedback to msearle@primagames.com.

Prima Games

An Imprint of Random House, Inc.
3000 Lava Ridge Court, Suite 100
Roseville, CA 95661
www.primagames.com

The Syndicate writers are:

Sean Stalzer, President/CEO, Byron-James Alcid, Cynthia Cheek (Team Lead), Daniel L. Bender, David Tomforde, Donald Corson, Donald Tye Calderwood, Gary Morrow, Harold Cheek, Joshua Kalpin, Mitchell J. Gross, Ray Mercier, Ron Wild (Team Lead), Travis Howeth

Visit The Syndicate® at www.LLTS.org.

CONTENTS

Navigating the Atlas 4

   The Zones 5

   Scenarios 5

   Dungeons 5

   Lairs 5

Dwarfs vs. Greenskins 6

Empire vs. Chaos 8

High Elves vs. Dark Elves 10

   Altdorf 12

      Docks District 13

      Emperor's Circle District 13

      Emperor's Palace District 14

      Slums District 15

      Market Square District 15

      Temple/Lord's Row District 16

      Temple District 16

      War Quarters District 17

   Avelorn 18

   Badlands 20

   Barak Varr 22

   Black Crag 24

   Black Fire Pass 26

   Blighted Isle 28

   Butcher's Pass 30

   Caledor 32

   Chaos Wastes 34

   Chrace 36

   Cinderfall 38

   Death Peak 39

   Dragonwake 40

   Eataine 42

   Ekrund 44

Ellyrion 46

Fell Landing 48

High Pass 50

Inevitable City 52

   Journey's End 53

   Apex District 53

   Death's Labyrinth 54

   Death's Labyrinth/Monolith District 54

   Dread Way 55

   Fate's Edge 55

   Fates Edge/Eternal Citadel 55

   Left of Undercroft (Slaanesh) 56

   Undercroft District 56

   Right of Undercroft District 57

   Lost Narrow 58

   Sacellum & Lost Narrows District 58

Isle of the Dead 59

Kadrin Valley 60

Marshes of Madness 62

The Maw 64

Mt. Bloodhorn 66

Nordland 68

Norsca 70

Ostland 72

Praag 74

Reikland 76

Reikwald 78

Saphery 80

The Shadowlands 82

Shining Way 84

Stonewatch 86

Talabecland 88

Thunder Mountain 90

Troll Country 92

West Praag 94

Scenarios..95

  Blackfire Basin...96

  Blood of Blackcairn.....................................98

  Caledor Woods...100

  Doomfist Crater..102

  Dragon's Bane...104

  Gates of Ekrund..106

  Gromril Crossing...108

  Grovod Caverns..110

  High Pass Cemetery.....................................112

  Howling Gorge..114

  Khaine's Embrace..116

  Logrin's Forge...118

  Lost Temple of Isha......................................120

  Maw of Madness...122

  Mourkain Temple..124

  Nordenwatch..126

  Phoenix Gate...128

  Reikland Hills..130

  Serpent's Passage...132

  Stone Troll Crossing.....................................134

  Talabec Dam..136

  Thunder Valley..138

  Tor Anroc...140

Dungeons..142

  Bastion Stair..142

    Bosses..142

    Monsters...144

  Bilerot Burrows...146

    Bosses..146

    Monsters...148

  Bloodwrought Enclave.................................150

    Bosses..150

    Monsters...152

  Gunbad...154

    Bosses..154

    Monsters...157

  The Lost Vale...160

    Bosses..160

    Monsters...164

  The Sacellum Location: Inevitable City.........166

    Bosses..166

    Monsters...170

  The Sewers...172

    Bosses..172

    Monsters...173

  Sigmar's Crypts..176

    Bosses..176

    Monsters...178

  Warpblade Tunnels

    Bosses..180

    Monsters...180

Lairs..182

  Lair of the Bandit Queen..............................182

  Lair of Nerx Gutslime...................................184

  Lair of Metoh..185

  Lair of Silveroak..186

  Lair of Tezakk Gnawbone.............................187

  Lair of Gorthlak..188

  Lair of Kelbrax..188

  Lair of Stinkfang the Vomitous.....................189

NAVIGATING THE ATLAS

At the touch of your fingers, you can be anywhere in the world. Want to know where Dwarfs chapter 15 begins? No problem. Need RvR schematics for Dragonwake? You've got it. Plan to infiltrate a dungeon like Gunbad or the lair of Nerx Gutswine? This atlas provides the tools you need to unlock the mysteries of the entire *WAR* experience. Before you lose yourself in the fascinations of *WAR* maps, here's a brief rundown of what to expect in this book.

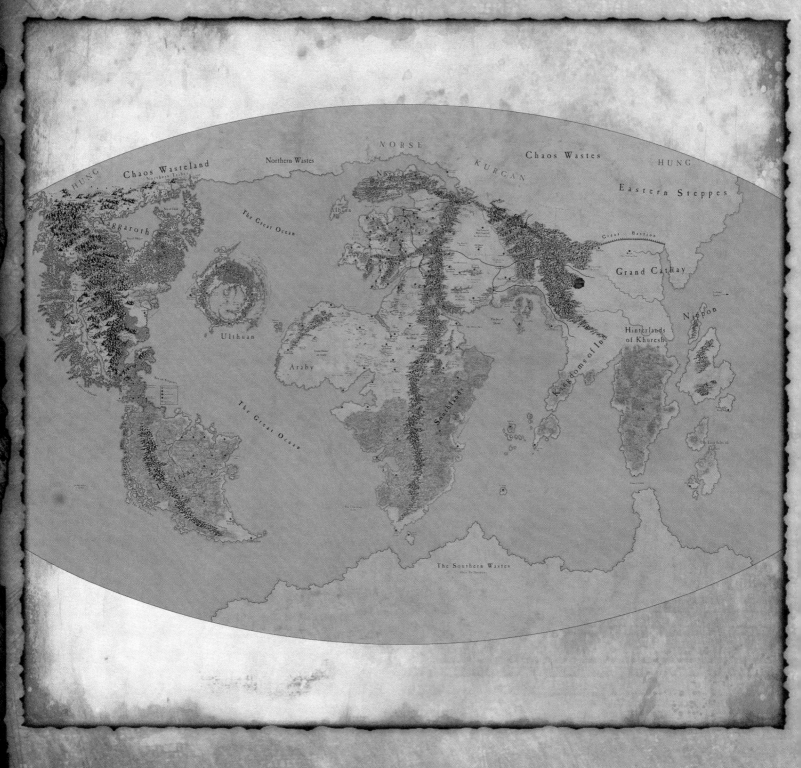

THE ZONES

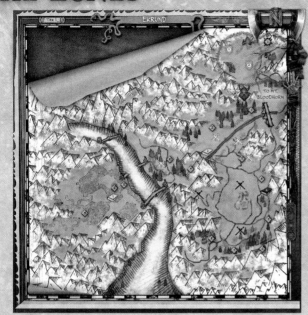

Everything you want to know about your current zone (and future ones yet discovered) is in this book. Each zone map covers the whole territory: every mountain, road, tree, and landmark. At a glance, you can see chapter unlocks, public quests, RvR areas, warcamps, and more. On the opposite page of the main zone maps, you'll find a deluxe RvR map that zooms in on the details of your RvR encounters, including keep maps, battlefield objectives, and tips on the most strategic skirmish points.

For a complete rundown on the Dwarfs and greenskins zones, flip to page 6. To learn the secrets of Empire and Chaos zones, turn to page 8. For details on the High Elves and Dark Elves zones, check out page 10.

SCENARIOS

As you adventure throughout world, you unlock scenarios in the zones you visit. A scenario is a queued-up battle zone or instance. To join a scenario, you can do two things: Go into an RvR area and get flagged, then wait for a window to pop up asking to join, or click on the scenario icon on the left side of the mini-map (in the top right of your screen). The latter option lets you quest while waiting for other players to fill up the scenario. Once enough players from both sides have signed up, a window pops open asking you if you're ready to join the scenario. When you enter the scenario, you temporarily disappear from your current location in the world, then reappear in the exact same spot once you exit the scenario. For the rundown on all 24 scenarios and detailed maps, turn to page 95.

DUNGEONS

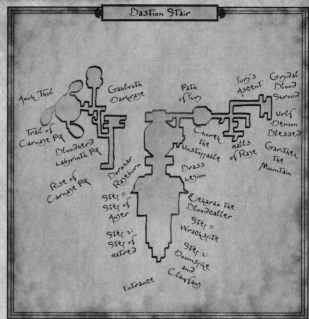

Dungeons aren't for cowards or loners. You need a party of six skilled, geared adventurers to best some of the toughest bosses in the game. As a warrior of Order, you may want to try out the Sewers under Altdorf to test your dungeon prowess, or wait until you band together with others and enter Gundbad for its trials and rewards. As a denizen of Destruction, seek out the Sacellum if you're in the Inevitable City or gain some expertise and battle through the Bastion Stair at later ranks. For the ultimate challenge, at Rank 40 gather your staunchest allies and journey to the Lost Vale in search of the missing Everqueen. To uncover the secrets of the most mysterious labyrinths in the game, turn to page 142.

LAIRS

There are 24 hidden lairs across the world of *WAR*, eight in each zone pairing. Some require feats of dexterity to uncover, others may be puzzles to solve, still others may take superior combat skills to dispatch the lair boss and gain its treasures. You may be able to solo some of the lair bosses, if you're advanced enough in rank, but for most lairs, it's recommended that you team up with a small party of two or three other players to vanquish the threat. More difficult lairs will require a full warband. In our special Lairs section, you'll find the lair's exact location in its zone, its relative rank, encounter type (dexterity, puzzle, or hack and slash), as well as strategy tips on how to enter the lair and defeat the lair boss. For the details, turn to page 182.

DWARFS VS. GREENSKINS

THE WARFRONT

Orcs and Goblins generally don't work well together. However, when a new tribe called the Bloody Sun Boyz grows in power, its leaders, the goblin Shaman Gazbag, providing the brains, and the towering brute Grumlok, supplying the muscle, pull the two races together as one. Under the sway of the Witch King Malekith's dark council, the allied greenskins march into the World's Edge Mountains and capture the Dwarf fortress of Karak Eight Peaks. The Orcs and Goblins are on the move.

The Dwarfs ache over the loss of Karak Eight Peaks. With vengeance in their hearts, the Dwarfs retaliate against the greenskins who have invaded their ancestral home. In the midst of the turmoil, Emperor Karl Franz sends word that the Chaos hordes have advanced on the Empire, and the Empire needs the Dwarfs' help. It is an impossible situation.

With civilization on the brink of war, the most powerful of the land's races choose sides. Trusty Dwarfs and wise High Elves join the Empire and become the forces of Order. Relentless greenskins and cunning Dark Elves join Chaos and become the forces of Destruction. The two sides shall battle, and the world shall sunder.

THE TIERS

There are three warfronts (race pairings) in *Warhammer Online*: Dwarfs vs. greenskins, Empire vs. Chaos, and High Elves vs. Dark Elves. Each of these warfronts breaks down into four tiers. There are two zones each in Tier 1, Tier 2, and Tier 3, and eight zones each in Tier 4

Tier 1 zones are where all characters begin. Generally, you'll spend approximately 10 ranks in each zone, so your early ranks, 1–10, will be spent in Tier 1, 11–20 in Tier 2, 21–30 in Tier 3, and 31–40 in Tier 4. Of course, there are exceptions to this rule, as you should rank up at your own pace and follow the paths set by your various quests. The RvR (realm vs. realm) areas in Tier 1, where you can fight against other players, are relatively small compared to the larger ones in Tier 4, so you won't get lost as you train up your player vs. player (PvP) skills.

Tier 2 zones bridge your advance between Tier 1 and Tier 3 zones. While in Tier 2, you should have gained all your fundamental abilities and you start mastering the paths that will define your career. RvR areas are a bit larger and more challenging than Tier 1. You certainly want to ally with other players from this point forward.

Tier 3 zones can be fierce battlegrounds as characters become more and more powerful. At this stage, you fine-tune your career before heading into the campaigns of Tier 4.

Tier 4 will become your home once you hit the 30s, and you'll stay locked in Tier 4 campaigns for the rest of your time in *Warhammer Online*. Because you will spend most of your time here, and the RvR areas are vast, you should learn each zone well before moving to the next. If you follow your race's chapter unlocks and complete as many regular quests and public quests as possible, each zone will be a memorable experience.

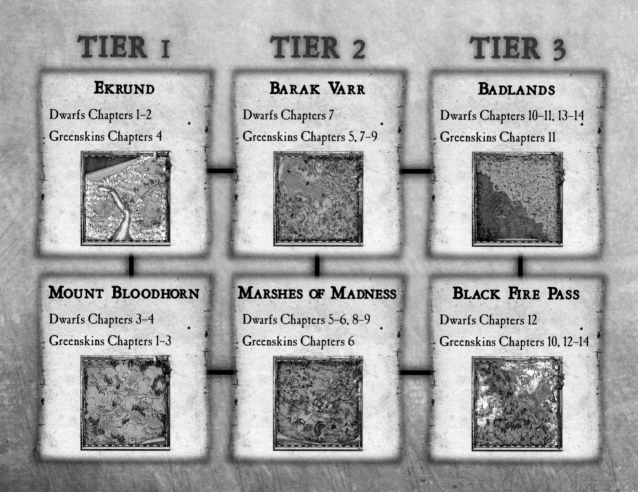

TIER 1

EKRUND

Dwarfs Chapters 1–2

Greenskins Chapters 4

MOUNT BLOODHORN

Dwarfs Chapters 3–4

Greenskins Chapters 1–3

TIER 2

BARAK VARR

Dwarfs Chapters 7

Greenskins Chapters 5, 7–9

MARSHES OF MADNESS

Dwarfs Chapters 5–6, 8–9

Greenskins Chapters 6

TIER 3

BADLANDS

Dwarfs Chapters 10–11, 13–14

Greenskins Chapters 11

BLACK FIRE PASS

Dwarfs Chapters 12

Greenskins Chapters 10, 12–14

NAVIGATING THE ATLAS

STONEWATCH

Dwarfs Campaign

Greenskins Campaign

REIKWALD

ALTDORF

KADRIN VALLEY

Dwarfs Chapters 15–16

Greenskins Chapters 20–22

TO BLACK FIRE PASS

CINDERFALL

Dwarfs Campaign

Greenskins Campaign

THUNDER MOUNTAIN

Dwarfs Chapters 17–19

Greenskins Chapters 17–19

DEATH PEAK

Dwarfs Campaign

Greenskins Campaign

BLACK CRAG

Dwarfs Chapters 20–22

Greenskins Chapters 15–16

TO BADLANDS

BUTCHER'S PASS

Dwarfs Campaign

Greenskins Campaign

THE MAW

INEVITABLE CITY

HOW TO USE THE MAPS

The maps in this guide are organized first by warfronts and then by tiers (in alphabetical order within each tier). The first section deals with Dwarfs and greenskins, the second section highlights Empire and Chaos, and the third section details the struggle between High Elves and Dark Elves. As you adventure, open the appropriate map section and follow along as you discover chapters. For example, as a Empire player, you would open to the start of the Empire vs. Chaos map section and turn to the Tier 1 zone, Nordland, the very first map in that section. Empire Chapters 1–3 take place in Nordland. To help you along on your journey, keep the Nordland map open until you're ready for Empire Chapter 4, which takes you to the Norsca map. For Empire Chapter 5, you travel to Troll Country, your first Tier 2 zone. Continue with your "Chapters of *WAR*" until you've completed Chapter 22 and conquered them all.

Each zone map contains a wealth of information. Important points are labeled right on the map: chapter unlocks, public quests, landmarks, dungeons, lairs, battlefield objectives, and more. To identify any map point for your race, see the map's legend.

The page next to each map summarizes that zone's chapters. At a glance, you can see what chapters are in the zone (and your enemy's chapters) and all the public quests in the area. Pay close attention to the public quest objective information, as this will give you a leg up on what to expect and arm you (or your warband) with clues about what gear, Morale abilities, and Tactics to equip before battle.

If you don't want to flip through the maps chapter by chapter, see the map index at the start of each warfront and look up exactly where the zone of your choice can be found.

primagames.com

EMPIRE VS. CHAOS

THE WARFRONT

In the midst of the Empire, a great and gruesome plague spreads. For weeks, victims suffer horrible symptoms until a fate worse than death befalls them—they transform into fiendish Chaos mutants, creatures that die by their own savagery or slaughter those around them. With each passing week the death toll climbs, and Emperor Karl Franz declares quarantines and martial law wherever the plague strikes hardest.

Meanwhile, far to the north, a huge warhost spawns seemingly out of the nothingness that is the Chaos Wastes. Grotesque creatures and armored warriors march side by side, led by the Chaos Lord Tchar'zanek wielding the flag of his god, the Changer of Ways, Tzeentch. The warhost crushes anyone and anything that defies it on its march into the heart of the Empire.

With civilization on the brink of war, the most powerful of the land's races choose sides. Trusty Dwarfs and wise High Elves join the Empire and become the forces of Order. Relentless greenskins and cunning Dark Elves join Chaos and become the forces of Destruction. The two sides shall battle, and the world shall sunder.

THE TIERS

There are three warfronts (race pairings) in *Warhammer Online*: Dwarfs vs. greenskins, Empire vs. Chaos, and High Elves vs. Dark Elves. Each of these warfronts breaks down into four tiers. There are two zones each in Tier 1, Tier 2, and Tier 3, and eight zones each in Tier 4.

Tier 1 zones are where all characters begin. Generally, you'll spend approximately 10 ranks in each zone, so your early ranks, 1–10, will be spent in Tier 1, 11–20 in Tier 2, 21–30 in Tier 3, and 31–40 in Tier 4. Of course, there are exceptions to this rule, as you should rank up at your own pace and follow the paths set by your various quests. The RvR (realm vs. realm) areas in Tier 1, where you can fight against other players, are relatively small compared to the larger ones in Tier 4, so you won't get lost as you train up your player vs. player (PvP) skills.

TIER 1

NORSCA

Empire Chapter 4

Chaos Chapters 1–2

NORDLAND

Empire Chapters 1–3

Chaos Chapters 3–4

TIER 2

TROLL COUNTRY

Empire Chapters 5–6

Chaos Chapters 6, 8, 9

OSTLAND

Empire Chapters 7–9

Chaos Chapters 5, 7

TIER 3

HIGH PASS

Empire Chapters 10–12

Chaos Chapters 13–14

TALABECLAND

Empire Chapters 13–14

Chaos Chapters 10–12

TIER 4

INEVITABLE CITY

Empire City Campaign

Chaos City Campaign

THE MAW

Empire Campaign

Chaos Campaign

CHAOS WASTES

Empire Chapters 20–22

Chaos Chapters 15–16

TO HIGH PASS

PRAAG

Empire Chapters 17–19

Chaos Chapters 17–19

WEST PRAAG

Empire Campaign

Chaos Campaign

REIKLAND

Empire Chapters 15–16

Chaos Chapters 20–22

TO TALABECLAND

ALTDORF

Empire City Campaign

Chaos City Campaign

REIKWALD

Empire Chapters

Chaos Chapters

Tier 2 zones bridge your advance between Tier 1 and Tier 3 zones. While in Tier 2, you should have gained all your fundamental abilities and you start mastering the paths that will define your career. RvR areas are a bit larger and more challenging than Tier 1. You certainly want to ally with other players from this point forward.

Tier 3 zones can be fierce battlegrounds as characters become more and more powerful. At this stage, you fine-tune your career before heading into the campaigns of Tier 4.

Tier 4 will become your home once you hit the 30s, and you'll stay locked in Tier 4 campaigns for the rest of your time in *Warhammer Online*. Because you will spend most of your time here, and the RvR areas are vast, you should learn each zone well before moving to the next. If you follow your race's chapter unlocks and complete as many regular quests and public quests as possible, each zone will be a memorable experience.

HOW TO USE THE MAPS

The maps in this guide are organized first by warfronts and then by tiers (in alphabetical order within each tier). The first section deals with Dwarfs and greenskins, the second section highlights Empire and Chaos, and the third section details the struggle between High Elves and Dark Elves. As you adventure, open the appropriate map section and follow along as you discover chapters. For example, as a Empire player, you would open to the start of the Empire vs. Chaos map section and turn to the Tier 1 zone, Nordland, the very first map in that section. Empire Chapters 1–3 take place in Nordland. To help you along on your journey, keep the Nordland map open until you're ready for Empire Chapter 4, which takes you to the Norsca map. For Empire Chapter 5, you travel to Troll Country, your first Tier 2 zone. Continue with your "Chapters of *WAR*" until you've completed Chapter 22 and conquered them all.

Each zone map contains a wealth of information. Important points are labeled right on the map: chapter unlocks, public quests, landmarks, dungeons, lairs, battlefield objectives, and more. To identify any map point for your race, see the map's legend.

The page next to each map summarizes that zone's chapters. At a glance, you can see what chapters are in the zone (and your enemy's chapters) and all the public quests in the area. Pay close attention to the public quest objective information, as this will give you a leg up on what to expect and arm you (or your warband) with clues about what gear, Morale abilities, and Tactics to equip before battle.

If you don't want to flip through the maps chapter by chapter, see the map index at the start of each warfront and look up exactly where the zone of your choice can be found.

HIGH ELVES VS. DARK ELVES

THE WARFRONT

Woe has embraced the world, and the Phoenix King of Ulthuan, Finubar, Ruler of the High Elves, will not stand idly by. With the threat mounting against his allies, the Empire and Dwarfs, Finubar sets sail with hundreds of warriors aboard their finest warships. They shall aid as best they can in this dire time.

Malekith, Lord of the Dark Elves, can sense the opportunity to seize the Throne of Ulthuan from his weak-bloodied cousins. Knowing that the High Elves will never abandon their allies against the looming Chaos invasion, Malekith commands all furnaces, forges, and blacksmiths to the crafting of weapons and machines of war. Witch Elves and Sorceresses join with ferocious creatures and fierce beasts as the kingdom of Naggaroth prepares for mighty bloodshed. When the High Elves depart to aid the Empire, the Dark Elves will strike.

With civilization on the brink of war, the most powerful of the land's races choose sides. Trusty Dwarfs and wise High Elves join the Empire and become the forces of Order. Relentless greenskins and cunning Dark Elves join Chaos and become the forces of Destruction. The two sides shall battle, and the world shall sunder.

THE TIERS

There are three warfronts (race pairings) in *Warhammer Online*: Dwarfs vs. greenskins, Empire vs. Chaos, High Elves vs. Dark Elves. Each of these warfronts breaks down into four tiers. There are two zones in Tier 1, Tier 2, and Tier 3, and eight zones in Tier 4 (in the Empire vs. Chaos warfront).

Tier 1 zones are where all characters begin. Generally, you'll spend approximately 10 ranks in each zone, so your early ranks, 1–10, will be spent in Tier 1, 11–20 in Tier 2, 21–30 in Tier 3, and 31–40 in Tier 4. Of course, there are exceptions to this rule, as you should rank up at your own pace and follow the paths set by your various quests. The RvR (realm vs. realm) areas in Tier 1, where you can fight against other players, are relatively small compared to the larger ones in Tier 4, so you won't get lost as you train up your player vs. player (PvP) skills.

Tier 2 zones bridge your advance between Tier 1 and Tier 3 zones. While in Tier 2, you should have gained all your fundamental abilities and you start mastering the paths that will define your career. RvR areas are a bit larger and more challenging than Tier 1. You certainly want to ally with other players from this point forward.

Tier 3 zones can be fierce battlegrounds as characters become more and more powerful. At this stage, you fine-tune your career before heading into the campaigns of Tier 4.

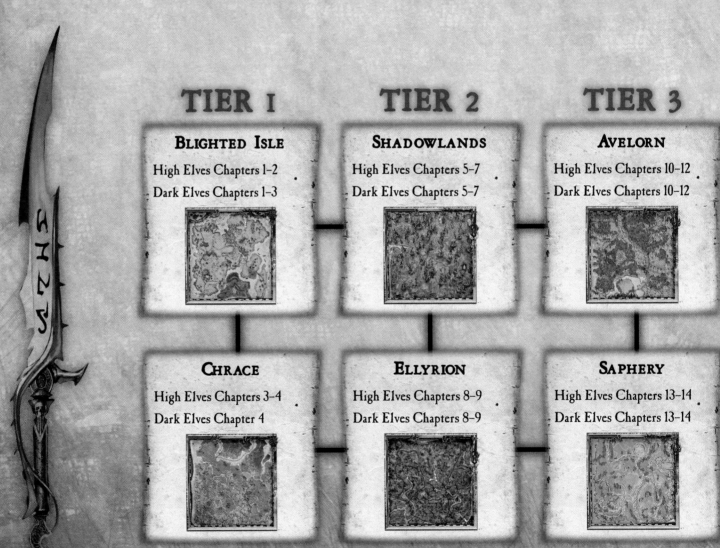

TIER 1

BLIGHTED ISLE
High Elves Chapters 1–2
Dark Elves Chapters 1–3

CHRACE
High Elves Chapters 3–4
Dark Elves Chapter 4

TIER 2

SHADOWLANDS
High Elves Chapters 5–7
Dark Elves Chapters 5–7

ELLYRION
High Elves Chapters 8–9
Dark Elves Chapters 8–9

TIER 3

AVELORN
High Elves Chapters 10–12
Dark Elves Chapters 10–12

SAPHERY
High Elves Chapters 13–14
Dark Elves Chapters 13–14

TIER 4

SHINING WAY

High Elves Campaign

Dark Elves Campaign

REIKWALD

ALTDORF

EATAINE

High Elves Chapters 15-16

Dark Elves Chapters 20-22

TO SAPHERY

DRAGONWAKE

High Elves Chapters 17-19

Dark Elves Chapters 17-19

ISLE OF THE DEAD

High Elves Campaign

Dark Elves Campaign

CALEDOR

High Elves Chapters 20-22

Dark Elves Chapters 15-16

TO SAPHERY

FELL LANDING

High Elves Campaign

Dark Elves Campaign

THE MAW

INEVITABLE CITY

Tier 4 will become your home once you hit the 30s, and you'll stay locked in Tier 4 campaigns for the rest of your time in *Warhammer Online.* Because you will spend most of your time here, and the RvR areas are vast, you should learn each zone well before moving to the next. If you follow your race's chapter unlocks and complete as many regular quests and public quests as possible, each zone will be a memorable experience.

HOW TO USE THE MAPS

The maps in this guide are organized first by warfronts and then by tiers (in alphabetical order within each tier). The first section deals with Dwarfs and greenskins, the second section highlights Empire and Chaos, and the third section details the struggle between High Elves and Dark Elves. As you adventure, open the appropriate map section and follow along as you discover chapters. For example, as a Empire player, you would open to the start of the Empire vs. Chaos map section and turn to the Tier 1 zone, Nordland, the very first map in that section. Empire Chapters 1–3 take place in Nordland. To help you along on your journey, keep the Nordland map open until you're ready for Empire Chapter 4, which takes you to the Norsca map. For Empire Chapter 5, you travel to Troll Country, your first Tier 2 zone. Continue with your "Chapters of *WAR*" until you've completed Chapter 22 and conquered them all.

Each zone map contains a wealth of information. Important points are labeled right on the map: chapter unlocks, public quests, landmarks, dungeons, lairs, battlefield objectives, and more. To identify any map point for your race, see the map's legend.

The page next to each map summarizes that zone's chapters. At a glance, you can see what chapters are in the zone (and your enemy's chapters) and all the public quests in the area. Pay close attention to the public quest objective information, as this will give you a leg up on what to expect and arm you (or your warband) with clues about what gear, Morale abilities, and Tactics to equip before battle.

If you don't want to flip through the maps chapter by chapter, see the map index at the start of each warfront and look up exactly where the zone of your choice can be found.

TIER 4

ALTDORF

LEGEND

Altdorf District Name
1 – War Quarters
2 – Emperor's Circle
3 – Lord's Row
4 – The Slums
5 – The Docks
6 – Market Square
7 – Palace Courtyard
8 – Emperor's Palace

Major Landmarks
1 – Mass Transit
2 – The Altdorf Library
3 – Temple of Sigmar
4 – Bright Wizard College

Public Quests (Order)
1 – Bank Robbery (Lord's Row near First Bank of Altdorf) (City Ranks 2-4)
2 – Pub Brawl (Blowhole Tavern) (City Ranks 2-4)
3 – Gargus the Unclean One (City Ranks 4-5)
4 – Delicate Work (City Ranks 3-5)
5 – Daemons of the Night (City Ranks 4-5)
6 – Cult of the Feathered Coin (City Ranks All)
7 – March of the Dead (City Ranks 1-2)
8 – Pale-Eye Hideout (City Ranks 3-5)

Instances / Dungeons
1 – Altdorf Sewer Entrance
2 – Entrance to Bright Wizard College
3 – Altdorf Sewer Entrance
4 – Main Entrance to Altdorf
5 – Warpblade Tunnels (inside the Reikland Arms Basement)

6 – Sigmar Crypts
7 – Warpblade Tunnels (inside the Mastiff's End Basement)
8 – Warpblade Tunnels (inside the Blowhole Basement)
9 – Warpblade Tunnels (inside the Screaming Cat Tavern Basement)

 Flight Master

 Banks

 Auctioneer

 Entrances to the City

DOCKS DISTRICT

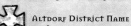

ALTDORF

LEGEND

◆ **Major Landmarks**
1 – Blowhole
2 – Screaming Cat
4 – Bright Wizard College

✠ **Altdorf District Name**
4 – The Slums
8 – The Docks

⚔ **Public Quests (Order)**
2 – Pub Brawl (Blowhole Tavern
and The Screaming Cat)
(City Ranks 2-4)
3 – Gargus the Unclean One
(City Ranks 4-5)
5 – Daemons of the Night
(City Ranks 4-5)
7 – March of the Dead
(City Ranks 1-2)
8 – Pale-Eye Hideout
(City Ranks 3-5)

△ **Quest Givers**
1 – Mad Matthias (The Proof is
in the Paws)
2 – Watchmen Terrence
(Spotting Trouble)
3 – Timoteo Amatangelo
(Ogre Bodyguard)
4 – Wanted Poster (Rat Men)

◇ **Instances / Dungeons**
1 – Mid-Level Sewer Entrance
2 – Entrance to Bright
Wizard College
3 – High-Level Sewer Entrance
8 – Warpblade Tunnels (inside
the Blowhole Basement)
9 – Warpblade Tunnels (inside
the Sreaming Cat Tavern
Basement)

◯ **Banks**

◯ **Auctioneer**

▣ **Trainers**

LEGEND

◆ **Major Landmarks**
1 – Golden Griffon Inn
2 – The Clank

✠ **Altdorf District Name**
2 – Emperor's Circle

△ **Quest Givers**
1 – John Richardson
(An Innocent Man)
2 – Sister Amalia (Morr's Bane)

◯ **Banks**

◯ **Auctioneer**

EMPEROR'S CIRCLE DISTRICT

ALTDORF

EMPEROR'S PALACE DISTRICT

ALTDORF

LEGEND

 Altdorf District Name
8 – Emperor's Palace
7 – Palace Courtyard

 Public Quests (Order)
2 – Pub Brawl (Blowhole Tavern
and The Screaming Cat)
(City Ranks 2-4)

△ Quest Givers
1 – General Albrecht
(Capture the Enemy Lair;
Shoulder of Heroes)
2 – Emperor Karl Franz
(Tchar'zanek; Orders Must
Be Followed)
3 – Councilor Zutzen
(An Empire Defiant)

 Instances / Dungeons
8 – Warpblade Tunnels (inside
the Blowhole Basement)

 Banks

○ Auctioneer

SLUMS DISTRICT

ALTDORF

LEGEND

 Altdorf District Name
6 – The Slums
5 – The Docks
7 – Palace Courtyard

 Major Landmarks
4 – Bright Wizard College

 Public Quests (Order)
2 – Pub Brawl (Blowhole Tavern and The Screaming Cat) (City Ranks 2-4)
3 – Gargus the Unclean One (City Ranks 4-5)
5 – Daemons of the Night (City Ranks 4-5)
7 – March of the Dead (City Ranks 1-2)
8 – Pale-Eye Hideout (City Ranks 3-5)

 Quest Givers
1 – Wanted Poster (Rat Men)
2 – Helena Bernhardt (Out of Their Hands)

 Instances / Dungeons
1 – Mid-Level Sewer Entrance
2 – Entrance to Bright Wizard College
3 – High-Level Sewer Entrance
8 – Warpblade Tunnels (inside the Blowhole Basement)

 Flight Master

Banks

Auctioneer

Trainers

LEGEND

 Altdorf District Name
4 – The Slums
6 – Market Square

Major Landmarks
1 – The Mastiff's End

 **Quest Givers**
1 – Hans the Sausage Vendor (Tasty Morsels)
2 – Collector Schmikt (Everyone Pays)
3 – Elise Strohmann (Poor Gustav!); Barkeep Olaf (Proof of Payment)
4 – Town Crier Kiosch (Center of the World) (Wanders between Hans the Sausage Vendor and the Flight Point)

 Instances / Dungeons
1 – Mid-Level Sewer Entrance

Flight Master

Banks

Auctioneer

Merchants / Vendors

Trainers
1 – Butcher, Cultivator, Apothecary
2 – Scavenger
3 – Renown

Flight Point

Healer

MARKET SQUARE DISTRICT

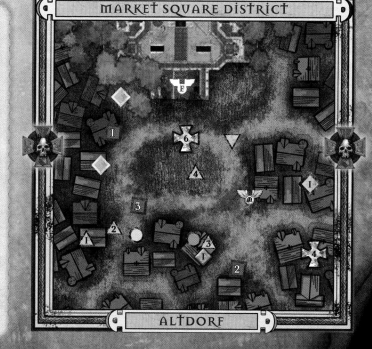

ALTDORF

LEGEND

 Altdorf District Name
3 – Temple of Sigmar
4 – Lord's Row

 Major Landmarks
1 – Grand Theogonist Volkmar

 Public Quests (Order)
6 – Cult of the Feathered Coin
(City Ranks All)

 Quest Givers
1 – Alrick Redwing
(Sky's the Limit)
2 – Glowing Grave Dust
(inside the Temple Crypts;
Rare Find)

 Instances / Dungeons
5 – Warpblade Tunnels
(inside Reikland Arms)
6 – Sigmar Crypts

 Auctioneer

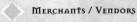 **Merchants / Vendors**

Trainers

TEMPLE DISTRICT

ALTDORF

TEMPLE/LORD'S ROW DISTRICT

ALTDORF

LEGEND

 **Altdorf District Name**
2 – Emperor's Circle
3 – Lord's Row

Major Landmarks
1 – Altdorf Library
2 – Reikland Arms
3 – The Bank of Altdorf

 Public Quests (Order)
1 – Bank Robbery (Lord's Row
near First Bank of Altdorf)
(City Ranks 2-4)
6 – Cult of the Feathered Coin
(City Ranks All)

 Quest Givers
1 – Barkeep Lothur
(Job Security)
2 – Rhysa Von Lucius
(Suspicious Characters)

 Instances / Dungeons
5 – Warpblade Tunnels
(inside Reikland Arms)
6 – Sigmar Crypts
7 – Warpblade Tunnels
(inside the Reikland Arms –
Enterance in the Basement)

 Banks

 Auctioneer

 Merchants / Vendors

 Trainers

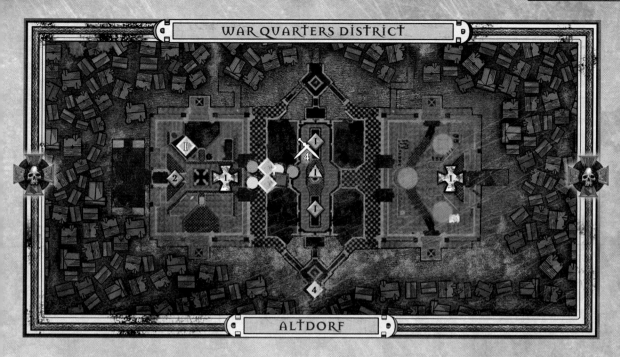

WAR QUARTERS DISTRICT

ALTDORF

LEGEND

 Altdorf District Name
1 – War Quarters

 Major Landmarks
1 – RvR Statues
2 – Guild Registrar

 Public Quests (Order)
4 – Delicate Work (City Ranks 3-5)

 Quest Givers
1 – Captain Lochner (Dogs of War; the Pale-Eye)

 Instances / Dungeons
4 – Unknown Portal

 Banks

 Auctioneer

 Merchants / Vendors
1 – Mount Vendor

 Trainers

TIER 3   AVELORN

TO ELLYRION

TO ELLYRION

TO SAPHERY

SITUATED ON THE RIVERBANK IN A SPRAWLING FOREST, MAIDEN'S LANDING GIVES A SLIGHT EDGE TO ITS DEFENDERS. JUST ACROSS A BRIDGE TO THE NORTHEAST IS A HIGH ELF CAMP, WHICH GIVES THE FORCES OF ORDER BETTER ACCESS.

FUNNELING INCOMING ATTACKERS GIVES THE DEFENSES A SLIGHT ADVANTAGE HERE, ALTHOUGH, ANY REINFORCEMENTS ALSO NEED TO PASS THROUGH THAT SAME FUNNEL. TREES PROVIDE LITTLE COVER FOR INCOMING ATTACKERS, MAKING IT ALMOST IMPOSSIBLE TO MASK ANY ASSAULT ATTEMPTS.

PLACED IN THE MIDDLE OF THE FOREST, AS WELL AS ON THE RIVER BANK, THIS HALF-COMPLETED FORT OFFERS LITTLE PROTECTION. MULTIPLE ENTRANCES TO THE WOOD CHOPPAZ FROM ALL SIDES MAKE IT ALMOST IMPOSSIBLE TO GUARD EVERYWHERE AT ONCE AND GIVES ATTACKERS A SLIGHT ADVANTAGE AS DEFENDERS WILL MOST LIKELY SPLIT UP.

LEGEND

WARCAMPS:

 1 = MAIDENGUARD

 1 = ISHA'S FALL

RvR AREA (OUTLINED)

 CHAPTER UNLOCK (DESTRUCTION)
10 – DARK ELF CHAPTER 10
11 – DARK ELF CHAPTER 11
12 – DARK ELF CHAPTER 12

 CHAPTER UNLOCK (ORDER)
10 – HIGH ELF CHAPTER 10
11 – HIGH ELF CHAPTER 11
12 – HIGH ELF CHAPTER 12

 MAJOR LANDMARKS
1 – HIGH ELF HIDEAWAY
2 – HANDMAIDENS APLENTY
3 – HOUSE ARKENETH
4 – JADE WIZARDS
5 – HIGH ELF CAMP
6 – DREADSTAFF'S CAMP
7 – ALTAR OF THE WINDS
8 – ARKENETH IN THE WOOD
9 – UTHORIN IN THE WOOD
10 – BIGHAMMA'S CAMP
11 – CHAOS IN THE PICTURE
12 – EVIL CROP
13 – WAYSTONE
14 – CAVE OF NARIELLE
15 – OAKENSTAFF'S HOUSE
16 – FOREST ALTAR
17 – CHEST OF ORMAGDIN
18 – BEASTMEN
19 – WOOD CHOPPAS
20 – HERALDS OF THE DARK HOST
21 – CAVE OF WHISPERS
22 – NECROMANCER AMBUSH
23 – ANULLI RUINS
24 – BARTHILAS CAMP
25 – EVERCOURT

 PUBLIC QUESTS (DESTRUCTION)
1 – SPIRITED RESISTANCE
2 – WAVESINGER
3 – QUYL-ISHA TEMPLE
4 – EVERSPRING
5 – POOL OF ELTHRAI
6 – DARTIAN FOREST
7 – WATCHTOWER OF AETHWYN
8 – SEA GUARD BEACHHEAD
9 – JADE STAND

 PUBLIC QUESTS (ORDER)
1 – SLASH AND BURN
2 – RITUAL OF CORRUPTION
3 – ROTTEN EMBRACE
4 – FALLS OF RENEWAL
5 – DEATHWIND PASS
6 – SHRIEKING MEADOW
7 – CORRUPTION
8 – WELL OF WHISPERS
9 – STORMRIVER'S END

 BATTLE OBJECTIVES
1 – THE WOOD CHOPPAZ
(ARTISAN'S GIFT)
2 – MAIDEN'S LANDING
(MERCHANT'S GIFT)

 1 – GHROND'S SACRISTY

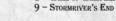 **FLIGHT MASTER**

GHROND'S SACRISTY IS WITHIN A FEW MINUTES'
TRAVEL TIME OF BOTH NEARBY BATTLEFIELD
OBJECTIVES, AS WELL AS BOTH SIDES' WARCAMPS.
THIS MAKES ATTACKING AND REINFORCING A
FAST-PACED BATTLE. THE EASE OF RETURNING TO THE
BATTLE CAN CREATE VERY LONG SIEGES AND KEEP
THE BATTLES RAGING FOR HOURS.

DESTRUCTION ENTRANCE

ORDER ENTRANCE

TO SAPHERY

RvR LEGEND

WARCAMPS:

 1 = MAIDENGUARD

 1 = ISHA'S FALL

RvR AREA (OUTLINED)

 BATTLE OBJECTIVES
1 – THE WOOD CHOPPAZ
(ARTISAN'S GIFT)
2 – MAIDEN'S LANDING
(MERCHANT'S GIFT)

 1 – GHROND'S SACRISTY

 FLIGHT MASTER

JUST BECAUSE THE ASSAULT BREAKS DOWN THE
FRONT DOOR DOESN'T MEAN LIFE WILL BE EASY.
ATTACKERS HAVE TO FUNNEL INSIDE THE MAIN
COURTYARD, GIVING THE DEFENSE A CHANCE TO
CENTRALIZE ALL THEIR ATTACKS.

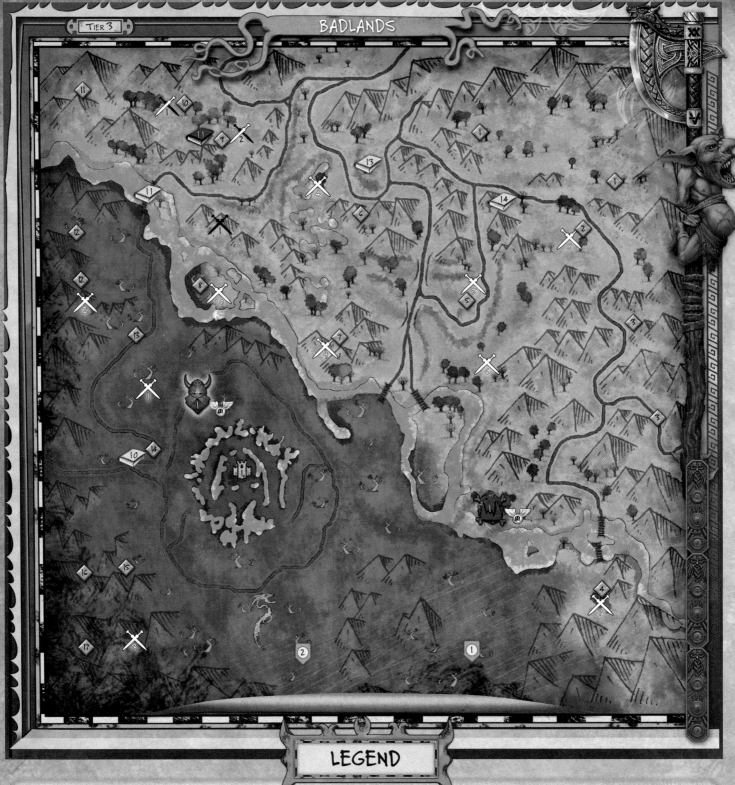

BADLANDS

TIER 3

LEGEND

Warcamps: 1 – Dour Guards   1 – Muggar's Choppa

RvR Area (Outlined)

Chapter Unlock (Destruction)
11 – Greenskin Chapter 11

Chapter Unlock (Order)
10 – Dwarf Chapter 10
11 – Dwarf Chapter 11
13 – Dwarf Chapter 13
14 – Dwarf Chapter 14

Major Landmarks
1 – Bloodgash Cave
2 – Bloody Savages
3 – Bloodmaw Cave
4 – Black Orc Slog
5 – Skullbreaker Ridge

6 – Olin's Hideout
7 – Tomb of Kali'Amon
8 – Troll Sunder
9 – Fireforge's Camp
10 – Enclave of the Withered
11 – Mount Gunbad (Dungeon)
12 – Blood Spike Cave
13 – Brokebone Pass
14 – Norrikson's Excavation
15 – Warpclaw Hideout
16 – Geyser Den
17 – Kazad Drung

Public Quests (Destruction)
1 – Mutant Exiles

Public Quests (Order)
1 – Savage Assault
2 – The Cauldron
3 – Kazad Drung
4 – Putrid Tar Pits
5 – Skullbreaker Ridge
6 – Skullsmasher's Boyz
7 – Black Orc Slog
8 – Bloody Savages
9 – Tomb of Kali'Amon
10 – Troll Island

Public Quests (Neutral)
1 – Revoltin Gobbos
2 – Fireforge's Camp

Battle Objectives
1 – Karagaz (Artisan's Gift)
2 – Goblin Artillery Range (Healing Gift)

1 – Thickmuck Pit

Flight Master

20

KARAGAZ WAS AN ENCLAVE OF THE BEST
ARTISANS IN THE DWARF KINGDOM.
THEIRS HAD BEEN A PEACEFUL LIFE UNTIL
DESTRUCTION CAME FROM MULTIPLE SIDES ALL
AT ONCE. THE ENCLAVE QUICKLY FELL AND
ALL THE BEAUTIFUL WORKS WERE DESTROYED
IN A BLOOD FRENZY. THE BOOK OF GRUDGES
CONTINUES TO GROW.

A HUGE FORTRESS WAS BUILT ON THE EDGE OF
DOOMFIST CRATER; THE GREENSKINS CALL IT
THICKMUCK PIT. IT STANDS IN DEFIANCE OF ALL
WHO TRANSGRESS INTO GREENSKIN LAND. HOW
THEY WERE ABLE TO BUILD SUCH A MASSIVE
FORTRESS ON A PIT OF MUCK DEFIES LOGIC.

THE REAL THREAT LIES NOT IN THE GOBLIN
ARTILLERY RANGE, BUT IN THE FORCES THAT
STALK THE NIGHT HERE. EVEN THE BRAVEST
WARRIORS HAVE BEEN KNOWN TO WAKE UP DEAD
WHEN THE FORCES OF CHAOS WALK THE NIGHT.

RvR LEGEND

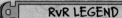

Warcamps:

1 – Dour Guardz

1 – Muggar's Choppa

RvR Area (Outlined)

Battle Objectives
1 - Karagaz
(Artisan's Gift)
2 – Goblin Artillery Range
(Healing Gift)

1 – Thickmuck Pit

Flight Master

ORDER
ENTRANCE

DESTRUCTION
ENTRANCE

ORDER
ENTRANCE

DESTRUCTION
ENTRANCE

DESTRUCTION
ENTRANCE

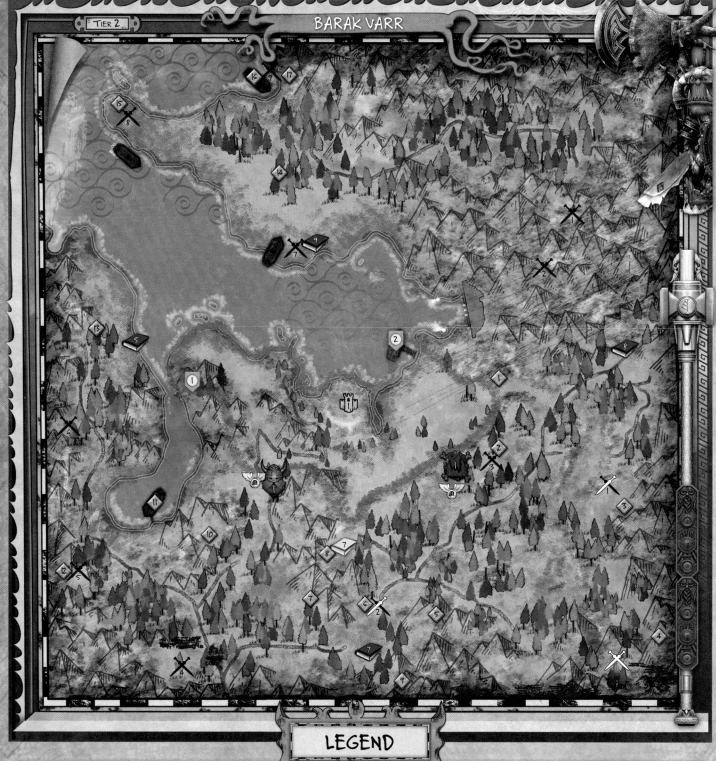

TIER 2

BARAK VARR

LEGEND

Warcamps: 1 – Foultooth's Warcamp   1 – Goldpeak's Overlook

RvR Area (Outlined)

Chapter Unlock (Destruction)
5 – Greenskin Chapter 5
7 – Greenskin Chapter 7
8 – Greenskin Chapter 8
9 – Greenskin Chapter 9

Chapter Unlock (Order)
7 – Dwarf Chapter 7

Major Landmarks
1 – Longbeard's Strand
2 – Mingol Vongal
3 – Steel Anvil Mine
4 – One-tusk Cave
5 – Rikkit Duk

6 – Bar Dawazbak
7 – Cave
8 – Gnol Garak Throng
9 – Rikkit Duk (Second Entrance)
10 – Thunder Ridge Tower
11 – Sea's Anvil
12 – Firebeard Duk
13 – Wetfang
14 – Mingol Ironside
15 – Ironrock Point Lighthouse
16 – Fair Fregar II
17 – Crazy Stunty Cove

Public Quests (Destruction)
1 – Fall of Firebrew
2 – Boarding the Seahammer

3 – Burn Rock Tower
4 – Up the Creek without a Battle
5 – Firebeard's Slayers
6 – Danurgi's Rangers
7 – When the Ship Hits the Sand
8 – Ironrock Point
9 – Long Drung and the Slayer Cove

Public Quests (Order)
1 – Korgoth's Raiders

Public Quests (Neutral)
1 – Gundrim's Veterans
2 – Bar Dawazbak

Battle Objectives
1 – Lighthouse (Artisan's Gift)
2 – Ironclad (Healing Boon)

1 – Dok Karaz Dwarf Keep

Flight Master

Map labels:

1

ORDER
ENTRANCE
(CAVE)

ORDER
ENTRANCE

DESTRUCTION
ENTRANCE

2

DESTRUCTION
ENTRANCE

ORDER
ENTRANCE

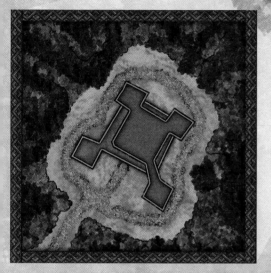

RvR LEGEND

RvR Area (Outlined)

Battle Objectives
1 – Lighthouse
(Artisan's Gift)
2 – Ironclad
(Healing Boon)

1 – Dok Karaz

Because the main path leads up to the front gates, you have to assault Dok Karaz from the front at some point. Note that you have more room on your left flank to maneuver around defenders if you can't make a great push for the doors.

Sitting on the only high ground around Dok Karaz gives the Dwarfs a tactical advantage. Their sharpshooters can target greenies from a great distance, and they use this advantage with deadly accuracy.

The Lighthouse on Port's Gate Coast stands as a testament of the oath given the manlings. It has shown safe passage for centuries, and now Destruction is climbing the only path to destroy it.

The pier to the Ironclad is the only way on the ship and is easily defended. It sits right outside the Port of Barak Varr, which contains Rank 55 Champions.

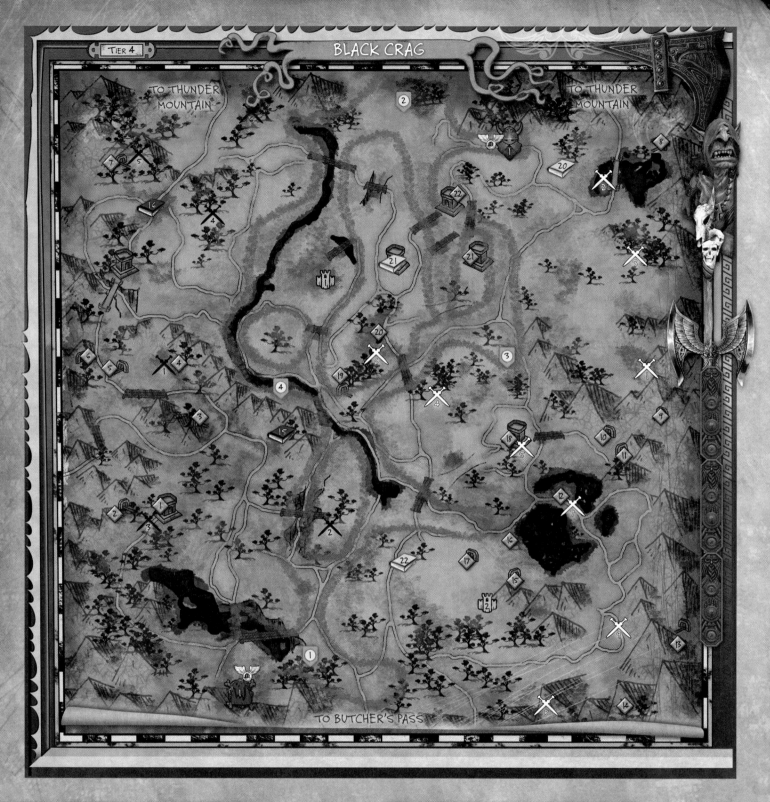

TIER 4

BLACK CRAG

TO THUNDER MOUNTAIN

TO THUNDER MOUNTAIN

TO BUTCHER'S PASS

HAMMERSTRIKER POINT WARCAMP IS THE BASE OF OPERATIONS FOR DWARFS IN THE BLACK CRAGS. DESTRUCTION WOULD BE WISE TO GIVE IT A WIDE BERTH. HOWEVER, IT HAS BUT A SINGLE PATH INTO THE BLACK CRAGS AND IS EASILY BLOCKED.

LOBBA MILL IS RIGHT OUTSIDE GUDMUD'S STRONG-HUTS WARCAMP. TO TAKE THE MILL, YOU MUST CONTAIN THE GREENIES AND THEIR ALLIES IN THE WARCAMP. THE BRIDGE IS A CHOKE POINT FOR LEAVING THE WARCAMP, THOUGH THEY CAN JUMP INTO THE WATER AND COME UP BEHIND THE MILL

LEGEND

Warcamps:

 1 – Hammerstriker Point

 1 – Gudmud's Strong-Hut's Warcamp

RvR Area (Outlined)

 Chapter Unlock (Destruction)
15 – Greenskin Chapter 15
16 – Greenskin Chapter 16

 Chapter Unlock (Order)
20 – Dwarf Chapter 20
21 – Dwarf Chapter 21
22 – Dwarf Chapter 22

 Major Landmarks
1 – Destroyed Tower
2 – Redmane Mine
3 – Bat Hollow
4 – Morkfang Camp
5 – Morkfang Cave
6 – Despair Pits
7 – Sulfur Caves
8 – Venom Cave
9 – Tunnel of Karak Dazh
10 – Lageredson's Brewery
11 – Festering Cave
12 – Da Big Stink
13 – Cliffrunner Den
14 – Redfang Ridge
15 – Poisonwing Tunnel (East Side)
16 – Ruins of Karak Dahz
17 – Poisonwing Tunnel (West Side)
18 – Vidian Tower
19 – Stonemane Mine
20 – Muck Pen
21 – Infested Tower
22 – Burnmaw Tower

 Public Quests (Destruction)
1 – Mokfang Da Mad
2 – Overtop Outpost
3 – Valley of the Rangers
4 – Ambush Canyon
5 – Wyvern in the Hand
6 – Skargor da Traitor

 Public Quests (Order)
1 – Da Great Smashin' Pit
2 – Venom Lake
3 – Bait and Hit
4 – Gobbo Canvas
5 – Magister Dhetal
6 – Muck Pen
7 – Defiled Anvil
8 – Dammaz Skar
9 – Poisonwing Canyon

 Battle Objectives
1 – Lobba Mill (Merchant's Gift)
2 – Squiggly Beast Pens (Healing Boon, Underground)
3 – Macap Pickins (Artisan's Gift)
4 – Rottenpike Ravine

 1 – Ironskin Scar
1 – Badmoon Hole (Underground)

 Flight Master

RvR LEGEND

Warcamps:

 1 – Hammerstriker Point

 1 – Gudmud's Strong

RvR Area (Outlined)

 Battle Objectives
1 – Lobba Mill (Merchant's Gift)
2 – Squiggly Beast Pens (Healing Boon, Underground)
3 – Macap Pickins (Artisan's Gift)
4 – Rottenpike Ravine

 1 – Ironskin Scar

 Flight Master

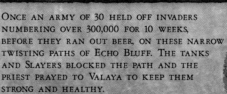

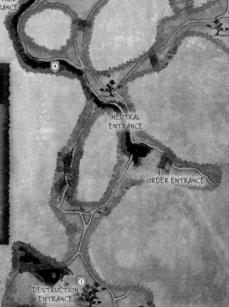

ONCE AN ARMY OF 30 HELD OFF INVADERS NUMBERING OVER 300,000 FOR 10 WEEKS, BEFORE THEY RAN OUT BEER, ON THESE NARROW TWISTING PATHS OF ECHO BLUFF. THE TANKS AND SLAYERS BLOCKED THE PATH AND THE PRIEST PRAYED TO VALAYA TO KEEP THEM STRONG AND HEALTHY.

ORDER ENTRANCE

NEUTRAL ENTRANCE

NEUTRAL ENTRANCE

NEUTRAL ENTRANCE

NEUTRAL ENTRANCE

ORDER ENTRANCE

DESTRUCTION ENTRANCE

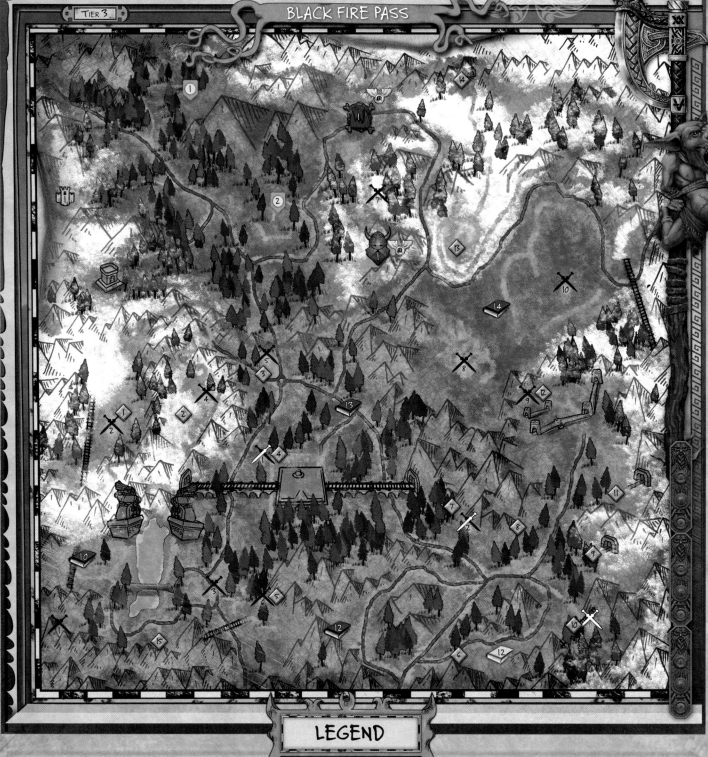

TIER 3

BLACK FIRE PASS

LEGEND

Warcamps: 1 – Odinator's Watch 1 – Blackteef's Boyz

RvR Area (Outlined)

Chapter Unlock (Destruction)
10 – Greenskin Chapter 10
12 – Greenskin Chapter 12
13 – Greenskin Chapter 13
14 – Greenskin Chapter 14

5 – Da Gassy Mines
6 – Khazad Bolg Tunnel
7 – Spida Hole
8 – Blackrock mine
9 – Warpclaw Cave
10 – Hindelburg
11 – Ebon Hollow
12 – Kolaz Umgal
13 – Ancient's Reach
14 – Black Fire Mine
15 – Lord Thardrik's Tower

3 – Statue of Inspiration
4 – Sigmarite Temple
5 – Altstadt
6 – Gassy Mine
7 – Kolaz Umgal Scouts
8 – FavoCult
9 – Kolaz Umgal
10 – Blighted Herd

Chapter Unlock (Order)
12 – Dwarf Chapter 12

Major Landmarks
1 – Priesterstadt
2 – Sigmarite Temple
3 – Altstadt
4 – Grimbeard Station

Public Quests (Destruction)
1 – Thardrik Smashin'
2 – Priesterstadt

Public Quests (Order)
1 – Hindelburg

Public Quests (Neutral)
1 – Grimbeard Station
2 – Moonfang Remnant

Battle Objectives
1 – Furrig's Fall (Defensive Boon)
2 – Bugman's Brewery (Merchant's Gift)

1 – Gnol Baraz

Flight Master

NEUTRAL ENTRANCE

DESTRUCTION ENTRANCE

ORDER ENTRANCE

ORDER ENTRANCE

Is a Dwarf fortress built to guard Black Fire Pass? Place your siege weapons and gather your forces, for this is the site of an epic battle. Whoever owns Gnol Baraz owns Black Fire Pass.

Bugman's Brew is the only place that will drive a Dwarf to fight as hard as they do for gold. This divine brew has properties that even scholars don't understand. It takes a Dwarf to appreciate it, though, since Elf and Manling just end up slumbering in their cups. There is no easy way to defend this site, so drink up and pray that Werner Bugman returns.

RvR LEGEND

Warcamps:

 1 – Odinator's Watch

 1 – Blackteef's Boyz

 RvR Area (Outlined)

 Battle Objectives
1 – Furrig's Fall (Defensive Boon)
2 – Bugman's Brewery (Merchant's Gift)

 1 – Gnol Baraz

 Flight Master

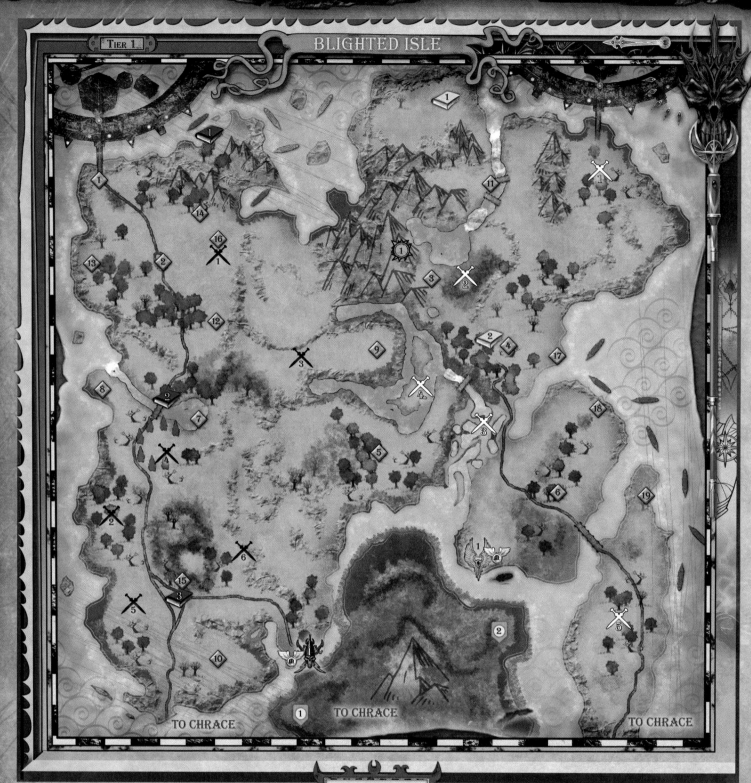

BLIGHTED ISLE

TIER 1

TO CHRACE

TO CHRACE

TO CHRACE

LEGEND

WARCAMPS: 1 – TOR AENDRIS   1 – CYNATHAI SPAN   RVR AREAS (OUTLINED)

CHAPTER UNLOCK (DESTRUCTION)
1 – DARK ELF CHAPTER 1
2 – DARK ELF CHAPTER 2
3 – DARK ELF CHAPTER 3

CHAPTER UNLOCK
1 – HIGH ELF CHAPTER 1
2 – HIGH ELF CHAPTER 2

MAJOR LANDMARKS
1 – BLACK ARK LANDING
2 – ISHA'S GARDEN
3 – FIRE CRYSTAL CAVERNS
4 – ADUNEI

5 – LACORITH VILLAGE
6 – STERNBROW'S LAMENT
7 – LAKE MENARHAIN
8 – LORE HOUSE
9 – GRIFFON'S NEST
10 – FOREST SPIRITS
11 – CALUMEL
12 – LIONWALK GROVE
13 – RUINS OF NARTHAIN
14 – SEAWIND GLADE
15 – POISONBLADE HEATH
16 – SPIRES OF NARTHAIN
17 – UTHORIN LANDING
18 – BLOODPRIEST CAMP
19 – FROSTRAGE KNIGHT CAMP

PUBLIC QUESTS (DESTRUCTION)
1 – SPIRES OF NARTHAIN
2 – WATCHTOWER
3 – MISTWOOD GROVE
4 – NIMOSAR
5 – DREAMSHADE FOREST
6 – GOLDEN TOR

PUBLIC QUESTS (ORDER)
1 – HOUSE ARKANETH
2 – THANALORN FOREST
3 – SWALE OF MIRALEI
4 – FORLORN ISLE
5 – RUINS OF ERRANETH

BATTLE OBJECTIVES
1 – ALTAR OF KHAINE (DEFENSIVE BOON)
2 – HOUSE OF LORENDYTH (HEALING BOON)

LAIRS
1 – GORTHLAK

FLIGHT MASTER

DEFENSIVELY CONTROLLING THE HOUSE OF LORENDYTH IS SIMPLE; THERE IS ONLY ONE WAY IN OR OUT OF THE OBJECTIVE. DEFENSIVE FORCES CAN SEE ANY ONCOMING ATTACKS FROM VERY FAR AWAY, AND CAN HOLD THEIR GROUND OR EVEN HIDE INSIDE WITH THE OBJECTIVE, FORCING THE ATTACKERS TO COME THROUGH A DOORWAY. HIGH ELVES WILL FIND IT EASY DEFENDING THE HOUSE OF LORENDYTH, BECAUSE THERE IS A WARCAMP DOWN THE HILL NEARBY.

IF OUTNUMBERED, DEFENSE MIGHT FIND IT EASIER TO DEFEND FROM WITHIN SO THAT THE ATTACKERS FUNNEL THROUGH THE DOOR.

THE LONG ROAD LEADING TO THE HOUSE OF LORENDYTH GIVES ITS DEFENSES A LONG TIME TO PREPARE FOR ANY INCOMING ATTACKS. KNOWING EXACTLY WHO AND HOW MANY ARE COMING WILL BE A KEEN ADVANTAGE.

RvR LEGEND

〜〜〜 RvR AREA (OUTLINED)

⬤ BATTLE OBJECTIVES
1 – ALTAR OF KHAINE (DEFENSIVE BOON)
2 – HOUSE OF LORENDYTH (HEALING BOON)

ORDER ENTRANCE

DESTRUCTION ENTRANCE

②

①

TO CHRACE

DEFENSE HAS AN EXCELLENT VIEW OF INCOMING ATTACKS FROM ALL SIDES STANDING ATOP THE TWIN TOWERS NEAR THE ALTAR OF KHAINE. OFFENSE HAS FIVE DIFFERENT APPROACHES IT CAN USE TO SPLIT DEFENSE OR TRY TO SNEAK BY UNNOTICED. DEFENSE CAN PLACE LOOKOUTS AT THE TOWERS WITH THEIR MAIN FORCES PROTECTING THE OBJECTIVE AT THE END OF THE PLATEAU. DARK ELVES WILL FIND IT EASY DEFENDING THE ALTAR OF KHAINE, BECAUSE THERE IS A WARCAMP DOWN THE HILL NEARBY.

ORDER WILL MOST LIKELY ENTER ON THIS SIDE BECAUSE DESTRUCTION WILL BE COMING UP FROM THE PATH ON THE OTHER SIDE OF THE TWIN TOWERS.

BUTCHER'S PASS

TO BLACK CRAG

LEGEND

RvR Area (Outlined)

 Portals
1 – To The Maw
2 – To Fell Landing

TO BLACK CRAG

NEUTRAL ENTRANCE

RVR LEGEND

RvR Area (Outlined)

Portals
1 – To The Maw
2 – To Fell Landing

THE BASTION OF GREENSKIN POWER, BUTCHER'S PASS STANDS IN DEFIANCE OF LOGIC AND SANITY. THE FORCE THAT TAKES THIS WILL BECOME LEGEND. THERE IS NO EASY WAY TO ASSAULT THIS HUGE FORTRESS BECAUSE THE GATES ARE A KILLING ZONE FROM THE SIDES AND THE DEFENDERS HAVE ALL THE ADVANTAGES.

THE INNER COURTYARD IS A KILLING GROUND FOR THOSE FOOLISH ENOUGH TO ASSAULT THE PINNACLE OF GREENSKIN POWER.

THE DWARFS WILL NEED A MIGHTY FORCE TO RECOVER BUTCHER'S PASS FROM THE GREENSKIN HORDE.

CALEDOR

Tier 4

LEGEND

WARCAMPS: 1 – Conqueror's Watch   1 – Conqueror's Descent   RvR Area (Outlined)

CHAPTER UNLOCK (DESTRUCTION)
15 – Dark Elf Chapter 15
16 – Dark Elf Chapter 16

CHAPTER UNLOCK (ORDER)
20 – High Elf Chapter 20 (Chapter Unlock in Dragonwake)
21 – High Elf Chapter 21
22 – High Elf Chapter 22

MAJOR LANDMARKS
1 – Dragon Shrine
2 – Giant Dragon Statue

PUBLIC QUESTS (DESTRUCTION)
1 – Battle of Avethir
2 – The Vault of the Dragon Princes
3 – Kelysian's Landing
4 – Loryndaal
5 – Malyro's Rest
6 – Fortress of Caledor

PUBLIC QUESTS (ORDER)
1 – Ulan Bel
2 – Shadowchasm
3 – Drakes Rest
4 – Shrine of the Dragontamer
5 – Shrine of Tethlis

6 – Exectuioner's Blade
7 – Tor Sethai
8 – Pure Power
9 – The Might of Ulthuan

PUBLIC QUESTS (NEUTRAL)
1 – Hatred's Way (RvR PQ)
2 – Wrath's Resolve (RvR PQ)

BATTLE OBJECTIVES
1 – Druchii Barracks
2 – Shrine of the Conqueror
3 – Sarathanan Vale
4 – Senlathain's Stand

1 – Hatred's Way
2 – Wrath's Resolve

FLIGHT MASTER

PORTALS
1 – Portal To Saphery

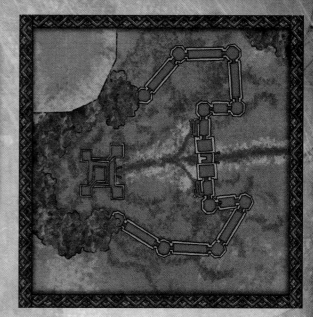

BERRAN VENOMTEAR BUILT WRATH'S RESOLVE AS A TRIBUTE TO HIS DARK LORDS, AND ANY WHO THINK THEY CAN TAKE IT WILL FEEL THE COLD STEEL OF HIS BLADE JUST BEFORE IT CARESSES THEIR HEART. THE FIELD IN FRONT OF THIS DARK FORTRESS IS FREE OF OBSTRUCTIONS, SO THERE IS NO PLACE TO HIDE AS THE ARCHERS RAIN DEATH ON THE ATTACKERS.

DESTRUCTION ENTRANCE

DESTRUCTION ENTRANCE

DESTRUCTION ENTRANCE

TO FELL LANDING

ORDER ENTRANCE

TO DRAGONWAKE

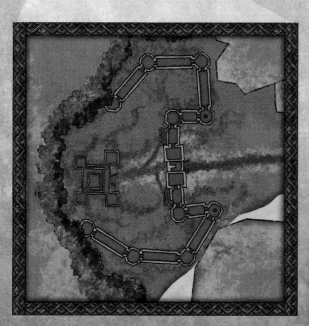

THERE ARE TWO PATHS INTO SARATHANAN VALE AND ONE OF THEM REQUIRES FORDING A MIGHTY RIVER. ATTACKERS ARE EXPOSED WHILE GETTING TO THE FIGHT AT THIS OBJECTIVE, AND THE DRAGON SKELETONS HINDER RANGED CLASSES WITH LINE-OF-SIGHT ISSUES.

RvR LEGEND

 RvR AREA (OUTLINED)

 CHAPTER UNLOCK (DESTRUCTION)
15 – Dark Elf Chapter 15

 PUBLIC QUESTS (NEUTRAL)
1 – Hatred's Way (RvR PQ)
2 – Wrath's Resolve (RvR PQ)

 BATTLE OBJECTIVES
1 – Druchii Barracks
2 – Shrine of the Conqueror
3 – Sarathanan Vale
4 – Senlathain's Stand

 1 – Hatred's Way
2 – Wrath's Resolve

 FLIGHT MASTER

 PORTALS
1 – To Saphery

THE DRUCHII BARRACKS ARE SECURE EXCEPT FOR THE THREE OPENINGS IN THE WALL. DEFENDERS SHOULD BLOCKADE THE OPENINGS WITH MELEE CLASSES AND HAVE HEALERS STAND OFF TO THE SIDE WHERE THEY CANNOT BE TARGETS. AOES WILL WORK THROUGH THE FENCE THOUGH, SO BE CAREFUL.

CHAOS WASTES

Tier 4

TO THE MAW

TO HIGH PASS

TO PRAAG

LEGEND

Warcamps: 1 – Tannenbach's Doom 1 – Seven Shades Creep   RvR Area (Outlined)

Chapter Unlock (Destruction)
15 – Chaos Chapter 15
16 – Chaos Chapter 16

Chapter Unlock (Order)
20 – Empire Chapter 20
21 – Empire Chapter 21
22 – Empire Chapter 22

Major Landmarks
1 – Bleakwind Wights
2 – Chaos Warband Encampment
3 – Grimclan Camp & nearby Cave
4 – Grimclan Camp & nearby Cave
5 – Grimclan Rune

6 – Nurgle Outpost
7 – Nurgle Outpost
8 – Twisted Caves
9 – Caves of Despair
10 – Tree of Souls
11 – Ancient Night
12 – Cave

Public Quests (Destruction)
1 – The Storm is Coming
2 – Reaping Pain
3 – Lonely Tower
4 – Sands of Time
5 – Fall of Grimclan
6 – Tower of Awakening

Public Quests (Order)
1 – Lost Artifacts
2 – Razing an Army
3 – Dance of Bones
4 – Madness
5 – Siren Sea
6 – Reaping Field
7 – Fall of Night
8 – Ebon Keep
9 – Altar of Madness

Battle Objectives
1 – Chokethorn Bramble (Merchant's Gift)
2 – Thaugamond Massif (Artisan's Gift)

3 – The Statue of Everchosen (Defensive Boon)
4 – The Shrine of Time (Healing Boon)

Lairs
1 – Tezakk Gnawbone

1 – Zimmeron's Hold
2 – Charon's Citadel

Flight Master

RvR Legend

Warcamps:

1 – Tannenbach's Doom

RvR Area (Outlined)

Battle Objectives

1 – Chokethorn Bramble (Merchant's Gift)
2 – Thavgamond Massif (Artisan's Gift)
3 – Statue of Everchosen (Defensive Boon)
4 – Shrine of Time (Healing Boon)

1 – Zimmeron's Hold
2 – Charon's Citadel

TO THE MAW

DESTRUCTION ENTRANCE

ORDER ENTRANCE

NEUTRAL ENTRANCE

TO PRAAG

To the east is the Empire's warcamp, Tannebach's Doom. Here you will find supplies, a healer, siege weapons merchant, Flight Master, and a mailbox. Take refuge here when necessary.

On the west side, adjacent to the Empire's warcamp, is the refuge for Destruction, Seven Shades Creep. Come here to load up on your siege weapons, because you're going to need them!

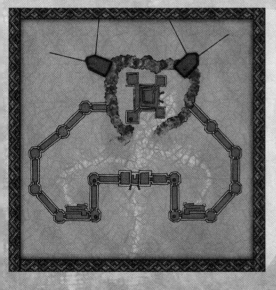

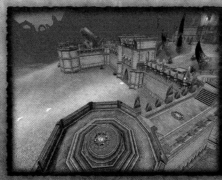

This objective is toward the north of the Chaos Wastes zone. Zimmeron's Hold has only one entrance, so it is easy to defend. There are heavy ranged pads all around the top of the hold walls, so use those to your advantage when defending. Don't forget to always have someone man the heavy oil pad right at the top of the entrance. On the attack, always man the heavy ram pad constantly to break the main entrance.

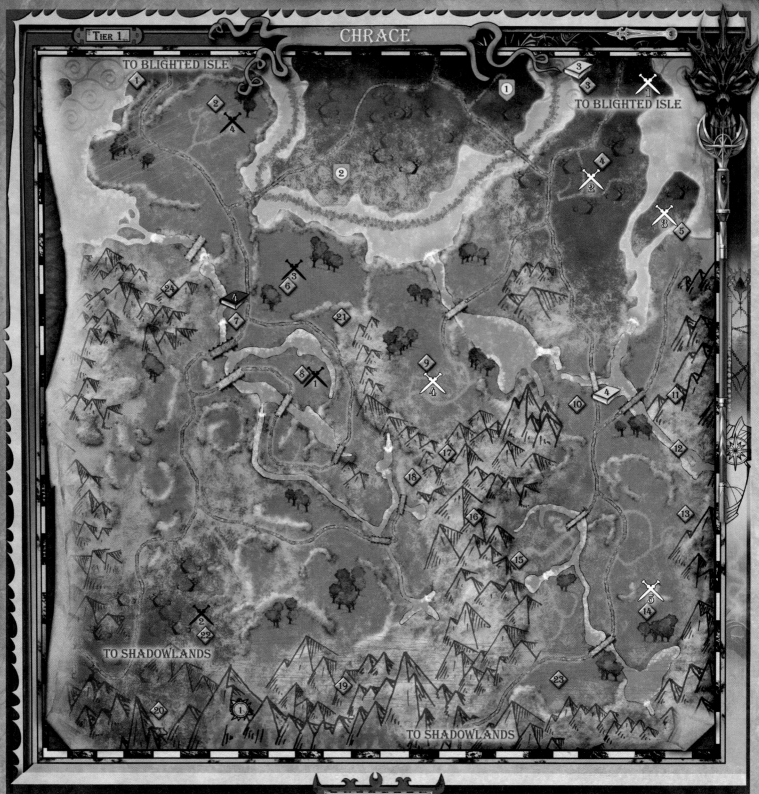

CHRACE

TIER 1

TO BLIGHTED ISLE

TO BLIGHTED ISLE

TO SHADOWLANDS

TO SHADOWLANDS

LEGEND

RvR AREA (OUTLINED)

 CHAPTER UNLOCK (DESTRUCTION)
3 – DARK ELF CHAPTER 3 (SEE BLIGHTED ISLE)
4 – DARK ELF CHAPTER 4

 CHAPTER UNLOCK (ORDER)
3 – HIGH ELF CHAPTER 3
4 – HIGH ELF CHAPTER 4

 MAJOR LANDMARKS
1 – SHADOWSONG LANDING
2 – GON'SERAPH

3 – BLIGHTSWARD
4 – YENLUI
5 – ELISIA
6 – TOR ACHARE
7 – MALAGURN'S CHARGE
8 – LIONHOME LODGE
9 – BLACKWOOD HILL GARRISON
10 – CLIFFS OF USHURU
11 – EVERSTAR STONE
12 – EVERSTAR LAKE
13 – LYRIANA'S MANSION
14 – STONE OF IMRATHIR
15 – LYRIANA'S REPOSE
16 – STONE OF MELANAR

17 – FLAMESCALE CAVERNS
18 – THANUIL'S RETREAT
19 – PRIDEHOME DEN
20 – DRAGONSCALE CAVERNS
21 – WHITECLAW CAVERN
22 – STONE OF VALETEAR
23 – DARK ELF CAMP
24 – EMLYRIA CAVERN

 PUBLIC QUESTS (DESTRUCTION)
1 – LIONHOME LODGE
2 – STONE OF VALETEAR
3 – TOR ACHARE
4 – GON'SERAPH

 PUBLIC QUESTS (ORDER)
1 – SHATTERED BEACH
2 – THRALLSEEKERS
3 – ELISIA
4 – BLACKWOOD HILL GARRISON
5 – STONE OF IMRATHIR

 BATTLE OBJECTIVES
1 – TOWER OF NIGHTFLAME
2 – SHARD OF GRIEF

 LAIRS
1 – KELBRAX

HIGH ROCKS AND WALLS SURROUND THE SHARD OF GRIEF, MAKING IT AN EXCELLENT AREA FOR DEFENDERS TO HIDE BEHIND IN AMBUSH. ATTACKERS MUST MANEUVER AROUND THESE OBSTACLES TO REACH THE BATTLEFIELD OBJECTIVE.

THE QUICKEST WAY TO THE BATTLEFIELD OBJECTIVE LIES ACROSS A LONG SLIVER OF A BRIDGE.

DEFENDERS WOULD BE WISE TO TAKE ADVANTAGE OF THIS BRIDGE. A FEW DEFENDERS COULD EASILY HOLD OFF COUNTLESS ATTACKERS IF DONE RIGHT.

TO BLIGHTED ISLE

TO BLIGHTED ISLE

RvR LEGEND

RvR AREA (OUTLINED)

BATTLE OBJECTIVES
1 – TOWER OF NIGHTFLAME
2 – SHARD OF GRIEF

ELEVATED ABOVE ITS SURROUNDING AREA, THE TOWER OF NIGHTFLAME HAS ONLY ONE ENTRANCE TO THE BATTLEFIELD OBJECTIVE. DEFENDERS DO NOT HAVE A LOT OF AREA TO SPREAD OUT IN, BUT ATTACKERS HAVE TO FUNNEL INTO THE AREA TO REACH THEM. NEARBY IS A VERY THIN BRIDGE WHERE A FEW DEFENDERS COULD EASILY STOP ANY CROSSING ATTACKERS.

ATTACKERS HAVE NO CHOICE BUT TO FUNNEL INTO THE BATTLEFIELD OBJECTIVE THROUGH THIS ONE ENTRANCE. HIGH GROUND ALL AROUND DETERS ALL OTHER WAYS IN.

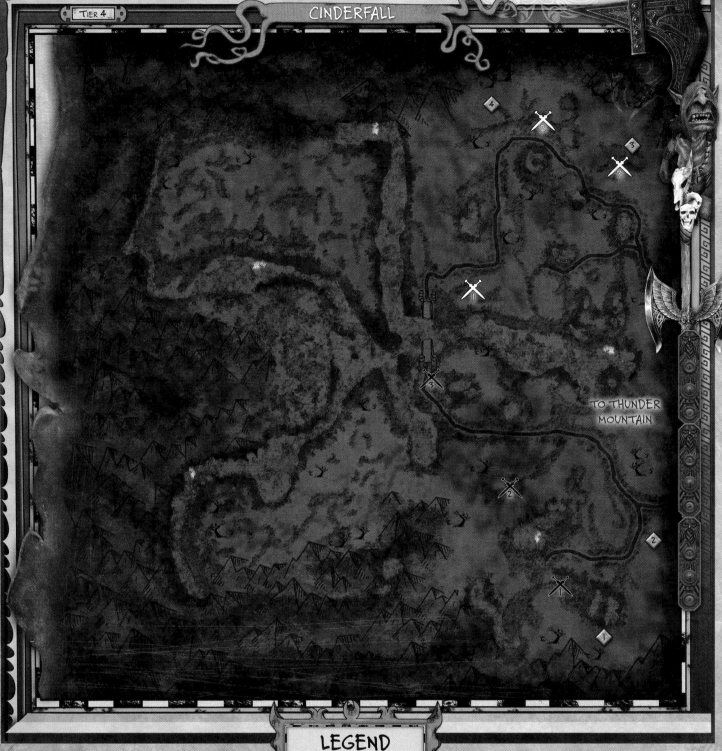

TIER 4

CINDERFALL

TO THUNDER
MOUNTAIN

LEGEND

RvR Area (Outlined)

Major Landmarks
1 – Cave
2 – Cave
3 – Cave
4 – Cave

Public Quests (Destruction)
1 – Gutbash Tribe Stronghold
2 – Flamerock Mine
3 – Da Drakk Cult

Public Quests (Order)
1 – Cult of Drakk
2 – Ashreaver Tribe Stronghold
3 – Emberlight Mine

TIER 4

DEATH PEAK

TO THUNDER MOUNTAIN

TO THUNDER MOUNTAIN

LEGEND

RvR Area (Outlined)

Major Landmarks
1 – Whoosha's Boyz
2 – Quimp's Cave
3 – Ashback Den
4 – Valley of Bones
5 – Webspun Hollow
6 – Skoragrim's Forge
7 – Ruins
8 – Ancestral Gates
9 – Sinar Orcstorm
10 – Ancestral Guardians

Public Quest (Destruction)
1 – Fallen Keep of Grom Rodrim
2 – Peak's Edge

Public Quests (Order)
1 – Whoosha's Boyz

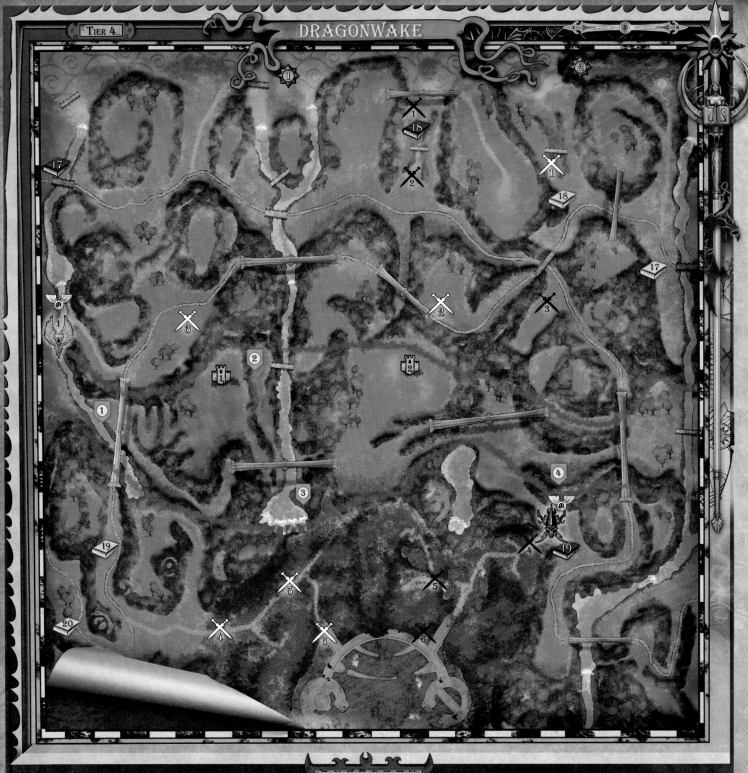

TIER 4

DRAGONWAKE

LEGEND

WARCAMPS: 1 – DRAKEWARDEN KEEP   1 – DRAKESLAYER HOLD

RvR AREA (OUTLINED)

CHAPTER UNLOCK (DESTRUCTION)
17 – DARK ELF CHAPTER 17
18 – DARK ELF CHAPTER 18
19 – DARK ELF CHAPTER 19

CHAPTER UNLOCK (ORDER)
17 – HIGH ELF CHAPTER 17
18 – HIGH ELF CHAPTER 18
19 – HIGH ELF CHAPTER 19
20 – HIGH ELF CHAPTER 20

PUBLIC QUESTS (DESTRUCTION)
1 – KEEPER'S VIGIL
(STARTS ON BRIDGES)
2 – DRAGONWATCH FALLS
3 – GALIRONS MOUTH
4 – CALADAIN STEPPE
5 – CALADAIN GATE
6 – CALADAIN'S FURNACE

PUBLIC QUESTS (ORDER)
1 – DRAGONWATCH
2 – KEEPER'S WATCH
3 – RESCUE OF AENARES
4 – CLIFFS OF VAUL
5 – BLOOD FOCUS
6 – DOMINION OF KHAINE

BATTLE OBJECTIVES
1 – FIREGUARD SPIRE
2 – MOURNFIRE'S APPROACH
3 – PELGORATH'S EMBER
4 – MILAITH'S MEMORY

COVENANT OF FLAME
1 – COVENANT OF FLAME
2 – DRAKEBREAKER'S SCOURGE

FLIGHT MASTER

PORTALS
1 – TO ISLE OF THE DEAD
2 – TO ISLE OF THE DEAD

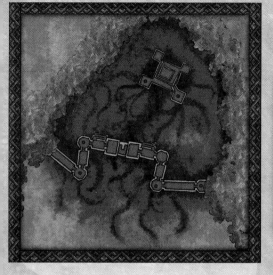

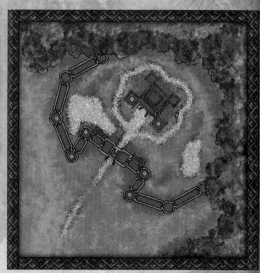

ON ONE SIDE OF THE ZONE LIES MILAITH'S MEMORY.
IT'S AT THE BOTTOM OF THE HILL, SO DEFENDERS
NEED TO WATCH EITHER DIRECTION SO THEY ARE
NOT SURPRISED BY INCOMING ATTACKS. WALLS AND
STONES PROTRUDING UP FROM THE GROUND PROVIDE
A LITTLE PROTECTION AND HIDING SPOTS FOR
DEFENDERS TO USE. THEY AREN'T MUCH, BUT HIDING
YOUR HEALERS DURING THE MELEE WILL HELP OUT.

ORDER
ENTRANCE
TO CALEDOR

DESTRUCTION
ENTRANCE

DESTRUCTION
ENTRANCE
TO EATAINE

DESTRUCTION
ENTRANCE

ORDER
ENTRANCE

RvR LEGEND

RvR AREA (OUTLINED)

BATTLE OBJECTIVES
1 – FIREGUARD SPIRE
2 – MOURNFIRE'S APPROACH
3 – PELGORATH'S EMBER
4 – MILAITH'S MEMORY

1 – COVENANT OF FLAME
2 – DRAKEBREAKER'S SCOURGE

AT THE BOTTOM OF A RAVINE, PELGORATH'S EMBER
WILL BE HEAVILY CONTESTED. DEFENDERS STATIONED
HERE SHOULD HAVE A CLEAR VIEW OF ANY
ATTACKERS COMING DOWN THE PATH. THIS ENSURES
THAT THEY HAVE PLENTY OF TIME TO CHOOSE
TARGETS PRIOR TO THEIR ARRIVAL.

A SMALL CORNER IN THE ROAD LEADS TO MOURNFIRE'S
APPROACH. BECAUSE IT'S NEAR A KEEP, THIS OBJECTIVE
WILL BE HEAVILY CONTESTED. STOPPING ANY ATTACKERS
ON THE BRIDGE AND FORCING THEM TO FUNNEL ACROSS
GIVES THE SPELLCASTERS AND RANGED DAMAGE PLAYERS
AN EXTREME ADVANTAGE HERE.

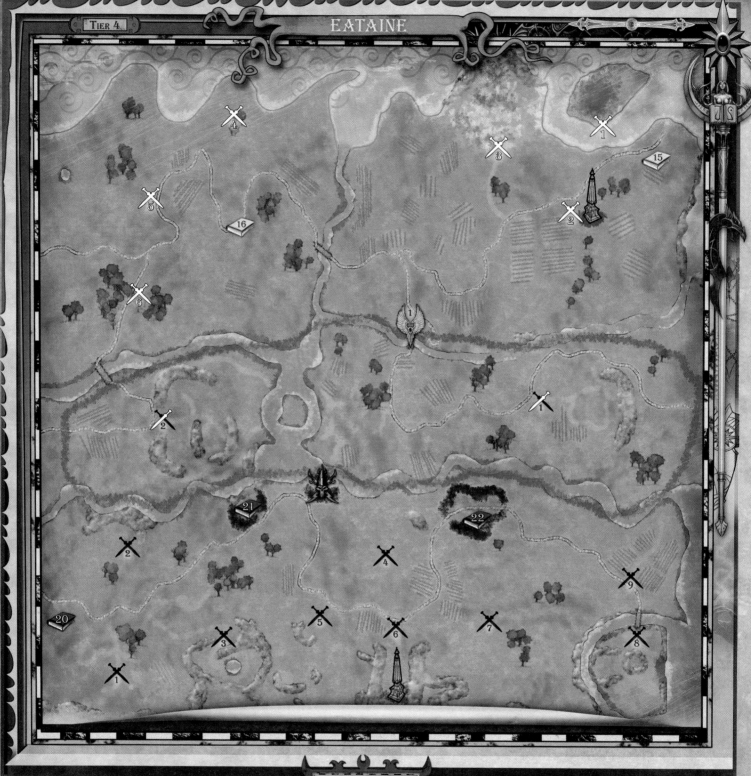

TIER 4

EATAINE

LEGEND

WARCAMPS: 1 – EATAINE MUSTERING   1 – EBONHOLD WATCH   RvR AREA (OUTLINED)

CHAPTER UNLOCK (DESTRUCTION)
20 – DARK ELF CHAPTER 20
21 – DARK ELF CHAPTER 21
22 – DARK ELF CHAPTER 22

PUBLIC QUESTS (DESTRUCTION)
1 – WOODSONG MANOR
2 – THE PHOENIX EYE
3 – SENTHOI POOL
4 – DAWNBREAK MANOR
5 – BLIND JUSTICE
6 – SPIRITS OF EATAINE
7 – LAST STAND
8 – GLITTERING CITADEL
9 – FOLLOW THE LIGHT

CHAPTER UNLOCK (ORDER)
15 – HIGH ELF CHAPTER 15
16 – HIGH ELF CHAPTER 16

PUBLIC QUESTS (ORDER)
1 – DA ORCWERKS
2 – CEYLNATH VINEYARDS
3 – SIEGE OF ANYERRIAL
4 – TOWER OF LYSEAN
5 – WELL OF SAR-SAROTH
6 – NEVERSONG

PUBLIC QUESTS (NEUTRAL)
1 – ARBOR OF LIGHT
2 – PILLARS OF REMEMBERANCE

SITUATED ON THE RIVERBANK IN THE HILLS BELOW PILLARS OF REMEMBRANCE, CHILLWIND MANOR WILL BE EASY TO DEFEND IF CONTROL OF THE KEEP IS SECURED. ONE SAVING GRACE THE DEFENSES HAVE IS THE ABILITY TO HUNKER DOWN INSIDE AND LET THE ATTACKERS FUNNEL THROUGH THE DOOR, WHICH ALLOWS FOR A SOLID DEFENSE EVEN WHEN OUTNUMBERED. OUTSIDE TERRAIN PROVIDES LITTLE PROTECTION FOR DEFENDERS OR WOULD-BE ATTACKERS; HOWEVER, WITH THE FLAG SITUATED INSIDE THE MANOR, GETTING THROUGH THE FRONT DOOR WILL BE THE CHALLENGE.

PLACED AT A CROSSROADS OF BRIDGES ON A SMALL ISLAND, BEL-KORHADRIS' SOLITUDE IS CENTRALLY LOCATED NEAR A COUPLE OTHER OBJECTIVES AND WILL MOST LIKELY CHANGE HANDS MANY TIMES. THE FOUR BRIDGES WILL BE WHERE MOST FIGHTS TAKE PLACE. DEFENSE WILL BE ABLE TO SEE ANYONE COMING PROVIDED THEY HAVE EYES AT EACH BRIDGE. LOTS OF TREES, STONES, AND STATUES GIVE THIS OBJECTIVE PLENTY OF HIDING SPOTS.

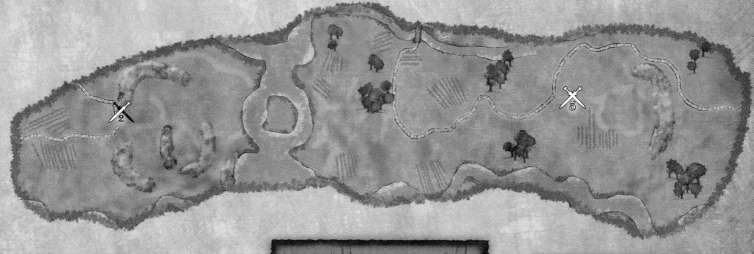

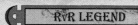

RvR LEGEND

RvR AREA (OUTLINED)

PUBLIC QUESTS (ORDER)
5 – WELL OF SAR-SAROTH

PUBLIC QUESTS (NEUTRAL)
2 – PILLARS OF REMEMBERANCE (RvR PQ)

THE SMALL, FORTIFIED SANCTUARY OF DREAMS IS CENTRALLY LOCATED. THIS BATTLEFIELD OBJECTIVE OFFERS A LITTLE PROTECTION FOR DEFENSES WITHOUT GIVING TOO MUCH. FORTIFIED WALLS ENSURE ATTACKERS CAN ENTER ONLY FROM ONE WAY, GIVING DEFENSE A SPOT TO FOCUS ON.

SITUATED ON THE OUTSKIRTS OF THE ZONE, ULTHORIN SIEGE CAMP OFFERS SOME PROTECTION FOR DEFENSES BUT ALSO GIVES ASSAULTERS A FEW ADVANTAGES. INSIDE PROVIDES LOTS OF AREAS FOR SPELLCASTERS AND HEALERS TO TAKE COVER AWAY FROM THE MELEE. STASHING YOUR HEALERS AWAY IN THE TENTS WHILE MELEE FIGHTS EASILY OUTSIDE COULD SWING THE BATTLE IN YOUR FAVOR.

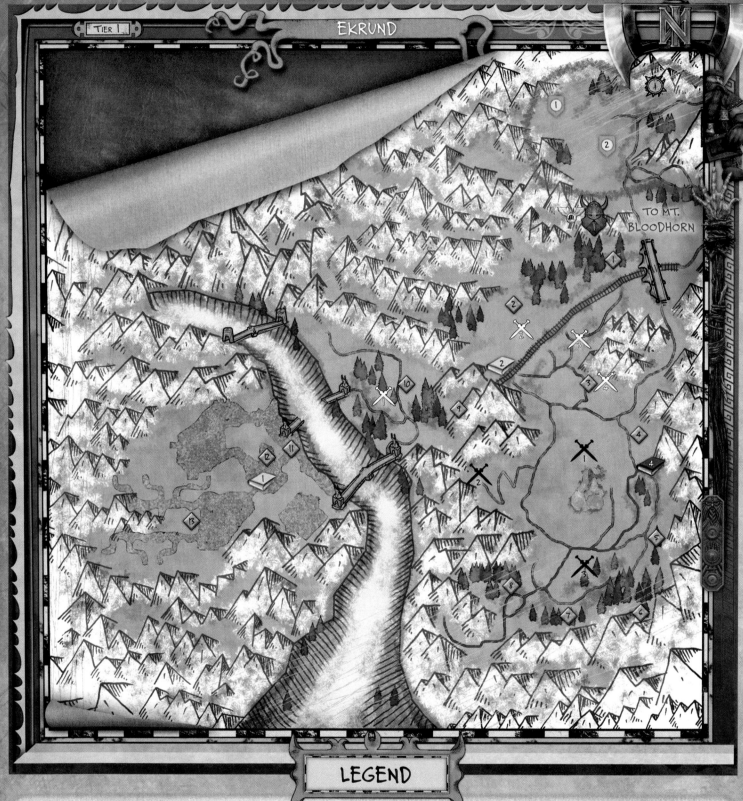

LEGEND

Warcamps: 1 – Grudgekeg's Guard

RvR Area (Outlined)

Chapter Unlock (Destruction)
4 – Greenskin Chapter 4

Chapter Unlock (Order)
1 – Dwarf Chapter 1
2 – Dwarf Chapter 2

Major Landmarks
1 – Norri's Tunnel
2 – Durak's Gate
3 – Durak's Mine
4 – Crawla Cave
5 – Goldfist's Tomb
6 – Wolf Den
7 – Broketoof Camp
8 – Njorinsson's Tomb
9 – Redhammer Tunnel
10 – Burguz's Boyz
11 – Ancestor's Watch
12 – Pick & Goggles
13 – Stonemane's Junction

Public Quests (Destruction)
1 – Goldfist Hole Recovery
2 – Raider's Haven
3 – Broketoof Camp

Public Quests (Order)
1 – Battle of Bitterstone
2 – Durak's Gate
3 – Engine Number Nine
4 – Murgluk's Gits

Battle Objectives
1 – Stonemine Tower
2 – Cannon Battery

Lairs
1 – Bandit Queen

Flight Master

THE TOWER IS EASILY ACCESSIBLE FROM THE NORTH SIDE THROUGH THE BROKEN WALL, AND ONCE UNDER YOUR CONTROL, IT IS DEFENSIBLE WITH RANGED DAMAGE FROM THE TOP.

NEUTRAL
ENTRANCE
(CAVE)

NEUTRAL
ENTRANCE

ORDER
ENTRANCE

RvR LEGEND

RvR Area (Outlined)

Battle Objectives
1 - Stonemine Tower
2 - Cannon Battery

MOUNT BLOODHORN IS A FIELD OF BONE AND MISERY
BETWEEN THE MARSHES OF MADNESS AND EKRUND.
ONLY THE GATES OF EKRUND STAND BETWEEN THE
DWARFS AND ANNIHILATION. THERE ARE NO KEEPS
OR FORTRESSES IN THE STARTING AREAS, BUT THE
GATES HAVE TWO OBJECTIVES.

THESE CANNONS WERE A GIFT FROM A WEALTHY
DWARF TO HELP SECURE THE DWARF LAND OF
EKRUND, AND THE GREENIES HAVE BEEN AFTER THEM
SINCE THEY FIRST BELCHED FORTH FLAME AND FIRE.
THEY CAN BE ATTACKED FROM MULTIPLE SIDES AND
ARE NOT EASILY DEFENSIBLE.

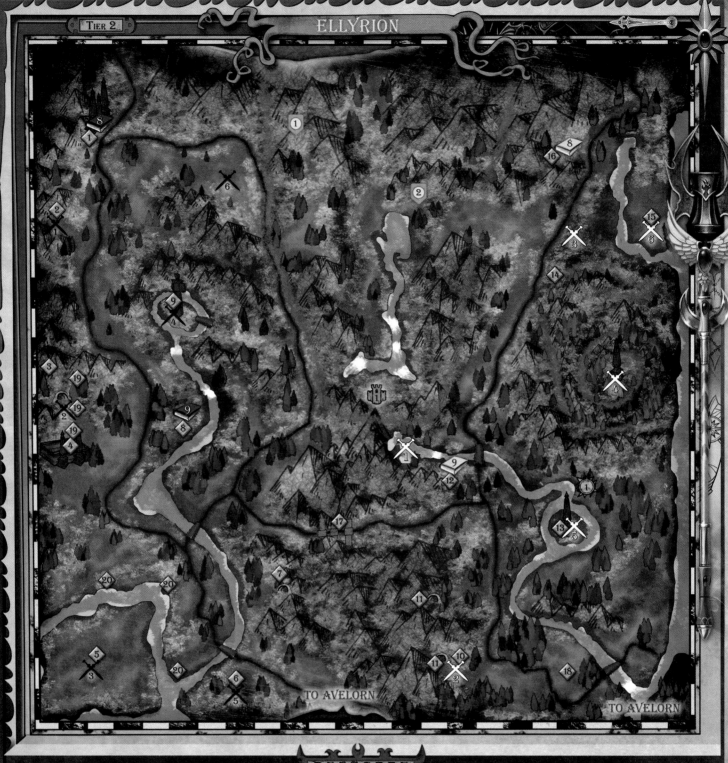

ELLYRION

TIER 2

TO AVELORN

TO AVELORN

LEGEND

RvR AREA (OUTLINED)

 CHAPTER UNLOCK (DESTRUCTION)
8 – DARK ELF CHAPTER 8
9 – DARK ELF CHAPTER 9

 CHAPTER UNLOCK (ORDER)
8 – HIGH ELF CHAPTER 8
9 – HIGH ELF CHAPTER 9

 MAJOR LANDMARKS
1 – BROKENBLADE
2 – BERHESSA
3 – SAVAGE CLAW CAVERN
4 – FORTRESS OF KORHANDIR
5 – TOR ELYR

6 – WHITEFIRE TOR
7 – HIGHVALE CAVERN
8 – GOLDMEAD
9 – MONUMENT TO NARIAELLE
10 – GATES OF ELTHRAI
11 – ELYR CAVERNS
12 – REAVER SPRING
13 – TOWER OF MILUNEN
14 – CONQUEROR'S ASCENT
15 – STARBROOK
16 – WINDRIDER PLAIN
17 – ELYR GATEHOUSE
18 – REAVER STABLES
19 – BEAR CAVES
20 – TOR ELYR TOWER / MANORS

 PUBLIC QUESTS (DESTRUCTION)
1 – TOWN OF BERHESSA
2 – REAVER'S END
3 – TOR ELYR
4 – MONUMENT OF NARIALLE
5 – WHITEFIRE TOR
6 – RESERVATION OF HONOR

 PUBLIC QUESTS (ORDER)
1 – WELL SPRINGS
2 – GATE OF ELTHRAI
3 – ELLYRIAN STABLES
4 – ALLIES OF WAR
5 – SHADY TOWER
6 – STARBROOK FALLS

 BATTLE OBJECTIVES
1 – NEEDLE OF ELLYRION
(HEALING BOOM)
2 – REAVER STABLES
(DEFENSIVE BOON)

 LAIRS
1 – STINKFANG THE VOMITOUS

 1 – CASCADES OF THUNDER

ORDER ENTRANCE
(FROM SHADOWLANDS
RvR AREA)

DESTRUCTION
ENTRANCE

DESTRUCTION
ENTRANCE

ORDER
ENTRANCE

- CAN GO AROUND THE FENCES AT
REAVER STABLES, BUT THEY DO FORCE
DIRECTION (IE CANT CROSS OVER THEM)

HIGH, ROCKY MOUNTAINS SURROUND THE NEEDLE OF ELLYRION, MAKING AN
ASSAULT FROM ANY DIRECTION BUT THE FRONT IMPOSSIBLE. DEFENSE HAS A
CLEAR VIEW OF ALL INCOMING ATTACKERS AND HAS A CHANCE TO EASILY
PREPARE. ALSO, DEFENSIVELY THERE ARE A COUPLE OF SPOTS FOR HEALERS
AND RANGE TO HIDE, ESPECIALLY THE ROCKS IN FRONT OF THE BATTLEFIELD
OBJECTIVE. THE ATTACKERS ALSO HAVE A NICE VIEW SITTING ATOP THE HIGH
MOUNTAIN SIDES AND CAN EASILY SEE ANY DEFENSIVE PLAYERS HIDING.

EVEN THOUGH IT IS SURROUNDED BY LOW MOUNTAINS, THE REAVER STABLES WILL BE
A CONSTANT CHALLENGE TO DEFEND. ATTACKERS CAN CHOOSE TO DROP FROM THE LOW
MOUNTAINS AROUND, APPROACH FROM THE FRONT, OR BOTH. DEFENSE HAS NO CLEAR
VIEW OF WHERE OR HOW MANY ATTACKERS IT WILL FACE, WHILE THE ATTACKERS CAN
EASILY LOOK DOWN UPON ANY POSSIBLE DEFENSE. EVEN A FRONTAL ATTACK IS MASKED
BY TREES AND A WINDING PATH.

RvR LEGEND

RvR AREA (OUTLINED)

BATTLE OBJECTIVES
1 – NEEDLE OF ELLYRION
(HEALING BOON)
2 – REAVER STABLES
(DEFENSIVE BOON)

1 – CASCADES OF THUNDER

TIER 4

FELL LANDING

TO CALEDOR

2
1 3

LEGEND

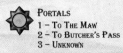

RvR Area (Outlined)

Portals
1 – To The Maw
2 – To Butcher's Pass
3 – Unknown

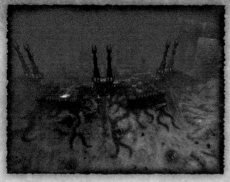

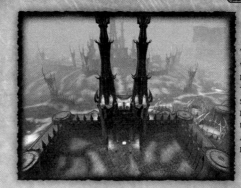

The Dark Elves were thinking when they made Fell Landing their home. Some say it sits on top of all the dead they have killed as they secured their hold over the area, but know this: attacking this position uphill will be costly, for the gates are mighty and the defenders are dangerous.

Attacks on the Inevitable City can be led in three regions. The Fell Landing region is guarded by the Dark Elves. The forces of Order can use long range pads and ram pads to attack in this region.

TO CALEDOR

RvR LEGEND

〜〜〜 RvR Area (Outlined)

✦ Portals
1 – To The Maw
2 – To Butcher's Pass
3 – Unknown

Lord Elethirean leads the defensive forces at Fell Landing. Should you be fortunate to reach him, you will, unfortunately, meet a swift death unless you enter with a powerful warband.

Your last step on your march through the Dark Elf lands ends with Fell Landing, a victory away from campaigning against the Inevitable City itself.

Tier 3

HIGH PASS

TO OSTLAND

TO CHAOS WASTES

TO TALABECLAND

LEGEND

Warcamps: 1 – Dogbite Ridge

RvR Area (Outlined)

Chapter Unlock (Destruction)
13 – Chaos Chapter 13
14 – Chaos Chapter 14

Chapter Unlock (Order)
10 – Empire Chapter 10
11 – Empire Chapter 11
12 – Empire Chapter 12

Major Landmarks
1 – Bonestomper Ogres
2 – Ogre Approach
3 – Oathbearer Camp
4 – Cultist Camp

5 – Horror Rifts
6 – Bonestomper Ogre Camps
7 – Vladesaul's Defense
8 – Cave
9 – Blood Marauders
10 – Cave
11 – Lost Miners (Cave)
12 – Brighthollow Tower
13 – Cave (Passage to Jaggedspine Ridge)

Public Quests (Destruction)
1 – Temple of Heimkell
2 – Beacon of Firengram
3 – Gut's Out

4 – Keep of Asavar Kul
5 – Tempest Horn
6 – Tower of the Elves

Public Quests (Order)
1 – Foetid Plains
2 – Tomb of the Traitor
3 – Chaos Ruins
4 – Lake of the Damned
5 – Cult of the Magus
6 – Temple of Change
7 – Echoes of War
8 – Grisly Herd
9 – Shrine of Tzeentch

Battle Objectives
1 – Feiten's Lock (Defensive Boon)
2 – Ogrund's Tavern (Healing Boon)
3 – Hallenfurt Manor (Artisan's Gift)

1 – Stoneclaw Castle

Flight Master

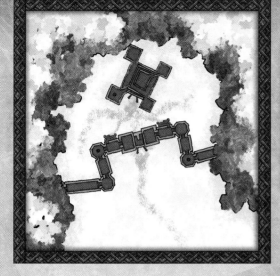

STONECLAW CASTLE IS AT THE MAP'S VERY LOWER LEFT CORNER. IT IS AN EXCELLENT LOCATION TO DEFEND, BECAUSE THERE IS ONLY A SINGLE ENTRANCE AND IT'S TUCKED AGAINST THE SNOWY MOUNTAINS. FOR DEFENDERS, MAN THAT MEDIUM OIL PAD AGAINST WOULD-BE RAM USERS. THERE ARE TWO MEDIUM RANGED PADS LOCATED ON BOTH SIDES OF THE CASTLE WALLS. GET SOME DEFENDERS TO KEEP THOSE ACTIVE AND PUSH BACK ATTACKERS. ATTACKERS, ON THE OTHER HAND, MUST MAN THE MEDIUM RAM PAD TO GAIN ACCESS TO THIS CASTLE. THERE ARE ALSO SOME MEDIUM RANGED PADS THAT WILL HELP KILL DEFENDERS WALKING AROUND THE CASTLE WALLS.

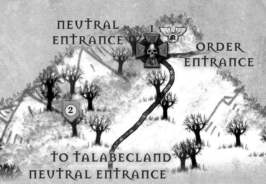

NEUTRAL ENTRANCE · ORDER ENTRANCE · ORDER ENTRANCE · NEUTRAL ENTRANCE · NEUTRAL ENTRANCE · TO TALABECLAND · NEUTRAL ENTRANCE · NEUTRAL ENTRANCE · NEUTRAL ENTRANCE

RvR LEGEND

WARCAMPS:

1 – DOGBITE RIDGE

RvR AREA (OUTLINED)

BATTLE OBJECTIVES
1 – FEITEN'S LOCK
   (DEFENSIVE BOON)
2 – OGRUND'S TAVERN
   (HEALING BOON)
3 – HALLENFURT MANOR
   (ARTISAN'S GIFT)

1 – STONECLAW CASTLE

FLIGHT MASTER

THIS POINT IS DIRECTLY SOUTH OF THE HALLENFURT MANOR AT THE VERY BOTTOM EDGE OF HIGH PASS ZONE. IT CONSISTS OF A GATED WALLED STRUCTURE THAT'S A PERFECT AREA TO DEFEND. MORE IMPORTANTLY, IT HAS A CAVE THAT LEADS TO THE TALABECLAND SIDE OF THE RvR AREA, MAKING IT EXCELLENT FOR QUICK ESCAPES OR EASY ACCESS TO THE LOWER PART OF THE RvR AREA. THIS CAVE SPILLS RIGHT INTO PASSWATCH CASTLE.

FEITEN'S LOCK IS SOUTHEAST OF THE STONECLAW CASTLE. THE FRONT ENTRANCE IS EASIER TO DEFEND THAN THE BACK. BE CAREFUL OF THE BACK AREA BECAUSE THIS HAS A HUGE OPENING. A CAVE ENTRANCE LEADS RIGHT OUTSIDE THE WALLS.

TIER 4

INEVITABLE CITY

11

2

10

3   9   4

1

2   5   1   3

5   6   8   12

4

4   2   7   1

7A

3

2

1A

1

LEGEND

Altdorf District Name

1 – Undercroft
1A – Undercroft, Northern Section
2 – Journey's End
3 – Dread Way
4 – Death's Labyrinth
5 – Monolith
6 – Apex
7 – Lost Narrows
7A – Lost Narrows, Eastern Section
8 – Sacellum
9 – Fate's Edge
10 – Breaking Grounds
11 – Eternal Citadel
12 – Fleshrot Alley

Landmarks

1 – Arena at Sacellum
2 – Viper Pit, Guild House

Public Quests (Destruction)

1 – Inevitable Rot
2 – Temple Of the Damned
3 – Disputable Power
4 – Hel'kar the Blood Lord
5 – The Bigger They Are...
6 – Toil and Trouble

Dungeon Entrances

1 – Bilerot Burrow
2 – Sacellum Holding Pits, Low Level
3 – Sacellum Holding Pits, Mid Level
4 – Sacellum Holding Pits, High Level

Banks

Auctioneer

Entrances to the City

Flight Master

APEX DISTRICT

INEVITABLE CITY

LEGEND

 Inevitable City District Name
4 – Death's Labyrinth
6 – Apex
7 – Lost Narrows
9 – Fate's Edge

 Major Landmarks
1 – The Char Bone

 Public Quests (Destruction)
3 – Disputable Power
4 – Hel'kar the Blood Lord

 Quest Givers
1 – Mivvar Blackshard (Pillar of Blood)
2 – Kuur Eightborn (Disputable Power; Ruinous Daemon)
3 – Vilhura Everseer (Enraged Souls)

 Banks

 Auctioneer

Merchants / Vendors
1 – Craft Supply Merchant
2 – Weapon Merchant
3 – Armor Merchant
4 – Renown Gear Merchant
5 – Camp Merchant

Trainers
1 – Career Trainer
2 – Scavenger Trainer
3 – Butcher Trainer
4 – Cultivator Trainer

JOURNEY'S END

INEVITABLE CITY

LEGEND

 Inevitable City District Name
2 – Journey's End
4 – Death's Labyrinth
7 – Lost Narrows

 Major Landmarks
1 – Soul Vault
2 – The Feast Hall

 Quest Givers
1 – Rotnog Onetoof (Mushroom Hunta)
2 – Lokur the Ravenhand (Inevitable Rot)

 Banks

 Auctioneer

 Merchants / Vendors

 Guards

Healer

LEGEND

DEATH'S LABYRINTH/MONOLITH DISTRICT

 Inevitable City District Name
5 – Monolith
10 – Breaking Grounds

 Major Landmarks
1 – The Grinning Skull

 Dungeon Entrances
1 – Bilerot Burrow

 Banks

 Auctioneer

 Merchants / Vendors
1 – Armor Merchant
2 – Camp Merchant
3 – Mount Vendor
4 – Weapon Merchant
5 – Disciple Everdamned
6 – Disciple Painbearer

Trainers
1 – Tome Trainer

INEVITABLE CITY

DEATH'S LABYRINTH

INEVITABLE CITY

LEGEND

 Inevitable City District Name
4 – Death's Labyrinth
5 – Monolith

 Dungeon Entrances
1 – Bilerot Burrow

 Auctioneer

DREAD WAY

INEVITABLE CITY

LEGEND

⬥ Inevitable City District Name
3 – Dread Way

△ Quest Givers
1 – Pleuress the Taker
(The Last Full Measure)

FATES EDGE/ETERNAL CITADEL

INEVITABLE CITY

LEGEND

⬥ Inevitable City District Name
II – Eternal Citadel

△ Quest Givers
1 – Tchar'zanek
(Taking the Offensive)
2 – Pheryx, Master of Change
(Enfold the Sty of Sigmar!;
The Other Ally)
3 – Hellebron
(Blood of the Vale)

⬤ Auctioneer

FATE'S EDGE

INEVITABLE CITY

LEGEND

⬥ Inevitable City District Name
6 – Apex
9 – Fate's Edge

◆ Major Landmarks
1 – The Viper Pit

✕ Public Quests (Destruction)
3 – Disputable Power
4 – Hel'kar the Blood Lord

△ Quest Givers
1 – Augur Verrimus
(The Inevitable City)
2 – Derl Iceheart
(Like Clockwork)

◯ Banks

◯ Auctioneer

▮ Guards

Flight Master

LEFT OF VNDERCROFT (SLAANESH)

INEVITABLE CITY

LEGEND

△ Quest Givers
I – Tivlas of the Kul (patrols)
(Petty Vengeance)

LEGEND

✦ Inevitable City District Name
I – Undercroft
IA – Undercroft, Northern Section

⬤ Entrances to the City

○ Banks

◐ Auctioneer

⬟ Guards

VNDERCROFT DISTRICT

IA

SLAANESH PORTION OF THE VNDERCROFT

BLOODWROVGHT ENCLAVE

I

INEVITABLE CITY

RIGHT OF UNDERCROFT DISTRICT

INEVITABLE CITY

LEGEND

△ Quest Givers
1 – Stavin Gutspiller
(Blood for the Blood God)

◇ Dungeon Entrances
1 – Bloodwrought Enclave

● Entrances to the City

LOST NARROW

LEGEND

Inevitable City District Name
7 – Lost Narrows

Major Landmarks
1 – Arena at Sacellum

Public Quests (Destruction)
1 – Inevitable Rot
2 – Temple Of the Damned
5 – The Bigger They Are...

Dungeon Entrances
1 – Bilerot Burrow

Guards

LEGEND

Inevitable City District Name
7A – Lost Narrows, Eastern Section
8 – Sacellum
12 – Fleshrot Alley

Major Landmarks
1 – Arena at Sacellum
2 – The Elysium
3 – Fleshrot Alley

Public Quests (Destruction)
1 – Inevitable Rot
2 – Temple Of the Damned
5 – The Bigger They Are...
6 – Toil and Trouble

Quest Givers
1 – Isanoro Winterheart (Grinding of Gears)
2 – Nollarr Rageborn (The Ever Ancient)
3 – Deavyr Lorzit (Book Return)
4 – Aekold Helbrass (Unity in Discord)

Dungeon Entrances
2 – Sacellum Holding Pits, Low Level
3 – Sacellum Holding Pits, Mid Level
4 – Sacellum Holding Pits, High Level

SACELLUM & LOST NARROWS DISTRICT

TIER 4

ISLE OF THE DEAD

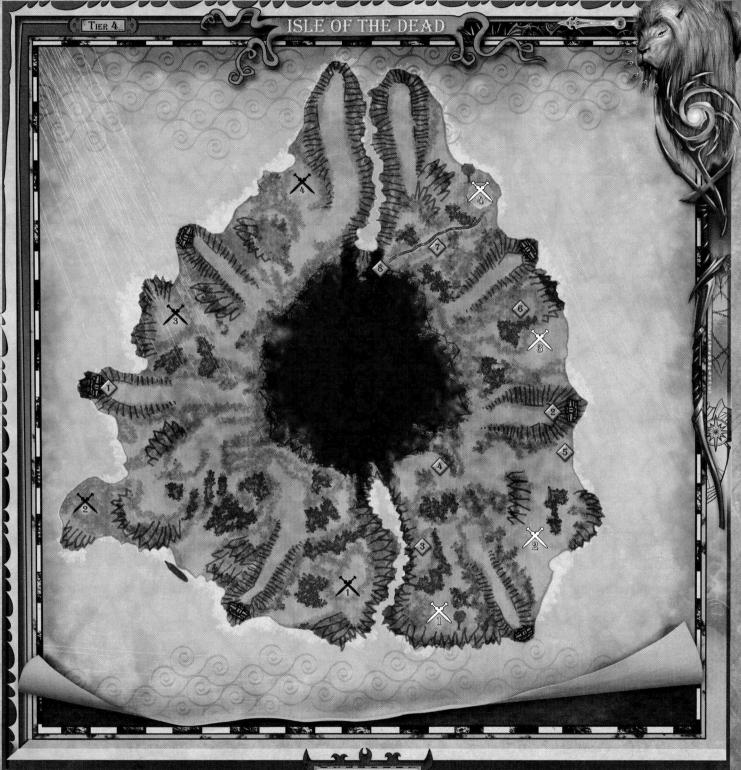

LEGEND

RvR Area (Outlined)

Chapter Unlock (Destruction)
17 – Dark Elf Chapter 17
(Unlock in Dragonwake)

Chapter Unlock (Order)
17 – High Elf Chapter 17
(Unlock in Dragonwake)

Major Landmarks
1 – Dark Elf (Entrance from Dragonwake)
2 – High Elf (Entrance from Dragonwake)
3 – Stone of Trials
4 – Scrying Pool
5 – Saruthil's Stand
6 – Savitha's Stand
7 – Watch of Althanis
8 – Chosen Path

Public Quests (Destruction)
1 – Ritual of Light
2 – Ritual of Fire
3 – Ritual of Metal
4 – Ritual of Shadow

Public Quests (Order)
1 – Ritual of Life
2 – Ritual of Death
3 – Ritual of the Heavens
4 – Ritual of Beasts

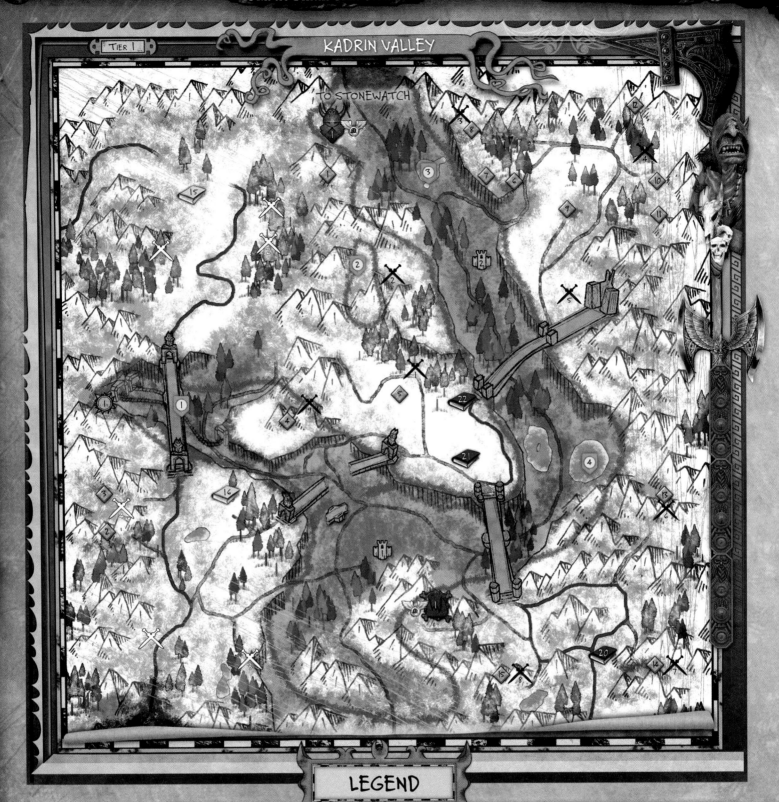

KADRIN VALLEY

TIER 1

TO STONEWATCH

LEGEND

Warcamps: 1 – Gharvin's Brace   1 – Krung's Scrappin' Spot   ~~~~ RvR Area (Outlined)

Chapter Unlock (Destruction)
20 – Greenskin Chapter 20
21 – Greenskin Chapter 21
22 – Greenskin Chapter 22

Chapter Unlock (Order)
15 – Dwarf Chapter 15
16 – Dwarf Chapter 16

Major Landmarks
1 – Shrine of Grimnir
2 – Tower of Grung Grimaz
3 – Mine of Grung Grimaz
4 – Clarion Tower

5 – Duraz Dok
6 – Gharvin's Tower
7 – Gharvin's Mine
8 – Crazy Stunty Drinking Place
9 – Peak Tower
10 – Duraz Deb
11 – Duraz Deb Mine
12 – Everpeak Mine
13 – Tunnel of Baradum
14 – Kazad Urbar
15 – Kloingar's Mine

Public Quests (Destruction)
1 – Duraz Dok
2 – Battlegut Ogres

3 – Beer Barrel Bash
4 – Duraz Deb
5 – Slayer Keep
6 – Baradum
7 – Kazad Urbar
8 – Burnbeard's Oath
9 – Clarion Tower

Public Quests (Order)
1 – Ambush Valley
2 – Evil Axis
3 – Sealed Tower
4 – Gates of Grung Grimaz
5 – Night Riders
6 – Plague Mist Vale

Battle Objectives
1 – Gromril Junction (Defensive Boon)
2 – Icehearth Crossing (Healing Boon, Underground)
3 – Kazad Dammaz
4 – Hardwater Falls (Artisan's Gift)

Lairs
1 – Fleshrender

1 – Dolgrund's Cairn (Merchant's Gift)
2 – Karaz Drengi

Flight Master

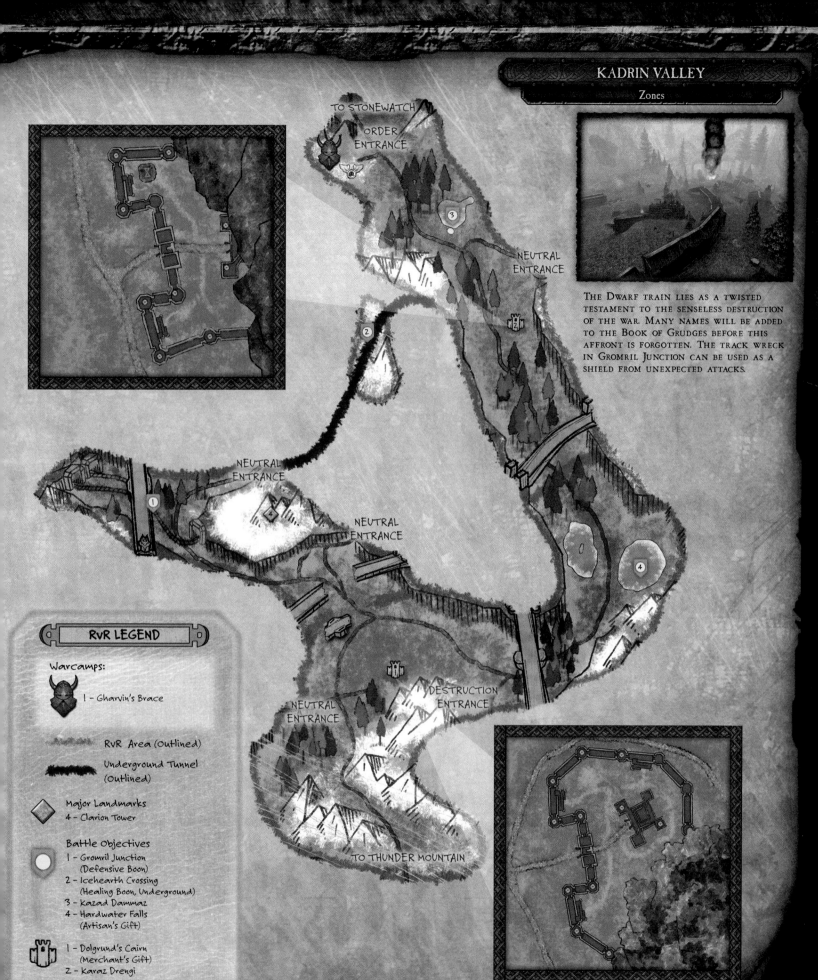

TO STONEWATCH

ORDER
ENTRANCE

3

NEUTRAL
ENTRANCE

2

THE DWARF TRAIN LIES AS A TWISTED
TESTAMENT TO THE SENSELESS DESTRUCTION
OF THE WAR. MANY NAMES WILL BE ADDED
TO THE BOOK OF GRUDGES BEFORE THIS
AFFRONT IS FORGOTTEN. THE TRACK WRECK
IN GROMRIL JUNCTION CAN BE USED AS A
SHIELD FROM UNEXPECTED ATTACKS.

NEUTRAL
ENTRANCE

1

NEUTRAL
ENTRANCE

4

NEUTRAL
ENTRANCE

DESTRUCTION
ENTRANCE

TO THUNDER MOUNTAIN

RvR LEGEND

Warcamps:

1 – Gharvin's Brace

RvR Area (Outlined)

Underground Tunnel
(Outlined)

Major Landmarks
4 – Clarion Tower

Battle Objectives
1 – Gromril Junction
(Defensive Boon)
2 – Icehearth Crossing
(Healing Boon, Underground)
3 – Kazad Dammaz
4 – Hardwater Falls
(Artisan's Gift)

1 – Dolgrund's Cairn
(Merchant's Gift)
2 – Karaz Drengi

Flight Master

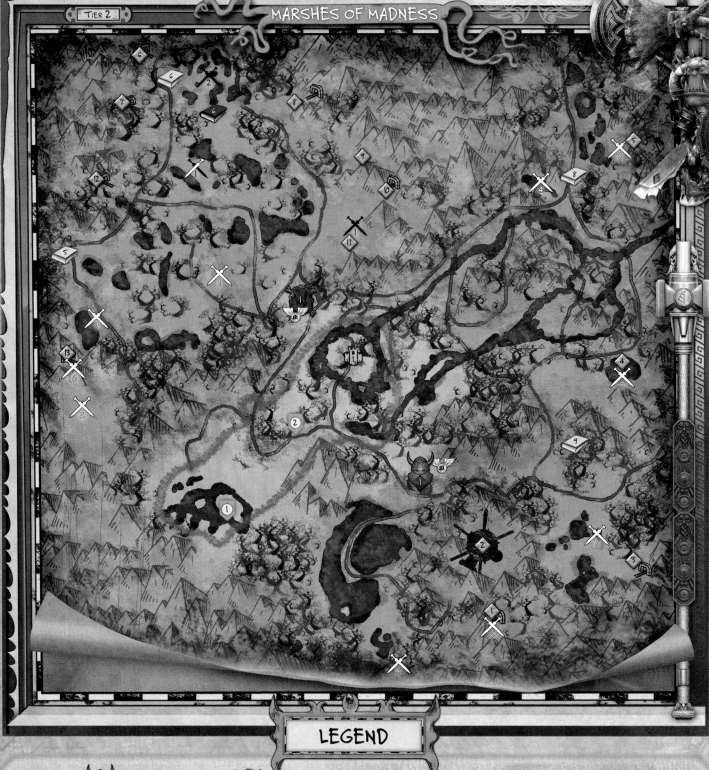

TIER 2

MARSHES OF MADNESS

LEGEND

Warcamps: 1 – Thurarikson's Warcamp   1 – Morth's Warcamp   RvR Area (Outlined)

Chapter Unlock (Destruction)
6 – Greenskin Chapter 6

Chapter Unlock (Order)
5 – Dwarf Chapter 5
6 – Dwarf Chapter 6
8 – Dwarf Chapter 8
9 – Dwarf Chapter 9

Major Landmarks
1 – Agymah's Lair
2 – Tower of Neborhest
3 – Falcon's Tomb

4 – Tree of Beards
5 – Nushtar's Tomb
6 – Hunk Grung
7 – Tainted Mines
8 – Marshfang Spider Cave
9 – Hargruk's Camp
10 – Dragon Eye Cavern
11 – Mingol Thag
12 – Mourkain Tomb
13 – Dawr Galaz Grung

Public Quests (Destruction)
1 – Spectre of Battle
2 – Battle at Blood Fen

Public Quests (Order)
1 – Assault on Coal Ridge Depot
2 – Axerust Peak
3 – Legacy of the Mourkain
4 – Dam Boglar
5 – Tree of Beards
6 – Tower of Neborhest
7 – Neborhest's Vanguard
8 – Agymah's Lair
9 – Foul Ruins
10 – Oathgold Burrow

Public Quests (Neutral)
1 – Marsh Conquest

Battle Objectives
1 – Goblin Armory (Merchant's Gift)
2 – Alcadizzaar's Tomb
      (Defensive Boon)

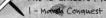 1 – Fangbreaka Swamp

 Flight Master

YOU CAN TRY ENCIRCLING THE GOBLIN ARMORY AND THEN PRESSING IN WITH FORCE. IF YOU CAN SNIPE DEFENDERS, PICK THEM OFF TO WEAKEN RESISTANCE.

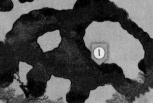

THE BRIDGE WILL BE A FOCAL POINT FOR FIGHTING WHEN ATTEMPTING THE GOBLIN ARMORY ANVIL. WITH THE TERRAIN OPEN IN SPOTS, EXPECT CASUALTIES AND BRING ALONG HEALERS TO RESURRECT COMPANIONS ON THE SPOT TO SPEED UP REINFORCEMENTS.

NEUTRAL ENTRANCE

NEUTRAL ENTRANCE

DESTRUCTION ENTRANCE

ORDER ENTRANCE

NOTE: LOT OF AREAS CAN JUMP DOWN INTO THE RVR AREA, BUT CAN ONLY GET OUT BY USING THE PASSAGES

INSTANCE ENTRANCE (CLOSED)

RvR LEGEND

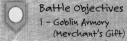

RvR Area (Outlined)

Battle Objectives
1 – Goblin Armory
    (Merchant's Gift)
2 – Alcadizzaar's Tomb
    (Defensive Boon)

1 – Fangbreaka Swamp

GREENIES HAVE DE A NICE PLACE TO CALL HOME IN THE SWAMP, IF THEY CAN CONTROL FANGBREAKA HOLD. WITH ONLY ONE BRIDGE, IT'S DIFFICULT TO INVADE THE FORTRESS.

TIER 4

THE MAW

ENTRANCES TO INEVITABLE CITY

TO CHAOS WASTES

LEGEND

Major Landmarks
1 – Career Trainers
2 – Small Camp (Merchant, Apothecary Trainer, Consumables Merchant)
3 – Small Camp (Salvaging Trainer, Scavenging Trainer, Talisman Trainer)
4 – Small Camp (Guild Registrar, Career Trainer)

5 – Door
6 – Door
7 – Door
8 – Door
9 – Door
10 – Door
11 – Door
12 – Door
13 – Migliod Menagerie (Lair)

RvR Area (Outlined)

Portals
1 – To Fell Landing
2 – To Butcher's Pass

Flight Master

RvR LEGEND

  RvR Area (Outlined)

Portals
1 – To Fell Landing
2 – To Butcher's Pass

TO CHAOS WASTES

NEUTRAL ENTRANCE

THE MAW STANDS AS THE LAST BASTION OF CHAOS BEFORE THE INEVITABLE CITY. THERE, THE LAWS OF PHYSICS AND SANITY ARE TWISTED BEYOND LOGIC AND SENSE. THERE IS NO EASY WAY IN AND EACH GATE MUST BE PAID FOR IN BLOOD, FOR THE TWIST OF CHAOS IS STRONG THIS FAR NORTH.

THE THREE GATES ARE EACH GUARDED BY HOUNDS OF KHORNE AND MUTANT HORRORS DRIVEN BY CHAOS WARRIORS.

GARRISON WARRIORS DEFEND THE MAW, AND THAT DOESN'T INCLUDE ANY DESTRUCTION PLAYERS WHO JOIN IN THE FUN. BRING A SMALL ARMY HERE IF YOU WANT ANY PRAYER OF ENTERING.

TIER 1

MT. BLOODHORN

LEGEND

Warcamps: 1 – Screeb's Stunty Killin' Camp

RvR Area (Outlined)

Chapter Unlock (Destruction)
1 – Greenskin Chapter 1
2 – Greenskin Chapter 2
3 – Greenskin Chapter 3

Chapter Unlock (Order)
3 – Dwarf Chapter 3
4 – Dwarf Chapter 4

Major Landmarks
1 – Mouth of Morngrim
2 – Old Dwarf Lookout Tower
3 – Old Stoneson Mine
4 – Da Gobbo Camp

5 – Broketoof Boyz
6 – Sharpthorn's Rock Mine
7 – Snout's Pens
8 – Lobber Hill
9 – Spore Rock
10 – Da Stumps
11 – Gran Thewn Watch
12 – Forgotten Hold
13 – Statue of the Oathbearer
14 – Glon Barak
15 – Forgehand's Workshop
16 – Crawla Cave
17 – Chompa's Cave

Public Quests (Destruction)
1 – Ironclaw Camp
2 – Sharpthorn Wud
3 – Urgog's Rage
4 – Sharpthorn's Rock Mine
5 – Sacred Grove
6 – Durak's Rest

Public Quests (Order)
1 – Siege of Komar
2 – Gutrot Mine
3 – Traitor's Watch
4 – Marghaz Bloodtoof Ritual

Public Quests (Neutral)
1 – Kron Komar Gap

Battle Objectives
1 – The Lookout (Artisan's Gift)
2 – Ironmane Outpost
(Healing Boon)

Flight Master

THE LOOKOUT GIVES THE GREENSKINS THE ADVANTAGE OF TERRAIN, ALTHOUGH HAVING TWO FRONTS TO DEFEND DETRACTS FROM THE ABILITY TO CONTROL THE SKIRMISH LINE.

NEUTRAL ENTRANCE
(QUEST ENTRANCE
GATES OF EKRUND)

NEUTRAL ENTRANCE
(CAVE FROM EKRUND;
NO MOBS)

NEUTRAL
ENTRANCE

NEUTRAL
ENTRANCE

DESTRUCTION
ENTRANCE

RvR LEGEND

Warcamps:
1 – Screeb's Stunty Killin' Warcamp

RvR Area (Outlined)

Battle Objectives
1 – Lookout (Artisan's Gift)
2 – Ironmane Outpost (Healing Boon)

Flight Master

IRONMANE BUILT THIS OUTPOST TO SUPPLY THE DWARFS WITH MUCH NEEDED ORE FOR DWARF STEEL. NOW HE IS ANOTHER PAGE IN THE BOOK OF GRUDGES. RANGED DEFENDERS SHOULD GATHER AT THE TOP OF THE OUTPOST, WITH THE MELEE OUT FRONT.

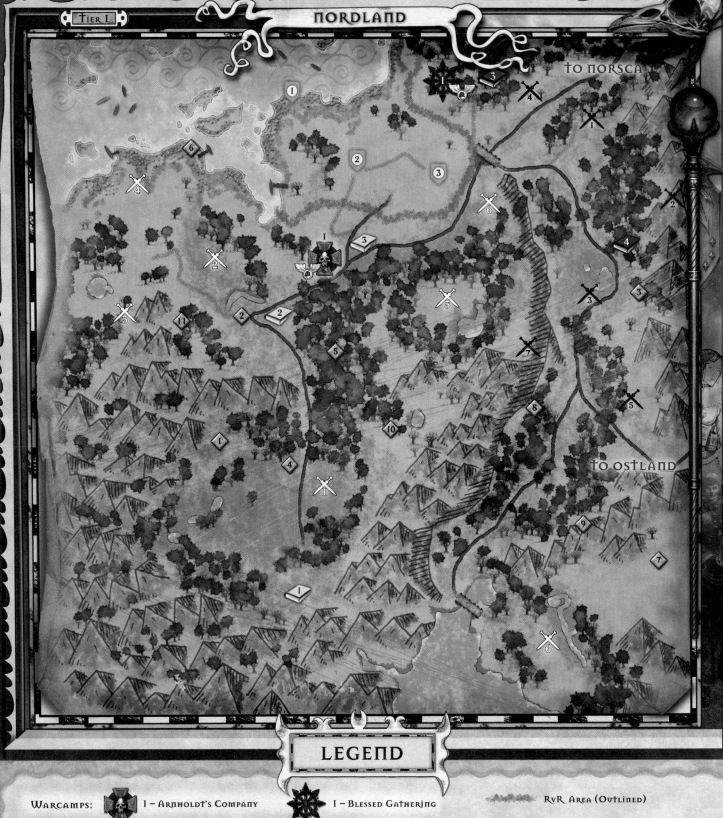

NORDLAND

Tier I

TO NORSCA

TO OSTLAND

LEGEND

WARCAMPS: I – Arnholdt's Company   I – Blessed Gathering

RvR Area (Outlined)

Chapter Unlock (Destruction)
3 – Chaos Chapter 3
4 – Chaos Chapter 4

Chapter Unlock (Order)
1 – Empire Chapter 1
2 – Empire Chapter 2
3 – Empire Chapter 3

Major Landmarks
1 – Grimmenhagen Barrows
2 – Grey Lady Coaching Inn

3 – Beeckerhoven Crypt
4 – Grimmenhagen Windmill
5 – Traitor's Crossing
6 – Norscan Longship
7 – Salzenmund Keep
8 – Gausser's Wilding
9 – Smugglers' Tunnel
10 – Murder Wood
11 – Abandoned Marauder Camp

Public Quests (Destruction)
1 – Pillage and Plunder
2 – Wilds of War
3 – Fields of Woe

4 – Macabre Fervor
5 – Sacred Ground
6 – Salzenmund

Public Quests (Order)
1 – Raven Host Vanguard
2 – Buring Windmill
3 – Ruins of Schloss von Rubendorff
4 – Norse Are Coming
5 – Faewulf's Rest
6 – Pillager's Approach
7 – Webworks

Battle Objectives
1 – Nordland docks
2 – Festenplatz Defense Boon
3 – Harvest Shrine

Flight Master

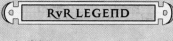
Blessed Gathering is the Chaos warcamp north of Nordland. It is filled with quest givers, Weapon and Armor Merchant, Healer, Flight Master, and more.

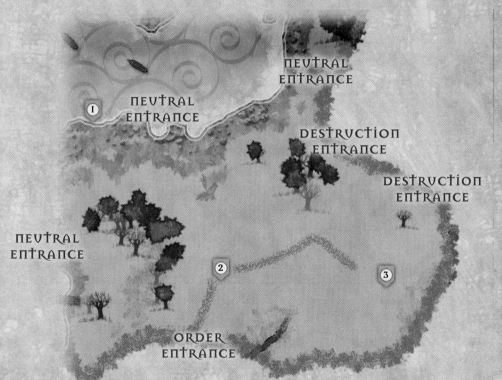

Arnholdt's Company is the Empire warcamp, filled with merchants, such as the Weapon and Armor Merchant, a Healer, Flight Master, and more. Get the supplies you need for your battles here.

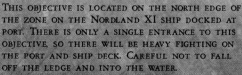

The Festenplatz Battlefield Objective is hidden inside a house. With only one floor for the flag there is not much cover for defense. One entrance makes it a little easier to concentrate your attacks.

This objective is located on the north edge of the zone on the Nordland XI ship docked at port. There is only a single entrance to this objective, so there will be heavy fighting on the port and ship deck. Careful not to fall off the ledge and into the water.

TIER I

NORSCA

TO TROLL COUNTRY

TO NORDLAND

LEGEND

RvR Area (Outlined)

Chapter Unlock (Destruction)
1 – Chaos Chapter 1
2 – Chaos Chapter 2

Chapter Unlock (Order)
4 – Empire Chapter 4

Major Landmarks
1 – Amund's Barrow
2 – Tomb of Ravenborne
3 – Skaldbjorn

4 – Charred Lands
5 – Watchtower of Selthis Lysk
6 – Gotland Forest
7 – Spindekraken
8 – Gotland
9 – Thorshafn Crypt

Public Quests (Destruction)
1 – Ruinous Powers
2 – Destruction of the Weak
3 – Superholm
4 – Holmstein Revisited

Public Quests (Order)
1 – Altar of Bloodbane
2 – Ulfenwyr
3 – Pit of the Forsaken

Battle Objectives
1 – Lost Lagoon

Lairs
1 – Silveroak

LOST LAGOON IS ON ITS OWN ISLAND SOUTH OF THE MAP IN THE NORSCA ZONE. IT CONSISTS OF TWO CAVE ENTRANCES AND THE FLAG RIGHT AT THE CENTER OF THE MOUNTAIN WALLS.

RVR LEGEND

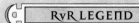 RVR AREA (OUTLINED)

Ⓘ BATTLE OBJECTIVES
I – LOST LAGOON

DEFENDERS NEED TO SPLIT IN HALF TO DEFEND BOTH ENDS. FOR ATTACKERS, SEND IN A DECOY PARTY AT ONE END WHILE YOUR MAIN PARTY ATTACKS THE OTHER.

TIER 2

OSTLAND

TO TROLL COUNTRY

TO TROLL COUNTRY

TO NORDLAND

TO HIGH PASS

LEGEND

WARCAMPS: 1 – Raven's Edge

 RvR Area (Outlined)

 Chapter Unlock (Destruction)
5 – Chaos Chapter 5
7 – Chaos Chapter 7

 Chapter Unlock (Order)
7 – Empire Chapter 7
8 – Empire Chapter 8
9 – Empire Chapter 9

Major Landmarks
1 – Ostland Troops
2 – Cleansing Flame Warriors
3 – Lost Cavern
4 – Gerstmann Crypt
5 – Wayshire of Ulric

6 – Forgotten Graveyard
7 – Hillsbottom Lake
8 – Badger's Nook and Luthor's Pond
9 – Shadow Lake Brigands
10 – Cave
11 – Catacombs
12 – Grim Monastery
13 – Altered Beasts
14 – Catacombs
15 – Lonely Farm
16 – Tower of Ruin
17 – Black Mire Bell Tower
18 – Ferlangen Cemetery

Public Quests (Destruction)
1 – Silkens
2 – Bells of War
3 – Spirits of the Shadow
4 – Krul Gor Herd
5 – Reapers Circle
6 – Wayshire of Sigmar
7 – Ragash's Last Stand

Public Quests (Order)
1 – Hochnar
2 – Siege of Bohsenfels
3 – Black Mire
4 – Nurenmir's Lancers
5 – Gore Wood

6 – Howling Vale
7 – Wolfenburg

 Battle Objectives
1 – Crypt of Weapons (Artisan's Gift)
2 – Kinshel's Stronghold (Healing Boon)

 1 – Mandred's Hold

 Flight Master

MANDRED'S HOLD IS IN A CLEARING WITHIN A THICK FOREST. THERE ARE NO WALLS FOR DEFENSE, THOUGH THERE IS A LIGHT OIL PAD OVER THE ENTRANCE AND TWO LIGHT RANGED PADS ON EACH TOWER. MAN THEM ALL, ESPECIALLY THE LIGHT OIL PAD. FOR ATTACKERS, THERE ARE SEVERAL LIGHT RANGED PADS LAID OUT IN FRONT OF THE HOLD, PLUS A LIGHT RAM PAD AT THE ENTRANCE. KEEP THE RAM PAD MANNED AT ALL TIMES TO GET INTO THE HOLD.

NEUTRAL ENTRANCE   NEUTRAL ENTRANCE

ORDER ENTRANCE

NEUTRAL ENTRANCE

②

DESTRUCTION ENTRANCE

DESTRUCTION ENTRANCE

①

NEUTRAL ENTRANCE

NEUTRAL ENTRANCE

RvR LEGEND

WARCAMPS:

1 – RAVEN'S EDGE

RvR AREA (OUTLINED)

BATTLE OBJECTIVES
1 – CRYPT OF WEAPONS (ARTISAN'S GIFT)
2 – KINSHEL'S STRONGHOLD (HEALING BOON)

1 – MANDRED'S HOLD

RAVEN'S EDGE WARCAMP IS JUST WEST OF MANDRED'S HOLD. IT IS THE PERFECT PLACE TO PLAN SIEGES. GATHER UP ALL OF YOUR SIEGE WEAPONS, ARMOR, AND OTHER SUPPLIES, THEN GET READY FOR SOME BATTLES.

SOUTH OF THE RAVEN'S EDGE, THE BATTLEFIELD OBJECTIVE IS INSIDE THE CRYPT OF WEAPONS. SURROUNDING THE CRYPT IS A CEMETERY. THERE'S NOT MUCH TO DEFEND HERE, THOUGH HAVING CONTROL OF MANDRED'S HOLD DOES MAKE IT EASIER.

KRAUSSNER'S GARRISON IS THE EMPIRE'S WARCAMP. HERE YOU WILL FIND ALL THE NECESSITIES SUCH AS ARMOR, SIEGE WEAPONS, CAREER TRAINER, RALLY MASTER, AND MORE. GET SOME REST HERE, THEN STOCK UP FOR SOME MORE BATTLES.

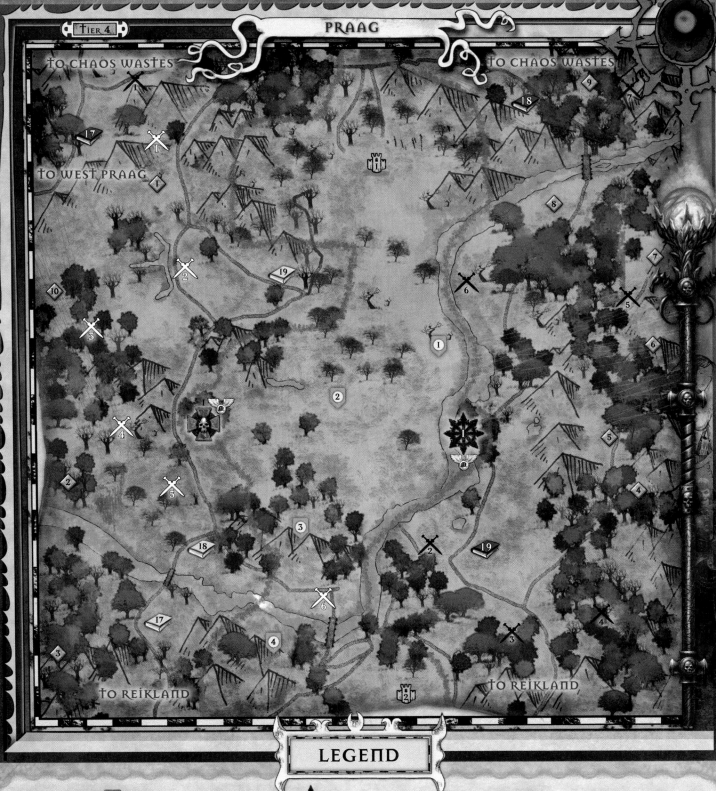

PRAAG

Tier 4

TO CHAOS WASTES

TO CHAOS WASTES

TO WEST PRAAG

TO REIKLAND

TO REIKLAND

LEGEND

WARCAMPS: 1 – WESTMARK BARRICADE GUARD   1 – RAVENSWORN   RvR AREA (OUTLINED)

CHAPTER UNLOCK (DESTRUCTION)
17 – CHAOS CHAPTER 17
18 – CHAOS CHAPTER 18
19 – CHAOS CHAPTER 19

CHAPTER UNLOCK (ORDER)
17 – EMPIRE CHAPTER 17
18 – EMPIRE CHAPTER 18
19 – EMPIRE CHAPTER 19

MAJOR LANDMARKS
1 – SUMMONING CIRCLE
2 – RAVEN HOST REINFORCEMENTS

3 – SKAVEN CAVE
4 – CAVE (STONECLAN DWARFS)
5 – GRIFFIN'S LAST STAND
6 – URSUN'S DEN
7 – CINDERASH TOWER
8 – KOSSARS & STRIKERS
9 – TALONPEAK
10 – BEAR SHRINE

PUBLIC QUESTS (DESTRUCTION)
1 – GATES OF PRAAG
2 – SOUTHERN BREACH
3 – THE END IS NIGH
4 – WINGS OF THE GRIFFIN

5 – CINDERASH ENCLAVE
6 – EASTERN BREACH
7 – TOMB OF DEATHSWORD

PUBLIC QUESTS (ORDER)
1 – HELL'S FALL
2 – GRIFFON'S LAST STAND
3 – BEASTS OF WAR
4 – EYES IN THE DARK
5 – BROKEN GROUND
6 – GOSPODAR SQUARE

BATTLE OBJECTIVES
1 – KURLOV'S ARMORY (DEFENSIVE BOON)
2 – MARTYR'S SQUARE (ARTISAN'S GIFT)
3 – MANOR OF ORTEL VON ZARIS (MERCHANT'S GIFT)
4 – RUSSENSCHELLER GRAVEYARD (ARTISAN'S GIFT)

1 – GARRISON OF SKULLS
2 – SOUTHERN GARRISON

FLIGHT MASTER

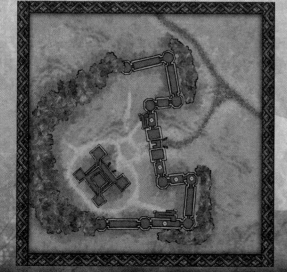

RvR LEGEND

WARCAMPS:

 I – Westmark
Barricade Guard

 I – Ravensworn

 RvR Area (Outlined)

 Major Landmarks
15 – Ouleg's Tower

 Public Quests (Order)
6 – Gospodar Square

 Battle Objectives
I – Kurlov's Armory
(Defensive Boon)
2 – Martyr's Square
(Artisan's Gift)
3 – Manor of Ortel von Zaris
(Merchant's Gift)
4 – Russenscheller Graveyard
(Healing Boon)

 I – Garrison of Skulls
2 – Southern Garrison

Flight Master

NEUTRAL
ENTRANCE

NEUTRAL
ENTRANCE

NEUTRAL
ENTRANCE

15

ORDER
ENTRANCE

1

2

ORDER
ENTRANCE

DESTRUCTION
ENTRANCE

I

3

ORDER
ENTRANCE

NEUTRAL
ENTRANCE

6

4

NEUTRAL
ENTRANCE

TO REIKLAND

NEUTRAL
ENTRANCE

2

REIKLAND

TIER 4

TO PRAAG

TO PRAAG

TO TALABECLAND

TO REIKWALD

TO REIKWALD

WILHELM'S FIST IS AT THE VERY CENTER OF REIKLAND ZONE. IT'S SURROUNDED BY A GIANT WALL WITH A HEAVY OIL PAD ABOVE THE MAIN ENTRANCE, AS WELL AS FOUR HEAVY RANGED PADS ON TOP OF THE WALL. INSIDE THESE WALLS LIES THE KEEP, DEFENDED WITH ANOTHER HEAVY OIL PAD AND TWO HEAVY RANGED PADS ON EITHER SIDE. ATTACKERS HAVE SEVERAL HEAVY RANGED PADS AND A HEAVY RAM AT THE MAIN ENTRANCE, BUT THEY NEED TO CONSTANTLY RELY ON THE HEAVY RAM TO BREAK THROUGH. DEFENDERS HAVE THE DOORS ALL AROUND FOR SNEAK ATTACKS AND EASY ESCAPES.

JUST SOUTHWEST OF REIKWATCH, RUNEHAMMER GUNWORKS IS SITUATED ON TOP OF A PLATEAU AND HAS TWO OPENINGS THAT REACH THE FLAG. DEFENDING THIS OBJECTIVE WILL BE DIFFICULT.

LEGEND

WARCAMPS: I – DEATHWATCH LANDING

 I – DARKSTONE VANTAGE

 RvR AREA (OUTLINED)

 CHAPTER UNLOCK (DESTRUCTION)
20 – CHAOS CHAPTER 20
21 – CHAOS CHAPTER 21
22 – CHAOS CHAPTER 22

CHAPTER UNLOCK (ORDER)
15 – EMPIRE CHAPTER 15
16 – EMPIRE CHAPTER 16

 MAJOR LANDMARKS
1 – CASTLE GRAVENBURG
2 – LORD'S PASS
3 – TROOP DEPLOYMENT
4 – WEST TEMPLE (MONASTERY)
5 – DISMAL HOLLOW
6 – RAVEN LANDING
7 – CAVE (THE DEPTHS OF DEPRAVITY)
8 – CAVE (BACK ENTRANCE TO
   HEINRICH ESTATE)
9 – CEMETARY
10 – TEMPLE OF REIKLAND
   (MONASTERY)
11 – CAVE
12 – FLAGELLANTS AND PILGRIMS
13 – CAVE
14 – RITTERBURG
15 – MORR'S MAZE
16 – CEMETARY
17 – SONS OF SIGMAR
18 – ELVEN EXPEDITION

PUBLIC QUESTS (DESTRUCTION)
1 – DARK RETRIBUTION
2 – RAIN OF FIRE
3 – VULGAR DISPLAY OF POWER
4 – STONECLAN'S DEMISE
5 – HUNTING THE HUNTERS
6 – REIKSGUARD, TRAINING GROUNDS
7 – ALL THE KINGS MEN
8 – FIELDS OF REIKLAND
9 – AMBUSH AT GARNSONBURG

PUBLIC QUESTS (ORDER)
1 – CASTLE GRAVENBURG
2 – THE ENEMY WITHIN
3 – REIK RIVER BANDITS
4 – ROOT OF REBELLION
5 – FIELDS OF RUIN
6 – HEINRICH ESTATE

 BATTLE OBJECTIVES
1 – FROSTBEARD'S QUARRY
   (ARTISAN'S GIFT)
2 – REIKWATCH (DEFENSIVE BOON)
3 – RUNEHAMMER GUNWORKS
   (HEALING BOON)
4 – SCHWENDERHALLE MANOR
   (MERCHANT'S GIFT)

 1 – WILHELM'S FIST, RENOWN TRAINER,
   CHAMPION EQUIPMENT
2 – MORR'S REPOSE, RENOWN TRAINER,
   CHAMPION EQUIPMENT

 FLIGHT MASTER

RvR LEGEND

 RvR AREA (OUTLINED)

BATTLE OBJECTIVES
1 – FROSTBEARD'S QUARRY
   (ARTISAN'S GIFT)
2 – REIKWATCH
   (DEFENSIVE BOON)
3 – RUNEHAMMER GUNWORKS
   (HEALING BOON)
4 – SCHWENDERHALLE MANOR
   (MERCHANT'S GIFT)

1 – WILHELM'S FIST, RENOWN
   TRAINER CHAMPION
   EQUIPMENT
2 – MORR'S REPOSE, RENOWN
   TRAINER, CHAMPION
   EQUIPMENT

Tier 4

REIKWALD

TO REIKLAND

TO REIKLAND

ENTRANCE TO
ALTDORF

ENTRANCE TO
ALTDORF

LEGEND

RvR Area (Outlined)

Major Landmarks
1 – Career Trainers
2 – Career Trainers

Portals
1 – To Shining Way
2 – To Stonewatch

NEUTRAL ENTRANCE TO REIKLAND

NEUTRAL ENTRANCE

NEUTRAL ENTRANCE

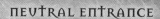

ENTRANCE TO ALTDORF ②

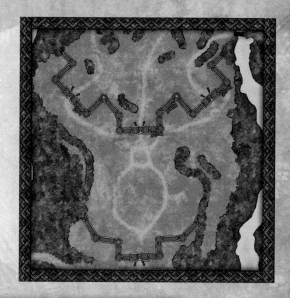

RvR LEGEND

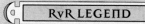

RvR Area (Outlined)

 Major Landmarks
2 – Career Trainers

REIKWALD GATEKEEPERS AND THEIR MASTIFFS GUARD THE GATES. IF YOU'RE ON THE SIDE OF DESTRUCTION, EXPECT TO GET DOUBLE-TEAMED BY THESE PAIRS SHOULD YOU GET TOO CLOSE.

REIKWALD IS THE PINNACLE OF THE EMPIRE'S STRENGTH, BUILT AFTER THE LAST INCURSION OF CHAOS. THE STREETS ARE A MAZE DESIGNED TO DRIVE EVEN THOSE INFLICTED WITH A STIGMATA OF INSANITY OVER THE EDGE. IT IS EASY FOR THOSE WHO DON'T KNOW THEIR WAY TO GET LOST IN THE WARREN OF STREETS. THE LAND OUTSIDE THE WALLS HAS BEEN CLEARED TO MAKE IT A KILLING FIELD. THE CENTER GATE GIVES THE BEST ATTACK ROUTE TO THE KEEP, BUT IT'S THE MOST HEAVILY DEFENDED.

ATTACKS ON THE CITY OF ALTDORF CAN BE LED IN THREE REGIONS, THOUGH REIKWALD HOLDS THE DIRECT ENTRANCE TO ALTDORF. THE REIKWALD REGION IS GUARDED BY THE EMPIRE. DESTRUCTION CAN USE LONG RANGE PADS AND RAM PADS TO ATTACK IN THIS REGION.

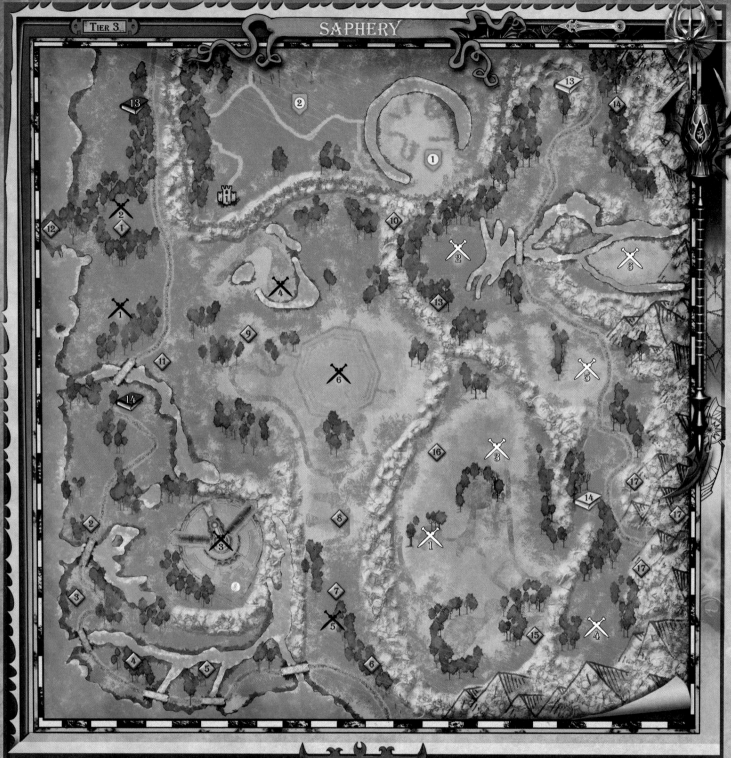

SAPHERY

TIER 3.

LEGEND

CHAPTER UNLOCK (DESTRUCTION)
13 – Dark Elf Chapter 13
14 – Dark Elf Chapter 14

CHAPTER UNLOCK (ORDER)
13 – High Elf Chapter 13
14 – High Elf Chapter 14

MAJOR LANDMARKS
1 – Whitemoon Manor
2 – Ransacked Caravan
3 – Arkaneth Devastator Camp
4 – Darkseer's Camp
5 – Stormweaver's Approach
6 – Turncoat's Hiding Place
7 – Arkaneth Officer Camp
8 – Starsight Mansion
9 – Mansion of Evermourn
10 – Gryphon Hatcheries
11 – Gryphon Training Camp
12 – Main Patroller Camp
13 – Stormfire's Tower
14 – Menhir Stone
15 – Dark Rider Patroller Camp

16 – Greenskin Encampment
17 – Mushroomin' Caverns

PUBLIC QUESTS (DESTRUCTION)
1 – Recompense
2 – Whitemoon Manor
3 – White Tower of Hoeth
4 – Trial by Fire
5 – House of Cards
6 – Ghyran's Embrace

RvR AREA (OUTLINED)

PUBLIC QUESTS (ORDER)
1 – Against All Odds
2 – Circle of the Winds
3 – Hall of the Crimson Shroud
4 – Sweating the Stone
5 – Ithilmar Tower
6 – Thanon Hall

BATTLE OBJECTIVES
1 – The Spire of Teclis (Healing Boon)
2 – Sari'Daroir (Defensive Boon)

1 – Well of Qhaysh

ORDER ENTRANCE
(FROM AVELORN
RvR AREA)

DESTRUCTION
ENTRANCE

DESTRUCTION
ENTRANCE

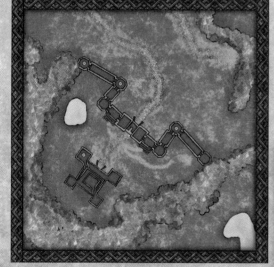

RvR LEGEND

 RvR Area (Outlined)

 Battle Objectives
1 – Spire of Teclis
   (Healing Boon)
2 – Sari'Daroir
   (Defensive Boon)

1 – Well of Qhaysh

Placed out in the middle of the forest, Sari' Daroir will be almost impossible to defend without either better tactics or raw numbers. It has no walls to hide behind and lies completely open to the world, so defending is challenging.

From above, attackers can choose different directions to enter the battlefield, splitting their forces and hopefully confusing its defenses. Attackers and defenders alike can come down the nice paths or possibly just fall down the small cliffs on the side for a shortcut. It won't be pretty but it won't kill you and might be quicker.

High walls and high hills surround the Well of Qhaysh, meaning any assaulters will pay for their efforts. It's outfitted generously by the High Elves, so any who undertake a siege on this keep better be ready to fight for it.

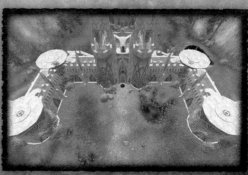

TIER 2

THE SHADOWLANDS

TO CHRACE

TO CHRACE

TO ELLYRION

TO ELLYRION

TO ELLYRION

LEGEND

WARCAMPS: 1 – BLADEWATCH   1 – OATH'S END

RvR AREA (OUTLINED)

CHAPTER UNLOCK (DESTRUCTION)
5 – DARK ELF CHAPTER 5
6 – DARK ELF CHAPTER 6
7 – DARK ELF CHAPTER 7

CHAPTER UNLOCK (ORDER)
5 – HIGH ELF CHAPTER 5
6 – HIGH ELF CHAPTER 6
7 – HIGH ELF CHAPTER 7

MAJOR LANDMARKS
1 – SHRINE OF REMEMBERANCE
2 – SEA CAVERN
3 – SERYNAL
4 – LAURILION CAVERNS
    (NORTH ENTRANCE)

5 – LAURILION CAVERNS
    (SOUTH ENTRANCE)
6 – DEATH'S WIND CAVERN
7 – DREAD LAKE
8 – ELBISAR
9 – SHADE ENCAMPMENT
10 – HARPIES
11 – DARK RIDER ENCLAVE
12 – WITCH ELF PRISONER CAMP
13 – CORSAIR BEACH CAMP
14 – ARKANETH TOWER
15 – PILLAGED HIGH ELF CAMP
16 – WILD COLD ONES
17 – SHADOW WARRIOR CAMP
18 – BLACKGUARD FORT

PUBLIC QUESTS (DESTRUCTION)
1 – OUT OF THE SHADOWS
2 – ROCK OF GALIRIAN
3 – RUINS OF ANLEC
4 – GLOOMRIDGE CLOPSE
5 – JAGGED COAST
6 – RUINS OF NAGARYTHE
7 – DAWN'S EARLY FIGHT
8 – STONE OF ECELSION
9 – GRIFFON GATE

PUBLIC QUESTS (ORDER)
1 – LAURILION CAVES
2 – MIRELEN
3 – COLD HEARTED PREDATORS
4 – FORGOTTEN FUTURE

5 – LAIR OF THE DEAD
6 – DRAGON GATE
7 – BROKEN DUNE
8 – BROKEN SPIRITS
9 – PREEMPTIVE STRIKE

BATTLE OBJECTIVES
1 – DRAGONSCALE TOWER
    (ARTISAN'S GIFT)
2 – DRAGON SIEGE CAMP
    (MERCHANT'S GIFT)

1 – SPITE'S REACH

FLIGHT MASTER

NEUTRAL ENTRANCE

NEUTRAL ENTRANCE

ORDER ENTRANCE

DESTRUCTION ENTRANCE

NEUTRAL ENTRANCE

TO ELLYRION

MULTIPLE PATHS INTO DRAGON SIEGE CAMP, PLUS THE HIGH MOUNTAIN PATHS SURROUNDING IT, MAKE THIS OBJECTIVE VERY HARD TO EFFECTIVELY DEFEND WITHOUT A GOOD-SIZED FORCE. IT LEAVES ANY DEFENSE WIDE OPEN WITH ALMOST NO TACTICALLY ADVANTAGEOUS SPOTS.

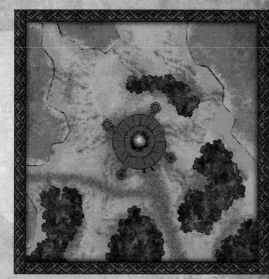

A SMALL SIDE CLIFF GIVES A SECOND OPTION FOR ATTACKERS BUT STILL DOES NOT PROVIDE MUCH IN THE LINE OF CONCEALMENT. DEFENSE SHOULD BE SMARTLY WATCHING BOTH ENTRANCES.

RvR LEGEND

WARCAMPS:

 1 = BLADEWATCH

 1 = OATH'S END

 RvR AREA (OUTLINED)

 BATTLE OBJECTIVES
1 – DRAGONSCALE TOWER (ARTISAN'S GIFT)
2 – DRAGON SIEGE CAMP (MERCHANT'S GIFT)

 1 – SPITE'S REACH

 FLIGHT MASTER

ONCE THE KEEP DOOR IS BREACHED, ATTACKERS NEED TO FUNNEL INTO THE MAIN CORRIDOR AND FACE THE KEEP'S NPC DEFENSES AS WELL AS THE OPPOSING FORCES. A BACK DOOR MAKES IT EASY FOR DEFENSES TO SLIP IN AND OUT WITHOUT RUNNING INTO THE ATTACKERS. ATTACK FORCES NEED TO KEEP AN EYE ON THIS DOOR, AS WELL TO HOLD OFF ANY ADDITIONAL DEFENSES GETTING INSIDE.

TIER 4

SHINING WAY

TO EATAINE

LEGEND

RvR Area (Outlined)

Portals
1 – To Stonewatch
2 – To Reikland
3 – To Stonewatch

DESTRUCTION
ENTRANCE

TO EATAINE

ORDER
ENTRANCE

RvR LEGEND

〰〰〰 RvR Area (Outlined)

◆ Portals
1 – To Stonewatch
2 – To Reikland
3 – To Stonewatch

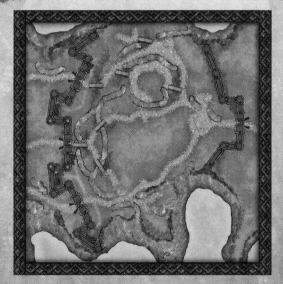

Attacks on the city of
Altdorf can be led in three
regions. The Shining Way
region is guarded by the
High Elves. The forces of
Destruction can use ranged
pads and ram pads to attack
in this region.

Shining Way seems to have been called
forth into existence simply to support
the elegant grace of the High Elves,
but these wall have the sturdiness of
the earth itself. You will find this
city set high overlooking the valley,
and attackers who are overly bold and
breach the walls will find the inside
a deadly funnel. There is little room
to stand before the keep gate, and the
bridges are choke points of death.

TIER 4

STONEWATCH

LEGEND

RvR Area (Outlined)

 Portals
1 – To Shining Way
2 – Cave Portal
3 – To Reikwald

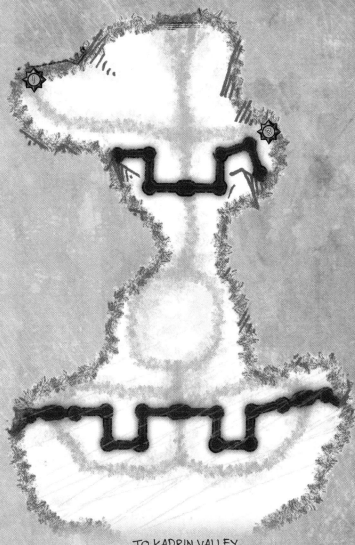

If you manage to brave the frostbite to reach this fortress, Stonewatch's massive walls will keep you at bay for a long while. The front gates are a force to be reckoned with.

TO KADRIN VALLEY

RvR LEGEND

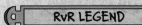 RvR Area (Outlined)

  Portals
1 – To Shining Way
3 – To Reikwald

Even should you penetrate Stonewatch's outer wall, you then have to deal with the very well-defended inner keep. Deal with all the outer defenses first before you attempt the final structure.

TO HIGH PASS

TO TROLL COUNTRY

TO REIKLAND

LEGEND

 WARCAMPS: 1 – Hellfang Ridge

RvR Area (Outlined)

Chapter Unlock (Destruction)
10 – Chaos Chapter 10
11 – Chaos Chapter 11
12 – Chaos Chapter 12

Chapter Unlock (Order)
13 – Empire Chapter 13
14 – Empire Chapter 14

Major Landmarks
1 – Griffin camps
2 – Join the Hunt
3 – Stags and Hounds

4 – Tower of the Fallen
5 – Road to Reikland
6 – Unterbaum
7 – Blackhorn Herdstone
8 – Chaos Landing
9 – Talabecland Troops
10 – Talabecland Bandits
11 – Horned Tower
12 – Ambushing Marauders
13 – Shrine of Sigmar
14 – Bell Tower
15 – Dortwald
16 – Bell Tower
17 – Bell Tower

Public Quests (Destruction)
1 – Serpent's Fang Bandits
2 – Army of Faith
3 – Suderheim
4 – Steinbruck Manor
5 – Mudflats
6 – Bitterspring
7 – Kruegerhaus
8 – Village Vermin
9 – Knightly Riders

Public Quests (Order)
1 – Meuselbach Farm
2 – Unterbaum Castle
3 – Unterbaum Cemetery

4 – Bitterschaum Swamp
5 – Witch Fire Glade
6 – Wagon Defense

 Battle Objectives
1 – Verentane's Tower
(Merchant's Gift)

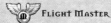 1 – Passwatch Castle

 Flight Master

Attackers at Passwatch Castle have a nicely set up medium ranged pads on top of a ridge with a good vantage point for killing the defenders.

Passwatch Castle is at the north part of Talabecland zone. A medium oil pad over the main entrance is perfect for defenders, along with medium ranged pads for additional support around the castle walls.

neutral entrance   **neutral entrance**   **neutral entrance**

destruction entrance   **destruction entrance**

destruction entrance

RvR Legend

Warcamps:

 I — Hellfang Ridge

RvR Area (Outlined)

Battle Objectives
I — Verentane's Tower (Merchant's Gift)

I — Passwatch Castle

Flight Master

Just when you think the hard work is over after dispatching the outer wall defenders, you have to tackle in the inner fortress. Watch which side the defenders are concentrated on, and circle around the outer edge of the plateau to attack from surprise.

This objective is just outside Passwatch Castle, so that makes it easier for the owner of the castle to occupy Verentane's Tower.

A winding stairwell leads toward the middle of the tower where the battlefield objective rests.

TIER 4

THUNDER MOUNTAIN

TO KADRIN VALLEY

TO CINDERFALL

TO DEATH PEAK

TO BLACK CRAG

LEGEND

Warcamps: 1 – Kagrund's Stand   1 – Mudja Warcamp

 RvR Area (Outlined)

Chapter Unlock (Destruction)
17 – Greenskin Chapter 17
18 – Greenskin Chapter 18
19 – Greenskin Chapter 19

Chapter Unlock (Order)
17 – Dwarf Chapter 17
18 – Dwarf Chapter 18
19 – Dwarf Chapter 19

Major Landmarks
1 – Nuffin' Eve
2 – Dragon's Breath Cave

3 – Ungdrin Ankor Tunnel
4 – Karak Palik
5 – Lava Flow Mine
6 – Moonfang Mine
7 – Ruins of Mingol Kurdak
8 – Field of Bone
9 – Bloodmaw Cave
10 – Ashhide Tunnel
11 – Nackrender's Warband

Public Quests (Destruction)
1 – Und-a-Runki
2 – Reichert's Raiders
3 – Gutbashed Goblins
4 – Ruins of Mingol Kurdak

Public Quests (Order)
1 – Dragon's Blessing
2 – Red with Envy
3 – Ungry Ungry Greenskins
4 – Ankul Grob

Battle Objectives
1 – Karak Palik (Merchant's Gift)
2 – Doomstriker Vein (Artisan's Gift, Underground)
3 – Thargrim's Headwall (Defensive Boon)
4 – Gromril Kruk (Healing Boon, Underground)

 1 – Blood-fist Rock
2 – Karak Karag

 Flight Master

Karak Palik has three paths leading up to it, and will be very hard to defend against a determined foe.

TO KADRIN VALLEY

NEUTRAL ENTRANCE

DESTRUCTION ENTRANCE

ORDER ENTRANCE

ORDER ENTRANCE

DESTRUCTION ENTRANCE

DESTRUCTION ENTRANCE

NEUTRAL ENTRANCE

TO BLACK CRAG

RvR LEGEND

Warcamps:

1 – Greymere Point

1 – Mudja Warcamp

RvR Area (Outlined)

Battle Objectives
1 – Karak Palik
   (Merchant's Gift)
2 – Doomstriker Vein
   (Artisan's Gift, Underground)
3 – Thargrim's Headwall
   (Defensive Boon)
4 – Gromril Kruk
   (Healing Boon, Underground)

1 – Bloodfist Rock
2 – Karak Karag

Flight Master

TROLL COUNTRY

Tier 2

TO TALABECLAND

TO OSTLAND

LEGEND

Warcamps: I – Brickbramble Hollow

Chapter Unlock (Destruction)
6 – Chaos Chapter 6
8 – Chaos Chapter 8
9 – Chaos Chapter 9

Chapter Unlock (Order)
5 – Empire Chapter 5
6 – Empire Chapter 6

Major Landmarks
1 – Suskarg Caves (cave)
2 – The Troll Rift (cave)
3 – Corrupted Wolflord
4 – Ragnhilder's Hut
5 – Den
6 – Plague Graves
7 – Eagle's Nests

8 – Deeprock Mine
9 – Grant's Lair
10 – Soulblight Cultists
11 – Shiver Hollow
12 – Iceflow Maw
13 – Frozen Cavern
14 – Ogre Hunters
15 – Blightgore

Public Quests (Destruction)
1 – Trovoler
2 – Plaguewood Thicket
3 – Lursa's Blight
4 – Blightstone Trolls
5 – Plague Altar
6 – Tearing the Portal
7 – Bog Hunters
8 – Griffon Outpost

Public Quests (Order)
1 – Welcome to Troll Country
2 – Plague on the Wind
3 – Deathstone Quarry
4 – Blighted Farm
5 – Grave Diggers
6 – Slayer's Demise
7 – Lissariel's Glade
8 – Plague Trolls

Battle Objectives
1 – Ruins of Greystone Keep (Merchant's Gift)
2 – Monastery of Morr (Defensive Boon)

RvR Area (Outlined)

Lairs
I – Metoh

I – Stonetroll Keep

Flight Master

BLACKBRAMBLE HOLLOW, THE EMPIRE WARCAMP, IS DIRECTLY EAST OF THE MONASTERY OF MORR. IT HAS MERCHANTS, A FLIGHT MASTER, AND SUPPLIES NEEDED FOR BATTLE. USE THIS AS A STAGING AREA FOR ATTACKS ON THE MONASTERY OF MORR.

THIS BATTLEFIELD OBJECTIVE LIES IN THE CENTER OF A CEMETERY. THE MONASTERY OF MORR IS IN A CLEARING WITH NUMEROUS WAYS TO GET IN. THIS OBJECTIVE WILL BE DIFFICULT TO DEFEND.

① ORDER ENTRANCE

NEUTRAL ENTRANCE

NEUTRAL ENTRANCE

DESTRUCTION ENTRANCE

NEUTRAL ENTRANCE

NEUTRAL ENTRANCE

②

TO OSTLAND

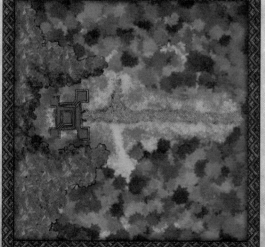

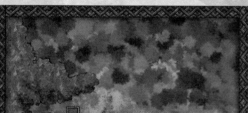

RvR LEGEND

WARCAMPS:

1 – BRICKBRAMBLE HOLLOW

 RvR AREA (OUTLINED)

 BATTLE OBJECTIVES
1 – RUINS OF GREYSTONE KEEP (MERCHANT'S GIFT)
2 – MONASTERY OF MORR (DEFENSIVE BOON)

 1 – STONETROLL KEEP

 FLIGHT MASTER

STONETROLL KEEP IS AT THE SOUTHWEST CORNER OF TROLL COUNTRY ZONE. IT HAS ONE LIGHT OIL PAD OVER THE ONLY MAIN ENTRANCE WITH TWO LIGHT RANGED PADS ON EITHER SIDE OF IT. WITHOUT ANY WALLS SURROUNDING THIS KEEP, IT WILL BE TOUGH TO DEFEND. ATTACKERS WILL HAVE AN EASIER TIME WITH THEIR SIEGE WITH ONE LIGHT RAM PAD AT THE ENTRANCE AND TWO LIGHT RANGED PADS TO KEEP THE PRESSURE ON THE DEFENDERS.

Tier 4

WEST PRAAG

LEGEND

 Major Landmarks
1 – Sundered Pistoliers
2 – Dwarf Mines
3 – Cave
4 – Dark Banner
5 – Blacktalon Camp
6 – Tower (Scouts/Olaf Bloodrunner)
7 – Cave

 Public Quests (Destruction)
1 – Sundered Fortress
2 – Chasing Shadows

 Public Quests (Order)
1 – Sundered Fortress
2 – Unlikely Allies
3 – Screaming Daemons

SCENARIOS

In seconds, the thrill of adrenalin will be pumping through your veins and glory is right around the corner. For those who love fast-paced, in-your-face, player vs. player combat, seek out scenarios for excitement, experience, and extra Renown points.

A scenario is a queued-up battle zone or instance. To join a scenario, you can do two things: Go into an RvR area and get flagged, then wait for a window to pop up asking to join, or click on the scenario icon on the left side of the mini-map (in top right of your screen). The latter option gives a zperson the ability to do quests while waiting for other

GATES OF EKRUND

players to fill up the scenario. Once enough players from both sides have signed up, a window pops open asking if you're ready to join the scenario. If you are, enter the scenario; you temporarily disappear from your current location in the world, then reappear in the exact same spot once you exit the scenario.

As you journey around the world, you will discover many different types of scenarios:

- Capture the Flag: Capture the enemy's flag and bring it back to your base.

- Death Match: Kill the other side.

- King of the Hill: Strategic areas where one has to gain control for a set amount of time.

- War Ball: This is similar to Capture the Flag, except there is one artifact that both teams must grab and hold. Some artifacts give bonus damage, which can prove to be fatal for the enemy.

GROMRIL CROSSING

NORDENWATCH

All scenarios end after a short time. Depending on the scenario, this can be anywhere from 10 minutes to 20 minutes. All scenarios are score-based up to 500 points. You gain points for your side by doing various things within the scenarios, such as killing players or possessing an artifact. You win if you have the most points at the end of the scenario time limit, or if your team gets to 500 points first.

All scenarios have a universal resurrection timer. In other words, when you die, you may be able to resurrect within a few seconds or you may have to wait a bit (up to 30 seconds). However, if a buddy resurrects you, you are back in action immediately.

Within the scenarios, realms are represented by colors. Red is Destruction. Blue is Order. White is Neutral. All scenarios are bracketed to pit you against players of relatively the same rank, and all scenarios have a population cap. For the most part, this ranges from 12-on-12 to 24-on-24.

So strap on your boots, sheathe your pointiest weapon, and use those fingers of yours to flip through the following pages. In this Scenarios chapter, you'll find detailed, labeled maps with everything from spawn points

REIKLAND HILLS

to artifact locations to attack routes. Read up on each side's scenario strategies and absorb some RvR tips to turn you into a formidable and fluid artisan of WAR.

HIGH PASS CEMETERY

Even at Rank 1, scenarios are great to join. What about balance and going against a Rank 10? Well, if you're a Rank 1, you advance to about Rank 8. A new character would have their health increased to that of a Rank 8, thus a Rank 1 becomes as powerful as a Rank 8 and can compete easily.

TALABEC DAM

BLACKFIRE BASIN

OVERVIEW

The Battle of Black Fire was a most important event. History saw the founding of the Empire through that great battle, with Sigmar anointed its first Emperor, and the oath sworn by the Dwarf king that the eastern borders of the lands of men would suffer no attack from an enemy force.

In the Age of Reckoning, Black Fire Basin will once again be the site of epic battles. Control of the pass is key to the defense of the Empire's southlands, now largely undefended as the bulk of the Empire's army has marched north to meet the onrushing Chaos warhost. The pass also figures into the plans of Warlord Grumlok, who wishes to secure it so that greenskin tribes to the north and west can join the *Waaagh!* without the need to cross over the mountains.

ORDER STRATEGY

This is a classic battle of Capture the Flag. You need to grab the enemy's flag and bring it back to your flag, which must be sitting in its home spot, to earn points. The number-one rule: Work together as a team. If you go running off on your own, you simply weaken the group's strength in numbers. You will either be staging a run on the enemy's flag or defending your own flag at all times; do not get caught in the middle of the map, Deadman's Dell, fighting other players, even though this avenue might seem the quickest. Your spawn point is in the southwest corner, so take the western ledge to reach the enemy's flag quickest. Always keep an eye out on what's going on around your flag and try to spot the enemy's position on the opposite ledges to alert your team of incoming attacks.

DESTRUCTION STRATEGY

This is a classic battle of Capture the Flag. You need to grab the enemy's flag and bring it back to your flag, which must be sitting in its home spot, to earn points. The number-one rule: Work together as a team. If you go running off on your own, you simply weaken the group's strength in numbers. You will either be staging a run on the enemy's flag or defending your own flag at all times; do not get caught in the middle of the map, Deadman's Dell, fighting other players, even though this avenue might seem the quickest. Your spawn point is in the northeast corner, so take the eastern ledge to reach the enemy's flag quickest. Always keep an eye out on what's going on around your flag and try to spot the enemy's position on the opposite ledges to alert your team of incoming attacks.

RvR TIP

Keep your distance from the front of the battle unless you are pure melee.

LOCATION: BLACK FIRE PASS (TIER 3)

ELIGIBLE RANKS: 20-30

SCENARIO TYPE: CAPTURE THE FLAG

SIZE: 12 ON 12

TIME LIMIT: 15 MINUTES

VICTORY CONDITIONS: 500 POINTS

SCORING: 1 POINT PER PLAYER KILL, 75 POINTS FOR CAPTURING ENEMY FLAG

BLACKFIRE BASIN

Use the side paths

Don't get stuck fighting in the middle!

BLOOD OF BLACKCAIRN

OVERVIEW

During the time of the Sundering, two sons of Lord Bloodcairn, Elthryril and Lothelryel, were divided on the decision of whom to follow. Elthryril supported the Phoenix King, while Lothelryel hungered after the power Malekith had promised his followers. Working closely with a hag, Morathi, at the Nagarythe court, Lothelryel was soon presented with a solution to his problem: a magical binding that, once triggered, would hold his brother outside of time, until the spell was undone.

No sooner had Lothelryel returned to his family's estate than he put his plan into action. Calling his brother to the practice ground, Lothelryel challenged him to a duel for control of the family. Elthryril agreed. Hidden among the carefully tended greenery surrounding the courtyard were the components of the ward.

Lothelryel struck first, opening a gash in his brother's side, followed so closely by Elthryril's answering thrust that the two brothers almost seemed to bleed as one. And with the spilling of blood, the ward flared into action, trapping both brothers within. For Lothelryel had been deceived; the ward Morathi had so thoughtfully designed was not in fact meant to serve his purposes, but hers. Instead of acting as a stasis prison the ward would trap the awareness, the soul, of its blood-bound victims. Worse still the spell had been constructed to magnify emotions, twisting and reflecting them back upon those trapped within. Not just a prison, but a breaking ground. And both brothers were powerless to stop it.

Fueled by the power of the initial binding, the spell continued to magnify the brothers' shared rage until the emotion was almost a living thing spreading eager claws out across the family lands. To this day, the Blackcairn estate is viewed as a place of ill omen, for none may pass through untouched by the brooding cloud of hatred that remains.

ORDER STRATEGY

There are three capture points in this scenario. Only one area will be active at a time, and it only stays active for two minutes before shutting down and another capture point becomes active. Capture points become active randomly. Because the only way to gain points is through control—player kills do not count—you should break into two strong teams and control two of the three capture points at all times. If you can, this will ensure that your chance of gaining points is greater than the enemy's. Order begins on the north side, so head south out of your three exit points and swarm the northeast (closest) and west capture points. If resistance seems weaker at the third capture point, you can swing around to capture that spot, but you don't want to get caught running around in circles without gaining points.

DESTRUCTION STRATEGY

There are three capture points in this scenario. Only one area will be active at a time, and it only stays active for two minutes before shutting down and another capture point becomes active. Capture points become active randomly. Because the only way to gain points is through control—player kills do not count—you should break into two strong teams and control two of the three capture points at all times. If you can, this will ensure that your chance of gaining points is greater than the enemy's. Destruction begins on the south side, so head north out of your three exit points and swarm the southeast (closest) and west capture points. If resistance seems weaker at the third capture point, you can swing around to capture that spot, but you don't want to get caught running around in circles without gaining points.

RvR TIP

Use max range on weapons. Do this and you will always attack your enemy, but they may not be able to attack you back.

LOCATION: HIGH ELVES VS. DARK ELVES (TIER 4)

ELIGIBLE RANKS: APPROXIMATELY 30–40

SCENARIO TYPE: KING OF THE HILL

SIZE: 12 ON 12

TIME LIMIT: 15 MINUTES

VICTORY CONDITIONS: 500 POINTS

SCORING: 2 POINTS EVERY 5 SECONDS FOR HOLDING AN ACTIVE CAPTURE POINT

BLACK CAIRN

Multiple spawn point exits

3 capture rotating king of the Hill

CALEDOR WOODS

LOCATION: CALEDOR

ELIGIBLE RANKS: TIER 4 (APPROXIMATELY RANK 30–40)

SCENARIO TYPE: KING OF THE HILL

SIZE: 12 ON 12

TIME LIMIT: 15 MINUTES

VICTORY CONDITIONS: 500 POINTS

SCORING: 2 POINTS PER PLAYER KILL, 3 POINTS EVERY 5 SECONDS FOR HOLDING THE ONLY CAPTURE POINT

OVERVIEW

Deep inside the zone of Caledor, with very lush patches of underbrush and large redwood trees, Caledor Woods stretches out magnificently. The conflict will take place mostly in the scenario's main valley, and a single capture point serves as the basis for a serious game of "King of the Hill."

ORDER STRATEGY

You have lots of cover options in this scenario. Trees, bluffs, bushes can all be used to conceal your location and block line of sight. If you rely on ranged attacks, you may have to be quick on your feet to keep a good angle on your opponent. Watch out for ambush spots; there are many hidden through the woods. As an organized group, hug the right border from your spawn point and head for the capture point in the middle of the battlefield. It's going to be one massive scrum for control, so whichever team coordinates the best will be victorious.

DESTRUCTION STRATEGY

You have lots of cover options in this scenario. Trees, bluffs, bushes can all be used to conceal your location and block line of sight. If you rely on ranged attacks, you may have to be quick on your feet to keep a good angle on your opponent. Watch out for ambush spots; there are many hidden through the woods. As an organized group, hug the left border from your spawn point and head for the capture point in the middle of the battlefield. It's going to be one massive scrum for control, so whichever team coordinates the best will be victorious.

RvR TIP

Use obstacles. Hide behind them so foes cannot attack you.

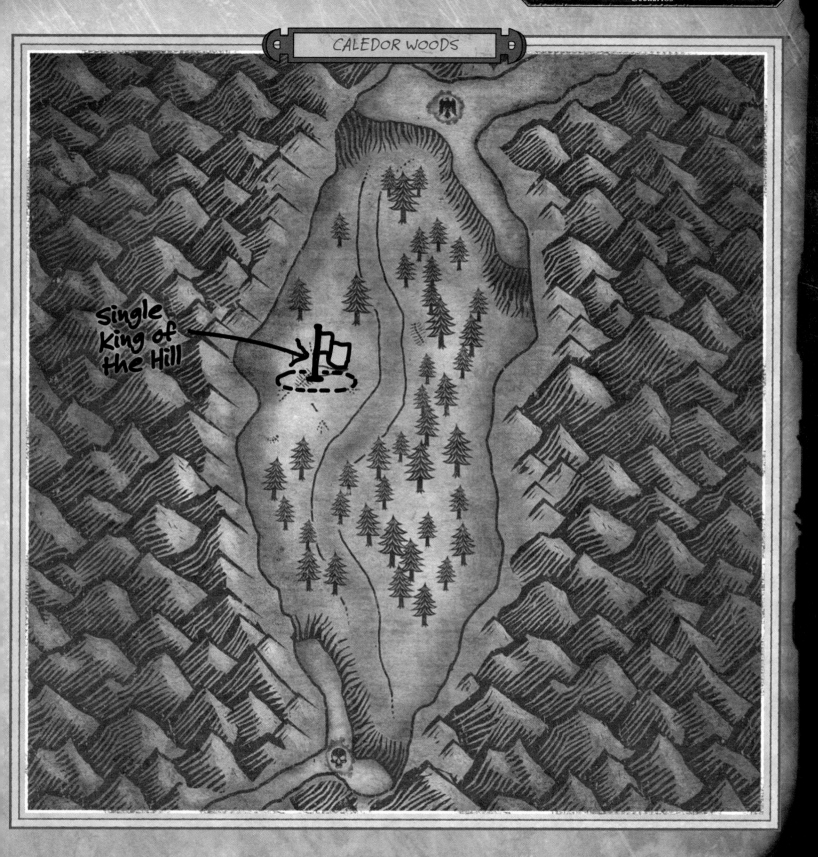

CALEDOR WOODS

Single King of the Hill

DOOMFIST CRATER

Overview

Doomfist Crater dominates the horizon in the southwest area of the Badlands; it is the ancient site of a pitched battle in which a powerful Chaos champion was slain. The resulting explosion as his body released all the stored up Chaos energy was large enough to level mountains. Deep within the crater, now filled with green, toxic waters, the champion's remains have rested for thousands of years, his bones infused with tiny bits of warpstone. Over the top of the crater's epicenter, goblins have constructed floating platforms, connected to the crater's edge by rickety bridges. From these platforms, the goblins are dredging up bits of warpstone for nefarious purposes.

The scenario mixes King of the Hill rules with War Ball. There is one central capture area, and if you can hold it, your team gains the most points over time. However, if your team controls the capture area, War Balls spawn for the other team around the cavern. These War Balls grant the bearer 25 percent more damage. Unfortunately, each player killed with a War Ball results in a 25 percent chance of the bearer dying as well. After one minute, no matter what, the player carrying the War Ball dies.

Order Strategy

Proceed to the center of the cavern as an organized unit. The only way to hold the central capture area is with coordinated tactics or raw superior numbers. The capture area is wide open, so attacks can come from any direction. If you're holding it, face outward, ready for anything, and work in small groups to repel invaders. Healers should stay in the middle and load available targets, specifically ones being targeted, with heal-over-time spells. If you're assaulting the capture area, grab the War Balls whenever they pop up; they may kill you quickly, but the extra damage is what you need to punch through the enemy's defenses and rout them. Finally, learn the map well. You don't want to waste time running around, and memorize that your spawn point is directly west of the capture point so that you can reach it in seconds should you resurrect.

Destruction Strategy

Proceed to the center of the cavern as an organized unit. The only way to hold the central capture area is with coordinated tactics or raw superior numbers. The capture area is wide open, so attacks can come from any direction. If you're holding it, face outward, ready for anything, and work in small groups to repel invaders. Healers should stay in the middle and load available targets, specifically ones being targeted, with heal-over-time spells. If you're assaulting the capture area, grab the War Balls whenever they pop up; they may kill you quickly, but the extra damage is what you need to punch through the enemy's defenses and rout them. Finally, learn the map well. You don't want to waste time running around, and memorize that your spawn point is directly north of the capture point so that you can reach it in seconds should you resurrect.

RvR Tip

Use height to your advantage. If there are stairs, go up them and shoot up there. It takes enemies longer to reach you.

LOCATION: BADLANDS (TIER 3)

ELIGIBLE RANKS: 23–40

SCENARIO TYPE: WAR BALL

SIZE: 12 ON 12

TIME LIMIT: 15 MINUTES

VICTORY CONDITIONS: 500 POINTS

SCORING: 3 POINTS EVERY 5 SECONDS FOR HOLDING CAPTURE AREA, 2 POINTS PER PLAYER KILL, 1 POINT PER PLAYER KILL IF YOU HOLD A WAR BALL, 1 POINT IF YOU KILL THE PLAYER CARRYING THE WAR BALL

Elevated capture point is very hard to capture without extra damage from Warballs.

Warballs spawn opposite of owner of capture point.

Center Area Captures

DRAGON'S BANE

LOCATION: DRAGONWAKE (TIER 4)

ELIGIBLE RANKS: APPROXIMATELY RANK 30–40

SCENARIO TYPE: KING OF THE HILL

SIZE: 18 ON 18

TIME LIMIT: 15 MINUTES

VICTORY CONDITIONS: 500 POINTS

SCORING: 3 POINTS PER PLAYER KILL, 1 POINT EVERY 2 SECONDS FOR HOLDING A CAPTURE POINT (THERE ARE 3 SEPARATE CAPTURE POINTS)

OVERVIEW

Are you ready to play with dragons? In this scenario, you can summon the power of a dragon down on your enemy! There are three capture points spread evenly through the map: Commorancy (north), Academy (center), and Summoning Tower (south). There are also two flags: one to the east of the Academy and one to the west, both directly in front of the teams' respective spawn points.

Teams earn points for holding the capture points. Unlike other scenarios where it's up to your team's own firepower to dislodge enemies from a capture point, Dragon's Bane gives you a little help. If you take a flag to one of the enemy capture points, you can call down a dragon to assist you in retaking the capture point. Let the fires begin!

ORDER STRATEGY

All your objectives lie to the east. You can follow the road to your right to seize the Summoning Tower, or take the road to the left to grab the Commorancy. The quickest route, however, will be straight ahead to the Academy, on the island at the map's center. Load up two strong teams and pick two objectives, or rush one with a huge group, control it, then move on to the next nearby capture point (leaving a competent defensive crew behind to guard the first capture point, of course). You must control two of the three capture points to ultimately win the scenario. If you fall behind, grab a flag and use the dragon power to your advantage to quickly storm another capture point.

DESTRUCTION STRATEGY

All your objectives lie to the west. You can follow the road to your right to seize the Commorancy, or take the road to the left to grab the Summoning Tower. The quickest route, however, will be straight ahead to the Academy, on the island at the map's center. Load up two strong teams and pick two objectives, or rush one with a huge group, control it, then move on to the next nearby capture point (leaving a competent defensive crew behind to guard the first capture point, of course). You must control two of the three capture points to ultimately win the scenario. If you fall behind, grab a flag and use the dragon power to your advantage to quickly storm another capture point.

RvR TIP

The only way to get experience or Renown is to kill, so try assisting players and whittle someone down quicker.

DRAGON'S BANE

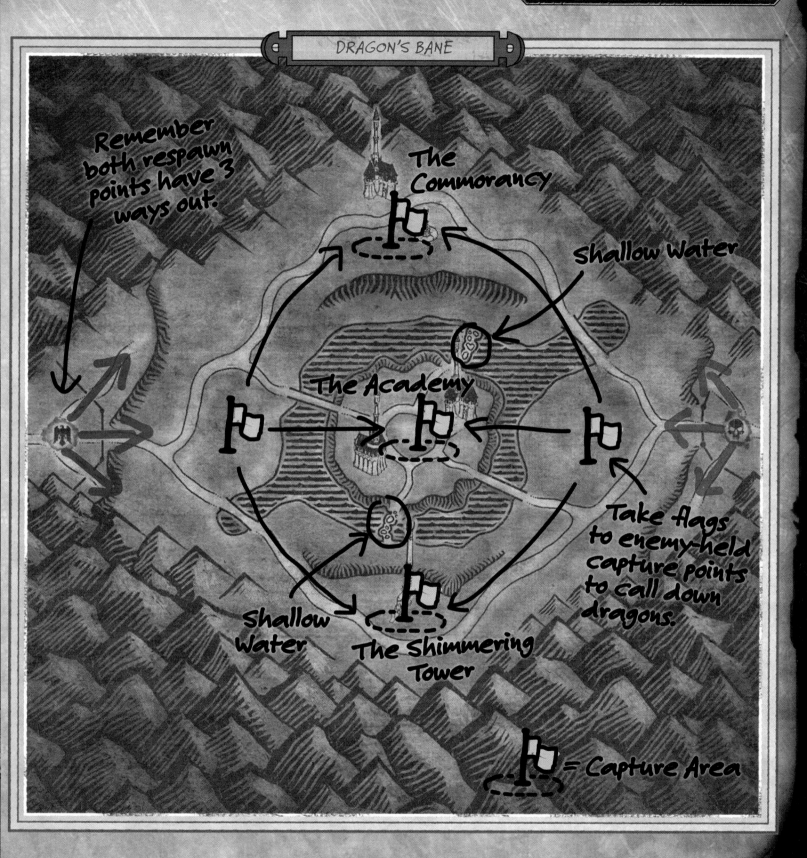

Remember both respawn points have 3 ways out.

The Commorancy

Shallow Water

The Academy

Take flags to enemy-held capture points to call down dragons.

Shallow Water

The Shimmering Tower

= Capture Area

GATES OF EKRUND

OVERVIEW

Ekrund has been overrun by greenskins. The Dwarfs have returned to Ekrund to take back their ancestral lands, but they must first secure the Gates to prevent more greenskins from flowing into the area. These ancient Gates guard the only mountain pass that is wide enough to accommodate an army. For the Dwarfs, recapturing these gates and sealing them shut is paramount to defeating the greenskin presence in Mount Bloodhorn. The Dwarfs have succeeded in repairing most of the damage to the Gates, but the greenskins remain relentless in their attempts to break through, if only to annoy the Dwarfs. The greenskins have no siege weaponry capable of damaging the doors, so they are forced to try to take control of the gate mechanism, located atop the gates. To accomplish this, the greenskins have erected siege towers that they use to climb to the top of the walls.

ORDER STRATEGY

There are three capture points, but your main priority is the central one: the Gate Switch. The huge gate lies between you and your opponent, so you won't know what they're up to right away. Your best bet is to gather one large force (or two if you plan on hitting two objectives simultaneously) and rush down the road to the stairs near the Ammo Cache. You can take the alternate route to the east and run along the path to reach the Supply Room too. When you reach the Gates, the path splits and you can go for the smaller capture point or drop down to the middle level to control the Gate Switch. Because the Gate Switch offers the most points, concentrate forces here if possible. With capture points secure, send out scouts to check on the enemy position and evaluate your next course of action without pulling valuable defenses away from an owned capture point.

DESTRUCTION STRATEGY

There are three capture points, but your main priority is the central one: the Gate Switch. The huge gate lies between you and your opponent, so you won't know what they're up to right away. Your best bet is to gather one large force (or two if you plan on hitting two objectives simultaneously) and rush down the road to the stairs near the Supply Room. You can take the alternate route to the west and run along the path to reach the Ammo Cache too. When you reach the Gates, the path splits and you can go for the smaller capture point or drop down to the middle level to control the Gate Switch. Because the Gate Switch offers the most points, concentrate forces here if possible. One trick the Destruction players can use is the mighty orcapults! Believe it or not, you can jump on them, release, and catapult onto the Gates!

RvR TIP

Keep enemy healers down and out of range of their teammates.

LOCATION: Ekrund

ELIGIBLE RANKS: I–II

SCENARIO TYPE: Capture the Flag

SIZE: 12 ON 12

TIME LIMIT: 15 MINUTES

VICTORY CONDITIONS: 500 POINTS

SCORING: HOLDING THE GATE SWITCH: 50 POINTS PER CAPTURE AND 2 POINTS EVERY 5 SECONDS, AMMUNITION CACHE: 50 POINTS PER CAPTURE AND 1 POINT EVERY 5 SECONDS, SUPPLY ROOM: 50 POINTS PER CAPTURE AND 1 POINTS EVERY 5 SECONDS, ENEMY KILLS: 1 POINT PER KILL PLUS MODIFIERS (+5 POINTS IF YOU CONTROL THE GATE SWITCH, +1 POINT FOR AMMUNITION CACHE, +1 POINT FOR SUPPLY ROOM)

GATES OF EKRUND

Alternate approach paths to get into the gate

3 Capture Locations

Use Orcapults to catapult onto the gate!

Alternate approach paths to get into the gate

GROMRIL CROSSING

OVERVIEW

The Gromril Spike is the name of the Dwarf train that runs through Kadrin Valley en route to the Empire. Greenskin ambushes along most of the major roads have made travel by cart more dangerous than usual, making the train one of the few reliable transportation methods still available.

Unfortunately, the greenskins have noticed the train regularly steaming through Kadrin Valley, and while they may fall short of actually understanding the true purpose of the massive locomotive, they do know that stopping it will anger the Dwarfs. That reason alone is more than good enough to explain why the greenskins have begun attacking the train.

To that end, the greenskins have set up several obstacles along the train's tracks, and they hope to slow the progress of the train enough that reinforcements arrive to help them capture the locomotive. The Dwarfs must defeat or bypass these obstacles before the greenskins can summon enough of their brethren to prevent the train from getting through at all.

ORDER STRATEGY

This is a traditional "Tug of War" battle. Both sides own two flags at the start, with the neutral Bridge flag in the middle. If you can take control of the Bridge, one of your enemy's flags becomes available, and if you take that, the flag farthest away, Da Camp, becomes your target. Capture that and you earn big points, plus steady points over time.

You have two exits from the spawn point: directly down into the fray, which takes you below the elevated Bridge flag, or through the tunnel, which wraps you around in a flanking position and deposits you near the Bridge flag. You definitely want to take the Bridge flag and push forward slowly, ensuring that you don't lose control of what you've gained. However, don't discount the player kills; they can add up, and will make the difference in a close match.

DESTRUCTION STRATEGY

This is a traditional "Tug of War" battle. Both sides own two flags at the start, with the neutral Bridge flag in the middle. If you can take control of the Bridge, one of your enemy's flags becomes available, and if you take that, the flag farthest away, Engine Number 9, becomes your target. Capture that and you earn big points, plus steady points over time.

You have two exits from the spawn point: directly down into the fray, which takes you below the elevated Bridge flag, or through the tunnel, which wraps you around in a flanking position and deposits you near the Bridge flag. You definitely want to take the Bridge flag and push forward slowly, ensuring that you don't lose control of what you've gained. However, don't discount the player kills; they can add up, and will make the difference in a close match.

RvR TIP

Better weapons mean more damage, and the more damage you do, the more experience and Renown you get.

LOCATION: KADRIN VALLEY (TIER 4)

ELIGIBLE RANKS: 30–40

SCENARIO TYPE: TUG OF WAR

SIZE: 18 ON 18

TIME LIMIT: 15 MINUTES

VICTORY CONDITIONS: 500 POINTS

SCORING: 5 POINTS PER PLAYER KILL, 50 POINTS FOR CAPTURING POINTS IN ENEMY TERRITORY, 40 POINTS FOR RECAPTURING POINTS IN YOUR TERRITORY, 1 POINT EVERY 2 SECONDS WHILE ORDER HOLDS DA CAMP, 1 POINT EVERY 2 SECONDS WHILE DESTRUCTION HOLDS ENGINE NUMBER 9

GROMRIL CROSSING

Remember that one capture point at a time is open!

Pile O' War Stuff

"Tug O' War" capture locations open in a chain one at a time.

Da' Base Camp

Use your tunnels to flank!

Bridge

Supply Depot

Engine Number 9

GROVOD CAVERNS

PER PLAYER KILL

Overview

You'll never look at Capture the Flag the same way again after playing through Grovod Caverns. It features the standard rules of Capture the Flag with one big twist. You still need to defend your flag while returning the enemy's flag to your home base to score points; however, when you return the enemy flag this time, one of the bridges spanning your home territory and the center of the map will crumble. Each side has five bridges, and with each flag capture, another bridge gets destroyed. This dramatically alters tactics. Attackers have a more difficult time assaulting your flag position with fewer bridges; at the same time, trying to cap an enemy flag will be tougher as you have fewer avenues to return and the enemy can camp them out better. If you get down to a single bridge, look out!

Order Strategy

Your battle plans should all be about quick, strategic moves, adjusting to the paths your enemy takes during the encounter and the paths that may suddenly vanish when one or more bridges collapse. A strong defense around your flag is always a good idea; just be careful not to wipe or your enemy will have an easy flag cap. Remember your side spawn paths, and use the outer paths as much as possible going to and from the flags because they offer the most cover. Avoid the center path because you're bound to run afoul of enemies. From your home vantage point you can see across the cavern to the flag on the west side.

Destruction Strategy

Your battle plans should all be about quick, strategic moves, adjusting to the paths your enemy takes during the encounter and the paths that may suddenly vanish when one or more bridges collapse. A strong defense around your flag is always a good idea; just be careful not to wipe or your enemy will have an easy flag cap. Remember your side spawn paths, and use the outer paths as much as possible going to and from the flags because they offer the most cover. Avoid the center path because you're bound to run afoul of enemies. From your home vantage point you can see across the cavern to the flag on the east side.

RvR Tip

Always think group first and not just go for points. Winning a scenario grants you double the experience of losing the scenario.

LOCATION: PRAAG (TIER 4)

ELIGIBLE RANKS: 30–40

SCENARIO TYPE: CAPTURE THE FLAG

SIZE: 12 ON 12

TIME LIMIT: 15 MINUTES

VICTORY CONDITIONS: 500 POINTS

SCORING: 75 POINTS FOR EACH FLAG CAPTURE, 2 POINTS

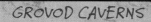

GROVOD CAVERNS

Grovod Caverns
CTF

Avoid zerging to
the center.

Alternate capture /
recapture route has lots
of cover.

Bridges destruct
on flag captures.

Remember your
other spawn point
exits!

HIGH PASS CEMETERY

LOCATION: HIGH PASS (TIER 3)

ELIGIBLE RANKS: 20–31

SCENARIO TYPE: KING OF THE HILL

SIZE: 12 ON 12

TIME LIMIT: 15 MINUTES

VICTORY CONDITIONS: 500 POINTS

SCORING: 75 POINTS IF BOTH CAPTURE POINT HELD, I POINT PER PLAYER KILL

OVERVIEW

Many decades ago, in a conflict for the ages, the soldiers of the Empire clashed with the barbarians of the north in a bloody battle. The leaders for each side strode through the melee to encounter one another. The combatants fell back to watch the mighty Champion and the courageous General engage in single combat, with each side cheering for its leader. After a hard-fought battle lasting for hours, the Champion of Chaos finally fell. The men of the Empire, inspired by the General's victory, surged forward and broke the enemy army.

Though he would live to see the victory, the General succumbed to his wounds later that day. His soldiers made camp and gathered stone. They buried their fallen comrades, marking each grave with a headstone. For their leader, the soldiers made a great cairn. Every man swore an oath that they would all return and build a proper cemetery to honor the dead and commemorate the victory. Many decades later, they did just that, and the High Pass Cemetery still stands as a rare landmark in the frozen wastes of the north.

Now, many years later, another battle is being fought in High Pass. The Order of the Griffon races north to capture the renegade Doctor Zumwald and learn the plans of his evil cult, which is responsible for the spread of the plague in the Empire. Zumwald seeks refuge in the lands of the Northmen, and the Changer of Ways sends his agents to protect the cult leader's retreat and drive back the soldiers of the Empire. At the High Pass Cemetery, the forces of Order and Destruction will clash, and they will find that in the Age of Reckoning, the spirits of the dead have been awakened by the winds of war.

ORDER STRATEGY

There are two capture points in this scenario: the Crypt to your far left and the Stag to your far right. You can choose from three paths when the start gate opens. Go either left or right as a group to take your first objective; never go straight or else you'll get distracted by constant fighting. Should you end up in a fight, there is very little room to maneuver around the tombstones. If you can, move to the first available open space to free up your options. It's one of the smaller arenas, so prepare for full-on combat; Ironbreakers, Swordmasters, and Warrior Priests will thrive in here.

DESTRUCTION STRATEGY

There are two capture points in this scenario: the Stag to your far left and the Crypt to your far right. You can choose from three paths when the start gate opens. Go either left or right as a group to take your first objective; never go straight or else you'll get distracted by constant fighting. Should you end up in a fight, there is very little room to maneuver around the tombstones. If you can, move to the first available open space to free up your options. It's one of the smaller arenas, so prepare for full-on combat; Black Orcs, Chosen, and Marauders will thrive in here.

RvR TIP

Bring potions, potions, and more potions. They can give you the extra edge against an evenly matched opponent.

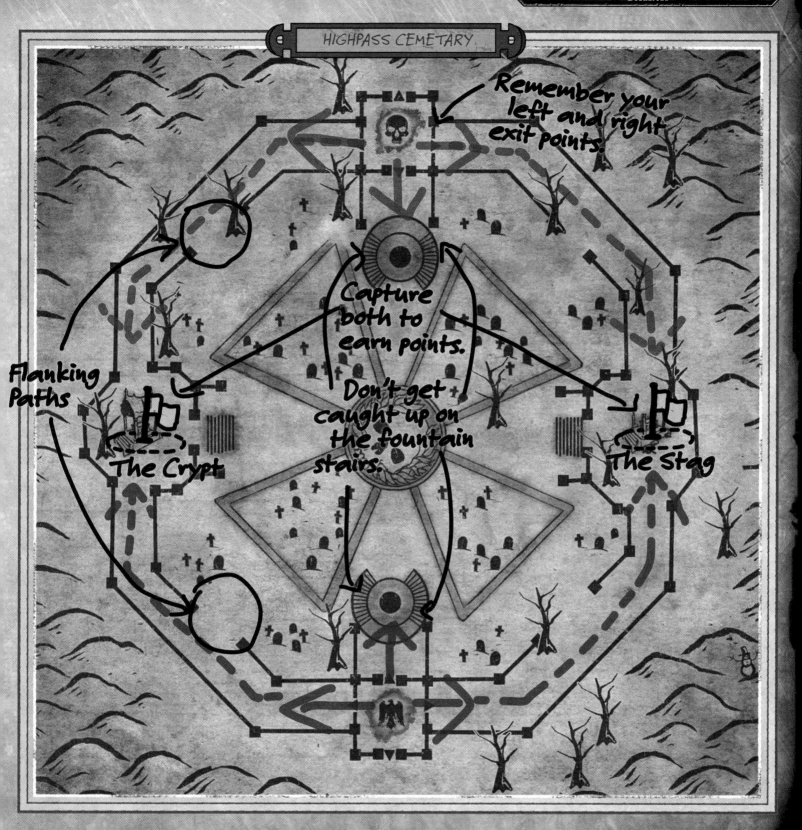

HIGHPASS CEMETARY

Remember your left and right exit points.

Capture both to earn points.

Don't get caught up on the fountain stairs.

Flanking Paths

The Crypt

The Stag

HOWLING GORGE

OVERVIEW

For some time, Dwarf Rangers have watched as the greenskins use the tunnels around Howling Gorge. One large tunnel mouth in particular is a vital thoroughfare for the Orcs and Goblins. If that could be sealed, the ambush would be prevented. The Dwarfs have gathered several barrels of black powder and traveled to the Howling Gorge to close the greenskins' main tunnel.

Upon seeing the Dwarfs arrive with their "boom-powder," the greenskins realize that they must act quickly. They draw up a hasty plan to turn the tables on the Dwarfs and use their enemies' black powder kegs to destroy a rock ledge above the road. The resulting avalanche will make the road completely impassable, and the Dwarf forces will be held up for weeks while they dig through, buying the greenskins valuable time to gather reinforcements.

As the Dwarfs enter the high cavern and prepare to do their work, Orcs and Goblins suddenly leap out from the shadows and cave mouths. The battle for Howling Gorge has begun!

ORDER STRATEGY

Initially, your team will have to decide to concentrate on offense or defense, but in the end, it takes a balance of both to succeed. You need to steal the bomb from the middle of the map and deposit it at the objective point almost due north near the Destruction spawn camp. Once you grab one of the black powder barrels, you have 90 seconds till it detonates, so get moving. The quickest route is taking the northeast bridge and heading straight up the path and around the bend to the left to reach the drop-off point. On defense, kill the guy with the bomb so it resets. You have to react quickly to offense or defense in this scenario, depending on who has the bomb. Communication is essential.

DESTRUCTION STRATEGY

Initially, your team will have to decide to concentrate on offense or defense, but in the end, it takes a balance of both to succeed. You need to steal the bomb from the middle of the map and deposit it at the objective point almost due south near the Order spawn camp. Once you grab one of the black powder barrels, you have 90 seconds till it detonates, so get moving. The quickest route is taking the southwest bridge and heading straight up the path and around the bend to the left to reach the drop-off point. On defense, kill the guy with the bomb so it resets. You have to react quickly to offense or defense in this scenario, depending on who has the bomb. Communication is essential.

RvR TIP

Love thy healer and maybe he'll love you back. Always watch for attacks on your healers.

LOCATION: BLACK CRAG (TIER 4)

ELIGIBLE RANKS: 30–40

SCENARIO TYPE: BOMBING RUN

SIZE: 12 ON 12

TIME LIMIT: 15 MINUTES

VICTORY CONDITIONS: 500 POINTS

SCORING: 75 POINTS FOR SUCCESSFULLY PLACING A BOMB.

HOWLING GORGE

This is a fast defense route to cut off would-be bombers!

Order Target

Fastest order bombing route

Deliver bomb to **X** locations.

Fastest Destruction bombing route

Destruction Target

Fastest defense route

KHAINE'S EMBRACE

LOCATION: BLIGHTED ISLE (TIER 1)

ELIGIBLE RANKS: 1–11

SCENARIO TYPE: KING OF THE HILL

SIZE: 12 ON 12

TIME LIMIT: 15 MINUTES

VICTORY CONDITIONS: 500 POINTS

SCORING: 75 POINTS FOR HOLDING BOTH CAPTURE POINTS, 1 POINT PER PLAYER KILL

OVERVIEW

The Blighted Isle holds many ancient treasures and ritual grounds in its broken lands. The ancient ritual area known as Khaine's Embrace is one such place. In the shadow of the Shrine of Khaine, the Embrace has long held dark secrets, for it is here that long ago rituals were performed to the god of murder. Some think there is great power still held in Khaine's Embrace and were it to be used, the power of a god could be harnessed. Others insist that the land is full of nothing more then malevolent evil ready to strike at a moment's notice.

You're about to test out those theories. In this version of King of the Hill, your team must control both capture points, the Dance of Swords to the west and Death's Charge to the east, to score points. However, once you control the shrines, the Will of Khaine builds up. This powerful effect increases in magnitude for 10 seconds and then detonates, destroying any players in proximity to the shrines. You'd best hit and run quickly.

ORDER STRATEGY

You begin on the western side, so it's natural for your team to tackle the Dance of Swords first. Secure it and then gradually test the enemy's defense as you pursue the second capture point, Death's Charge. Without losing the Dance of Swords, you must outflank and outthink the Destruction team to grab Death's Charge.

As soon as you do, prepare for the big blast. You have 10 seconds to escape, and two possible havens. First, you can duck in the cave between the two capture points; it's safe from the Will of Khaine. Second, you can run to the center of the map, where a Khaine's Reprieve NPC has spawned to protect you from the blast. Get as close as you can to survive the shockwave and begin your assault again.

DESTRUCTION STRATEGY

You begin on the eastern side, so it's natural for your team to tackle Death's Charge first. Secure it and then gradually test the enemy's defense as you pursue the second capture point, the Dance of Swords. Without losing Death's Charge, you must outflank and outthink the Order team to grab the Dance of Swords.

As soon as you do, prepare for the big blast. You have 10 seconds to escape, and two possible havens. First, you can duck in the cave between the two capture points; it's safe from the Will of Khaine. Second, you can run to the center of the map, where a Khaine's Reprieve NPC has spawned to protect you from the blast. Get as close as you can to survive the shockwave and begin your assault again.

RvR TIP

Feel free to double back to find friends and take a new area, especially if you are outnumbered on the frontlines.

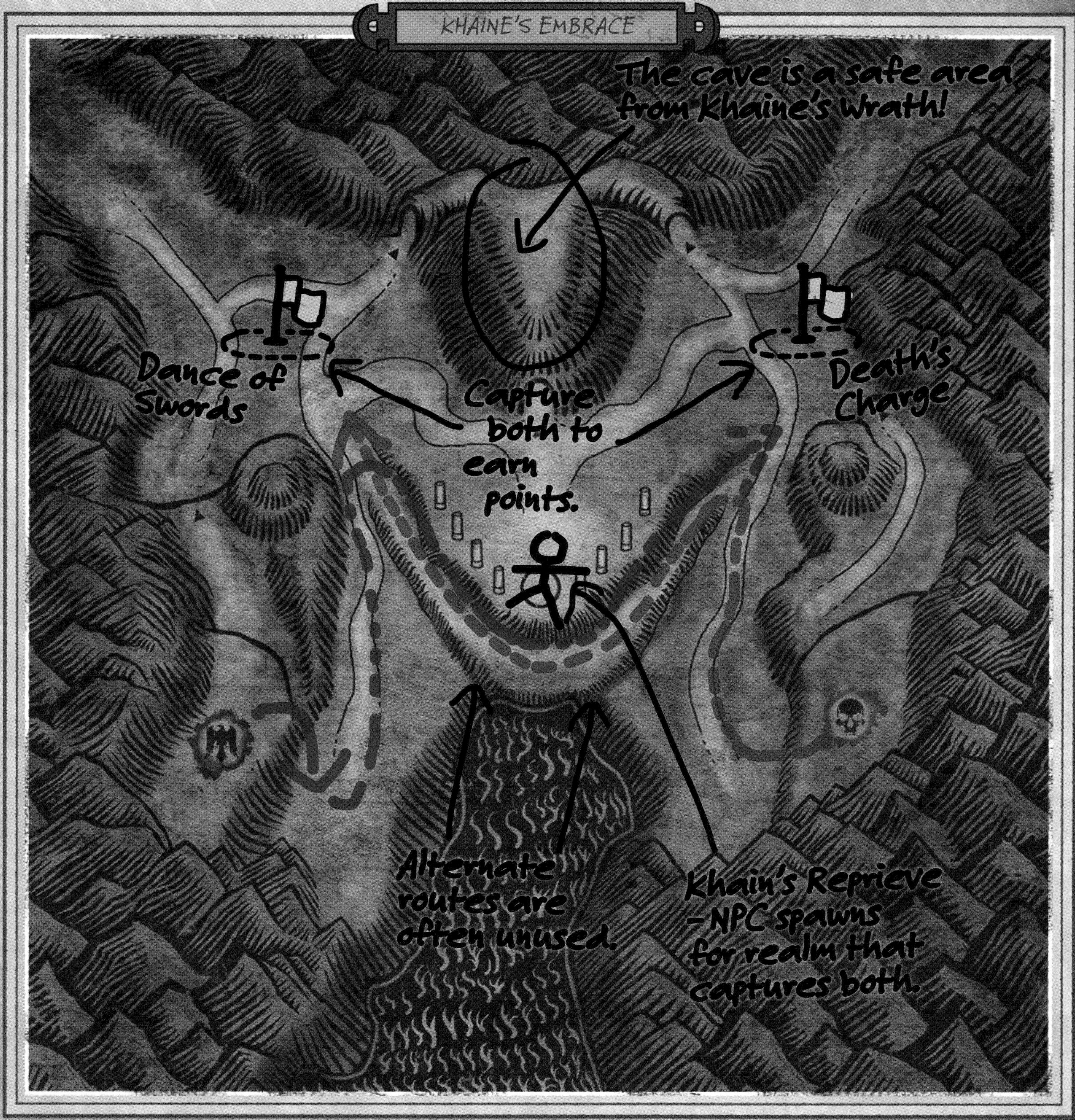

KHAINE'S EMBRACE

The cave is a safe area from Khaine's wrath!

Dance of Swords

Death's Charge

Capture both to earn points.

Alternate routes are often unused.

Khain's Reprieve —NPC spawns for realm that captures both.

LOGRIN'S FORGE

OVERVIEW

Logrin's Forge will test your skill at King of the Hill with two capture points and some difficult terrain to navigate. The two capture points, Logrin's Hammer to the west and Logrin's Anvil to the east, flank the center expanse. Main walkways connect the capture points to the center, and on either side of these are a pair of narrow passages. They make great shortcuts, as long as you mind that they can suddenly become choke points at any moment when a brawny enemy steps in your way.

ORDER STRATEGY

You begin on the north side. You have multiple exit routes from your spawn point. Head to the far right or left if you want to go straight for the objectives. Controlling the middle between the capture points cuts off fast access between them and also allows your team to send smaller groups out to capture lost points. Melee bashers, such as Swordmasters and Ironbreakers, should cut off any enemies using the thin passages; you can really bottle the enemy up if have a competent fighter or two with an Archmage or Rune Priest behind them.

DESTRUCTION STRATEGY

You begin on the south side. You have multiple exit routes from your spawn point. Head to the far right or left if you want to go straight for the objectives. Controlling the middle between the capture points cuts off fast access between them and also allows your team to send smaller groups out to capture lost points. Melee bashers, such as Chosen and Marauders, should cut off any enemies using the thin passages; you can really bottle the enemy up if have a competent fighter or two with a Shaman or Zealot behind them.

RvR TIP

Save instant cast spells until you need to move. Instant spells can be cast while on the run and usually have a longer recovery time than spells with a cast time.

LOCATION: THUNDER MOUNTAIN (TIER 4)

ELIGIBLE RANKS: APPROXIMATELY RANK 30–40

SCENARIO TYPE: KING OF THE HILL

SIZE: 12 ON 12

TIME LIMIT: 15 MINUTES

VICTORY CONDITIONS: 500 POINTS

SCORING: 75 POINTS FOR HOLDING BOTH CAPTURE POINTS, 5 POINTS PER PLAYER KILL

LOGRIN'S FORGE

Multiple spawn point exits

Narrow Thru-ways

Controlling the middle cuts off fast access between capture points.

Logrin's Hammer

Logrin's Anvil

Capture both to earn points.

LOST TEMPLE OF ISHA

Overview

Prepare to battle for the Temple of Isha. It's the lone capture point in the scenario, and as such, whichever team holds it the longest wins. Both teams start on the northern end of the map; the Temple is in the cul-de-sac to the far south. Because it may be difficult to wrest control from an opponent who has the Temple, a War Ball spawns in front of the centermost path between the two team spawn points. The War Ball grants you five percent more damage per hit, but the carrier also receives five percent damage. Use the War Ball to force the other team off Temple grounds, for it won't be yours after you gain control.

Order Strategy

There are several exits from your spawn point, but unless you're going for the War Ball, take the southeast slope, which drops you closest to the capture point. Head toward the southern Temple battleground. If you stay down low, you will run into a serious bottleneck in front of the capture area. Instead, look for a path to your right that runs up behind the objective. You can assault the Temple from behind by dropping down this slope and sneaking up unannounced.

Destruction Strategy

There are several exits from your spawn point, but unless you're going for the War Ball, take the southwest slope, which drops you closest to the capture point. Head toward the southern Temple battleground. If you stay down low, you will run into a serious bottleneck in front of the capture area. Instead, look for a path to your left that runs up behind the objective. You can assault the Temple from behind by dropping down this slope and sneaking up unannounced.

RvR Tip

In a group, healers should be healing at all times, no exceptions.

LOCATION: AVELORN (TIER 3)

ELIGIBLE RANKS: APPROXIMATELY RANK 20–30

SCENARIO TYPE: KING OF THE HILL/WAR BALL

SIZE: 12 ON 12

TIME LIMIT: 20 MINUTES

VICTORY CONDITIONS: 500 POINTS

SCORING: 25 POINTS FOR CAPTURING THE CENTER, 3 POINTS EVERY 5 SECONDS FOR HOLDING THE CAPTURE POINT, 2 POINTS PER PLAYER KILL (1 POINT PER PLAYER KILL IF YOU CARRY THE WAR BALL).

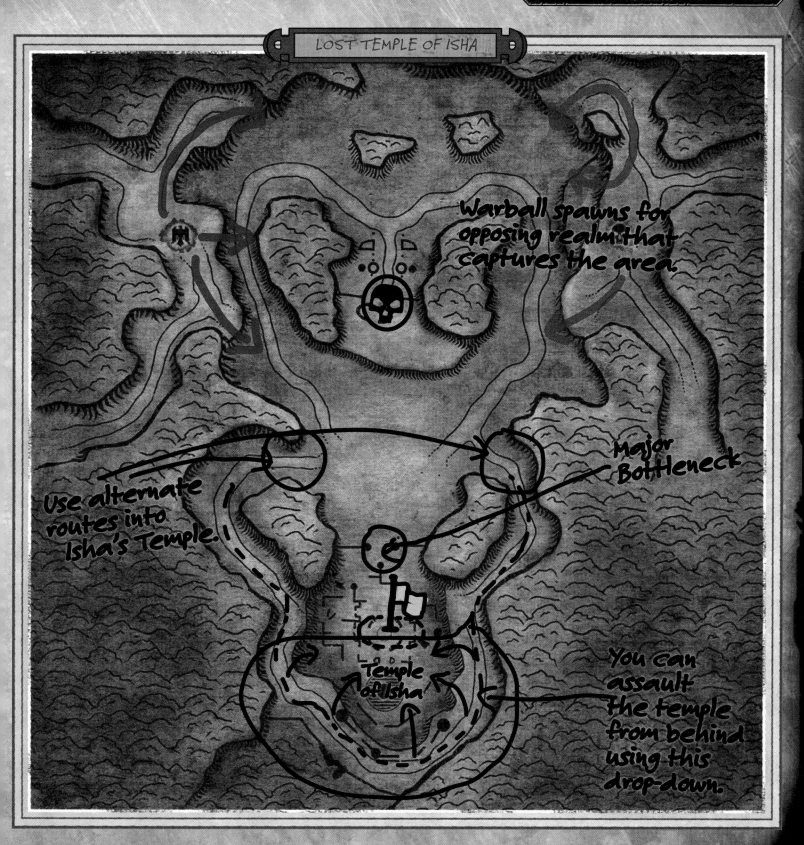

LOST TEMPLE OF ISHA

Warball spawns for opposing realm that captures the area.

Major Bottleneck

Use alternate routes into Isha's Temple.

Temple of Isha

You can assault the temple from behind using this drop-down.

MAW OF MADNESS

LOCATION: CHAOS WASTES (TIER 4)

ELIGIBLE RANKS: 23–40

SCENARIO TYPE: DEATH MATCH/WAR BALL

SIZE: 12 ON 12

TIME LIMIT: 15 MINUTES

VICTORY CONDITIONS: 500 POINTS

SCORING: 10 POINTS PER PLAYER KILL, +10 POINTS PER PLAYER KILL IF YOU CARRY A WAR BALL, +10 POINTS PER PLAYER KILL IF YOU KILL THE WAR BALL CARRIER, 3 POINTS EVERY 5 SECONDS FOR CARRYING A WAR BALL.

OVERVIEW

Are you ready for a giant free-for-all? The object of this scenario is to kill as many of the other team as possible. Of course, you probably want a bit more fun than that, so the center of the play area spawns a War Ball to increase the onslaught. The map is shaped like a giant bowl. The spawn points are on opposite ends of the zone, with ledges running around a pit in the middle. Your battle skills will be challenged!

ORDER STRATEGY

You don't have to worry about capture points, so go out and slay some enemies. Of course, wielding the War Ball improves your kill percentage, but a well-coordinated team will always win the day here. Stick to the outer paths for maximum movement speed; the middle is full of obstacles that impede movement and block line of sight. Melee specialists, such as Witch Hunters, Shadow Warriors, and Ironbreakers, should definitely seek the center's protection and wrestle for the War Ball. Ranged nukers, such as Engineers, Bright Wizards, and Archmages, should stay on the fringe to take out targets moving into the center or along the edges; you don't want to be anywhere near the center. Rune Priests and other healers need to stay out of harm's way, yet be close enough to help out their melee comrades.

DESTRUCTION STRATEGY

You don't have to worry about capture points, so go out and slay some enemies. Of course, wielding the War Ball improves your kill percentage, but a well-coordinated team will always win the day here. Stick to the outer paths for maximum movement speed; the middle is full of obstacles that impede movement and block line of sight. Melee specialists, such as Black Orcs, Chosen, and Witch Elves, should definitely seek the center's protection and wrestle for the War Ball. Ranged nukers, such as Magi and Sorceresses, should stay on the fringe to take out targets moving into the center or along the edges; you don't want to be anywhere near the center. Disciples and other healers need to stay out of harm's way, yet close enough to help out their melee comrades.

RvR TIP

Use up all your action points before hitting Flee, because it takes away all remaining action points.

MAW OF MADNESS

There are multiple ways into the play space for both realms.

= Warball(s)

MOURKAIN TEMPLE

Overview

The Mourkain Temple is a remnant of the defunct Mourkain civilization. All that remains of the once-mighty complex are half-sunken ruins. Pillars, collapsed buildings, and large swamp trees surround the temple ruin, obscuring it from the rest of the swamp. The temple itself has no interior (players cannot enter it). However, a wide ledge runs around its circumference with five sets of stairs winding down into the brackish swamp water; one set at each corner and a set at rear center. The entire area is knee-deep in water and a broken bridge spans (or rather, fails to span) the gap reaching from the short cliff face where the players enter the scenario to the temple doors.

A crafty Goblin Shaman of the Black Skull tribe recently discovered a strange artifact near the temple. He learned that while he carried this glowing artifact, he and all the other greenskins around him became more powerful in battle, as long as they did not stray too far from the temple. The Dwarfs, who have clashed with the Shaman and his band more than once, have pieced together that the artifact is a source of magical power and must be taken from the greenskins. The two sides now square off in a battle around the ancient temple to fight for control of the artifact.

Order Strategy

Both sides start at opposite ends of the map with the War Ball in the middle. Use Sprint to reach the War Ball as fast as possible; whichever team holds it gains the combat advantage. Work together as a team, coordinate your tactics, and you'll do well. Healers should protect the War Ball carrier. There is a lot of open-field terrain here, so be sure to out-flank your opponents. Ranged attackers, such as Engineers and Shadow Warriors, or even White Lions with their lion pets, should clean up.

Destruction Strategy

Both sides start at opposite ends of the map with the War Ball in the middle. Use Sprint to reach the War Ball as fast as possible; whichever team holds it gains the combat advantage. Work together as a team, coordinate your tactics, and you'll do well. Healers should protect the War Ball carrier. There is a lot of open-field terrain here, so be sure to out-flank your opponents. Ranged attackers, such as Sorceresses and Magi, or even Squig Herders with their squig pets, should clean up.

RvR Tip

Keep your window view all the way out so that you can see flanking enemies.

LOCATION: MARSHES OF MADNESS (TIER 2)

ELIGIBLE RANKS: 10–21

SCENARIO TYPE: DEATH MATCH/WAR BALL

SIZE: 12 ON 12

TIME LIMIT: 15 MINUTES

VICTORY CONDITIONS: 500 POINTS

SCORING: 10 POINTS PER PLAYER KILL, 3 POINTS EVERY 5 SECONDS FOR HOLDING WAR BALL, 20 POINTS PER PLAYER KILL IF HOLDING WAR BALL, 20 POINTS TO OPPOSING TEAM IF WAR BALL CARRIER KILLED

MOURKAIN TEMPLE

Single WarBall

NORDENWATCH

OVERVIEW

This imposing edifice, recently constructed on an island of rock just off the shore of Nordland, is the cornerstone of the province's coastal defenses. Numerous batteries of cannons bristle from the storm-lashed walls of Nordenwatch, safeguarding the nearby town of New Emskrank from assault by the black ships of the Northmen.

Knowing that the fort will pose a threat to his fleets, Tchar'zanek, lord of the Chaos Warhost, decides to first attack by land, drawing out the soldiers stationed in the sea fort. His plan proves successful, and when the garrison at Nordenwatch sails ashore to defend New Emskrank from assault by the ravaging warhost, the dread warlord gives the signal for his fleets to assault the fort and seize control of its guns.

Now, the remaining soldiers in the fort fight desperately to fend off the attack from the black warships of the enemy. Knowing that they must hold at all costs, they dispatch a messenger to the shore calling for reinforcement.

ORDER STRATEGY

There are three control points: Lighthouse (closest to Order spawn), Fortress (farthest away in the middle), and Barracks (closest to Destruction spawn). You need two of the three capture points to win, and, of course, the Fortress is the most valuable. At the start, use your Flee ability to sprint directly to the Fortress. You can drop one person behind to capture the Lighthouse, but everyone else should attack the Fortress as a coordinated mass. Secure the Fortress and then decide on the next course of action based on Destruction's movements. If they've left the Barracks lightly guarded, send a team down to gain control. Lost the Lighthouse already? Send a team to gain it back. Whichever team adjusts the best and keeps track of the other team's movement will win the scenario.

DESTRUCTION STRATEGY

There are three control points: Barracks (closest to Destruction spawn), Fortress (farthest away in the middle), and Lighthouse (closest to Order spawn). You need two of the three capture points to win, and, of course, the Fortress is the most valuable. At the start, use your Flee ability to sprint directly to the Fortress. You can drop one person behind to capture the Barracks, but everyone else should attack the Fortress as a coordinated mass. Secure the Fortress and then decide on the next course of action based on Order's movements. If they've left the Lighthouse lightly guarded, send a team down to gain control. Lost the Barracks already? Send a team to gain it back. Whichever team adjusts the best and keeps track of the other team's movement will win the scenario.

RvR TIP

If you have a ranged weapon and the enemy healers don't make easy targets, engage an enemy tank. They are weak to ranged attackers and you can usually drop them before they reach you.

LOCATION: NORDLAND (TIER 1)

ELIGIBLE RANKS: 1–11

SCENARIO TYPE: KING OF THE HILL

SIZE: 12 ON 12

TIME LIMIT: 15 MINUTES

VICTORY CONDITIONS: 500 POINTS

SCORING: LIGHTHOUSE: 5 POINTS PER PLAYER KILL, 15 POINTS FOR A CAPTURE THEN 2 POINTS EVERY 7 SECONDS, BARRACKS: 15 POINTS FOR A CAPTURE THEN 2 POINTS EVERY 7 SECONDS, FORTRESS: 30 POINTS FOR A CAPTURE THEN 2 POINTS EVERY 7 SECONDS

NORDENWATCH

3 Capture Areas

The Barracks

Sneaky Hidden Back Route

Go to the Fortress first...then work backward!

Fort

Lighthouse

PHOENIX GATE

Overview

This is another classic battle of Capture the Flag, with each side holding a single flag. You need to grab the enemy's flag and bring it back to your flag, which must be sitting in its home spot, to earn points. You can gain victory points with player kills, but it takes flag captures to win before the time limit expires. The terrain is set up so the direct route to its flag is down the middle (very risky because everyone can see you and it's easy for them to engage you). Side routes along the borders offer unique opportunities and challenges.

Order Strategy

The number-one rule: Work together as a team. If you go running off on your own, you simply weaken the group's strength in numbers. You will either be staging a run on the enemy's flag or defending your own flag at all times; do not get caught in the middle of the map, even though this avenue might seem the quickest. Your spawn point is in the southeast corner, so take the eastern ledge to reach the enemy's flag quickest. Use that same route to return, unless the enemy has it bottled up; in that case, run along the western path. Always keep an eye on what's going on around your flag and try to spot the enemy's position on the opposite paths to alert your team of incoming attacks.

Destruction Strategy

The number-one rule: Work together as a team. If you go running off on your own, you simply weaken the group's strength in numbers. You will either be staging a run on the enemy's flag or defending your own flag at all times; do not get caught in the middle of the map, even though this avenue might seem the quickest. Your spawn point is in the northwest corner, so take the western ledge to reach the enemy's flag quickest. Use that same route to return, unless the enemy has it bottled up; in that case, run along the eastern path. Always keep an eye out on what's going on around your flag and try to spot the enemy's position on the opposite paths to alert your team of incoming attacks.

RvR Tip

Don't be afraid of dying in scenarios. You will, but there's no penalty if you're killed by a player.

LOCATION: ELLYRION (TIER 2)

ELIGIBLE RANKS: APPROXIMATELY RANK 11–20

SCENARIO TYPE: CAPTURE THE FLAG

SIZE: 12 ON 12

TIME LIMIT: 15 MINUTES

VICTORY CONDITIONS: 500 POINTS

SCORING: 75 POINTS FOR EACH FLAG CAPTURE, 2 POINTS PER PLAYER KILL

PHOENIX GATE

Alternate Exit Point

Good capture route for Order

Direct path, but very risky.

Good capture route for Destruction

Alternate routes from spawn point.

REIKLAND HILLS

OVERVIEW

This is a rotating King of the Hill match where one or two of three locations will be available for capture at specific times during the scenario. The three capture locations are the Broken Bridge, the Mill, and the Factory. The first location to open is always the Broken Bridge, but from there it's entirely random as to which capture location will open next. To capture these locations, you need to interact with the flag and keep the opposing team from doing the same for about 30 seconds. If successful, your side starts earning points for holding the area. After three to four minutes, another capture area opens. The time these locations stay open overlap slightly and force a decision upon defenders: leave to assault the new location, or stay to protect the currently captured location.

ORDER STRATEGY

When you enter this scenario, you can head straight to the Bridge or flank left and right. The Broken Bridge is a flat, open location that is readily assaulted from all angles. Of all the capture locations in this scenario, it is the hardest to hold. To the sides are the Mill and Factory. Each has a main path that leads to the flag, but each is also reached by a tunnel. Use the tunnels to approach from the back and take these locations by surprise. Keep scouts out watching for the new capture areas to become active and give you a head start on your opponents.

DESTRUCTION STRATEGY

When you enter this scenario, you can head straight to the Bridge or flank left and right. The Broken Bridge is a flat, open location that is readily assaulted from all angles. Of all the capture locations in this scenario, it is the hardest to hold. To the sides are the Mill and Factory. Each has a main path that leads to the flag, but each is also reached by a tunnel. Use the tunnels to approach from the back and take these locations by surprise. Keep scouts out watching for the new capture areas to become active and give you a head start on your opponents.

RvR Tip

Talk to your teammates and coordinate your tactics. The team that works together the best, unless vastly outnumbered, should win.

LOCATION: REIKLAND (TIER 4)

ELIGIBLE RANKS: 30–40

SCENARIO TYPE: KING OF THE HILL

SIZE: 18 ON 18

TIME LIMIT: 15 MINUTES

VICTORY CONDITIONS: 500 POINTS

SCORING: 5 POINTS PER PLAYER KILL, 10 POINTS EVERY 5 SECONDS FOR HOLDING A CAPTURED AREA

REIKLAND HILLS

Rotating King of the Hill

The Mill

Bridge jumping is fast but deadly.

Fallen Bridge

The Factory

Center bridge is always the first one open...then it's random.

SERPENT'S PASSAGE

Overview

Two vessels are forced ashore from violent storms and have massive hull damage. Both Dark Elves and High Elves are forced to battle each other over spare parts from other storm-wrecked ships. The goal of the scenario is to bring back salvage to your home base (essentially single-flag Capture the Flag). The only problem? The enemy wants to do the same thing.

Order Strategy

Both teams start along the north coast, with you on the east side. The only points scored are for capturing salvage, so what are you doing standing around? Sprint to the salvage ship in the far south. Ranged damage-dealers, such as Bright Wizards or Shadow Warriors, should seek out high ground to ambush the unwary and maximize your range capabilities. Look for high ground at the central plateau and near the flag. The passes between spawn points provide quick access side to side in the fray.

Destruction Strategy

Both teams start along the north coast, with you on the west side. The only points scored are for capturing salvage, so what are you doing standing around? Sprint to the salvage ship in the far south. Ranged damage-dealers, such as Magi or Squig Herders, should seek out high ground to ambush the unwary and maximize your range capabilities. Look for high ground at the central plateau and near the flag. The passes between spawn points provide quick access side to side in the fray.

RvR Tip

Remember to switch your gear and Tactics for RvR play before entering a scenario.

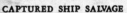

LOCATION: HIGH ELVES VS. DARK ELVES (TIER 4)

ELIGIBLE RANKS: APPROXIMATELY 30–40

SCENARIO TYPE: CAPTURE THE FLAG

SIZE: 12 ON 12

TIME LIMIT: 15 MINUTES

VICTORY CONDITIONS: 500 POINTS

SCORING: 2 POINTS PER PLAYER KILL, 75 POINTS PER CAPTURED SHIP SALVAGE

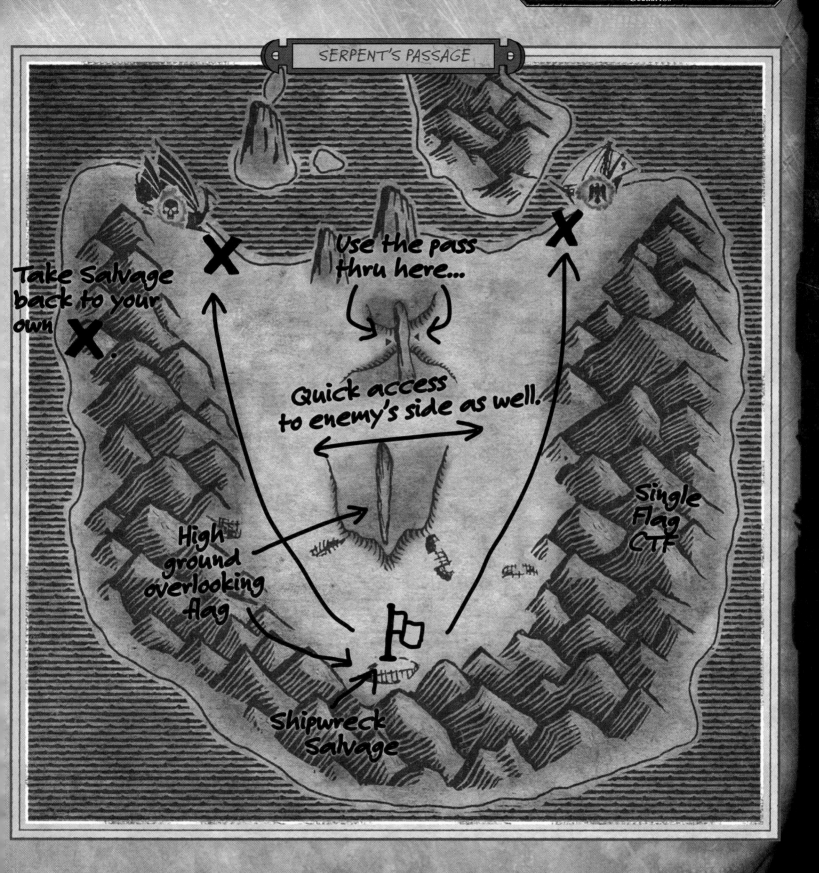

SERPENT'S PASSAGE

Take Salvage back to your own

Use the pass thru here...

Quick access to enemy's side as well.

High ground overlooking flag

Single Flag CTF

Shipwreck Salvage

STONE TROLL CROSSING

OVERVIEW

This match is pretty straight forward: kill or be killed, but avoid the trolls! That's right, trolls. You're fighting on their turf, and they're not too keen on either side being in the area. Because you're trespassing, the not-so-friendly trolls hurl large boulders into the area from time to time. These boulders aren't lethal, but they cause a hefty knockback to anyone they hit. This throws a bit of variety into the scenario.

ORDER STRATEGY

When you first enter the scenario you can go straight ahead or cut to the right to take an alternate path out of the spawn area. Most of the play area is lowlands with large boulders breaking up the space, but a large tree mound in the middle has spiraling walkways up both sides for an elevated fight. Gain the high ground, and you can do some damage by forcing the enemy to come to you. The disadvantage to being in this elevated position is knockback vulnerability. Don't get too comfortable on your perch because it's just a matter of time before you get knocked off. Once you've thinned opposition around the tree, grab the flag and run to one of the troll positions to score points.

DESTRUCTION STRATEGY

When you first enter the scenario you can go straight ahead or cut to the right to take an alternate path out of the spawn area. Most of the play area is lowlands with large boulders breaking up the space, but a large tree mound in the middle has spiraling walkways up both sides for an elevated fight. Gain the high ground, and you can do some damage by forcing the enemy to come to you. The disadvantage to being in this elevated position is knockback vulnerability. Don't get too comfortable on your perch because it's just a matter of time before you get knocked off. Once you've thinned opposition around the tree, grab the flag and run to one of the troll positions to score points.

RvR TIP

Scenarios can range from tight quarters—great for melee fighters—to wide open spaces. Learn the scenario, so you'll know when to take chances and how to surprise the enemy best.

LOCATION: TROLL COUNTRY (TIER 2)

ELIGIBLE RANKS: 10–21

SCENARIO TYPE: CAPTURE THE FLAG

SIZE: 12 ON 12

TIME LIMIT: 15 MINUTES

VICTORY CONDITIONS: 500 POINTS

SCORING: 2 POINTS PER PLAYER KILL, 25 POINTS PER CAPTURED AREA, 100 POINTS FOR CAPTURING ALL 3 AREAS BEFORE TIME RUNS OUT

STONE TROLL CROSSING

Trolls throw rocks, which do AE knockback.

Alternate spawn point exit

Boulder Fist Trolls

Gravel Botatom Trolls

X

X

Alternate spawn point exit

Double spiral access to top of "tree" where the flag is.

Chuck Rock Trolls

X

Take a flag to each X

to earn points.

TALABEC DAM

OVERVIEW

Much of the Empire's commerce flows along its rivers. In a land where travel by wagon is often fraught with danger and the roads are not always well-kept, the Empire's many waterways make for swifter, safer passage.

Among the Empire's rivers, the Talabec is certainly one of the most important. As the invading warhost presses deeper in the Empire, the strategic importance of the Talabec grows. Knowing this, the forces of Chaos have set out to disrupt the shipping of supplies and troops that flows to and from the front lines along the river's course.

Near the village of Esselfurt, the Talabec forks into two branches before rejoining a short distance away. The villagers have built a dam across one of the forks, and the forces of Chaos intend to destroy this dam and flood the area. Using foul magic, they have erected a temple with a magical altar. Those who touch the altar are blessed with the power to blast apart whatever they touch. A garrison of soldiers at the nearby village must stop the invaders from wrecking the dam, and they'll need all the help they can get.

This bomb run scenario features a single bomb that both realms have to deliver to their intended bomb targets. In this case, Order is trying to blow up a large Chaos sigil that is infecting Talabec Dam, and Destruction is trying to blow up a windmill that is a major production engine for a local town off of Talabec River.

LOCATION: TALABECLAND (TIER 3)

ELIGIBLE RANKS: 20–31

SCENARIO TYPE: BOMB RUN

SIZE: 12 ON 12

TIME LIMIT: 15 MINUTES

VICTORY CONDITIONS: 500 POINTS

SCORING: 75 POINTS PER SUCCESSFUL BOMB DETONATION, 2 POINTS PER PLAYER KILL

ORDER STRATEGY

When you start this scenario, you're near your respective opponent's target (Destruction spawns near the Dam and Order spawns near the Windmill). You can hop down in a few spots to either defend or go on the assault. As you approach the central location where the bomb is, you'll notice four ways into this location (two from each side). You can either stay and defend this location for bomb respawns, or take the bomb and run. When the bomb is picked up, you have 60 seconds to get to your target or you blow up and anyone around you gets knocked back. Bombs are deadly, but you also amass a hefty point gain for successful bomb runs.

Let one player grab the bomb and another run escort. Don't send everyone; the rest stay behind and control the Bridge. Why? If the bomb runner is killed and the bomb not picked up by his escort in five seconds, the bomb will respawn in the center of the Bridge. Someone else can then grab it and take off toward the Dam. On defense, watch and see how many enemies go with the bomb runner. If they just send a few, dispatch a group after them and destroy them before they can reach their target. If the majority goes on the run, stay and gain control of the Bridge and grab the bomb next time it spawns.

Each of the bomb locations can be defended fairly well because you can only approach them from two sides; however both locations are highly susceptible to knockback. You won't die if you get knocked back into the river below, but any extra firepower that comes your way may make life difficult!

DESTRUCTION STRATEGY

When you start this scenario you're near your respective opponent's target (Destruction spawns near the Dam and Order spawns near the Windmill). You can hop down in a few spots to either defend or go on the assault. As you approach the central location where the bomb is, you'll notice four ways into this location (two from each side). You can either stay and defend this location for bomb respawns, or take the bomb and run. When the bomb is picked up, you have 60 seconds to get to your target or you blow up and anyone around you gets knocked back. Bombs are deadly, but you also amass a hefty point gain for successful bomb runs.

Let one player grab the bomb and another run escort. Don't send everyone; the rest stay behind and control the Bridge. Why? If the bomb runner is killed and the bomb not picked up by his escort in five seconds, the bomb will respawn in the center of the Bridge. Someone else can then grab it and take off toward the Dam. On defense, watch and see how many enemies go with the bomb runner. If they just send a few, dispatch a group after them and destroy them before they can reach their target. If the majority goes on the run, stay and gain control of the Bridge and grab the bomb next time it spawns.

Each of the bomb locations can be defended fairly well because you can only approach them from two sides; however both locations are highly susceptible to knockback. You won't die if you get knocked back into the river below, but any extra firepower that comes your way may make life difficult!

RvR TIP

In general, a ranged attacker should have freedom to use ranged abilities. Most scenarios have several spots from which to fire safely. Learn the scenario, so you'll know where to ambush the enemy or support your side.

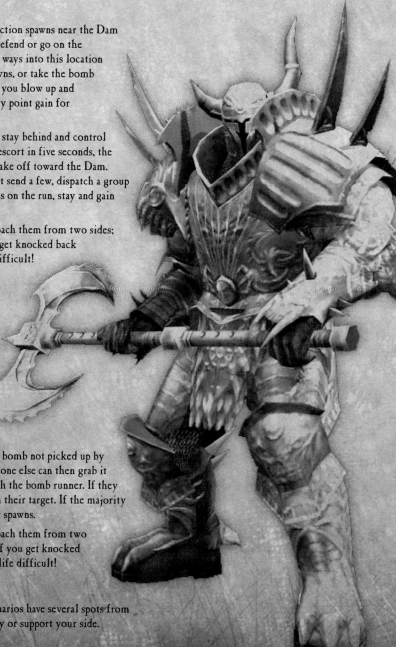

TALABEC DAM

Fastest route to bomb

Defensive choke points

Destruction Target: "The Mill"

Legit side routes

Best bombing route for Order

Best bombing route for Destruction

Use this ledge if you get knocked off.

Use this ledge if you get knocked off.

Legit side routes

Order Target: "The Dam"

Fast route to bomb

Take bomb to "X".

Defensive choke points

THUNDER VALLEY

OVERVIEW

The Dwarf Engineers Guild has long maintained a testing ground near Thunder Mountain. There, they fashion new weapons and test them out in (relative) safety. When the *Waaagh!* marches into the lands around Thunder Mountain, greenskin scouts discover the testing grounds and move quickly to attack the Engineers. The outnumbered Engineers send for reinforcements, for if the greenskins overrun the testing grounds and destroy the mad inventions that the half-crazed (or half genius?) Engineers have created, decades of research and meticulous craftsmanship will be undone.

There are five capture areas to gain on this map. In the center of the battlefield, Gyrocopter Hanger gives the most points per capture. The other four—Fireball Mortar, Gungnir's Fist, Blasting Cart and Firing Range—all grant equal points per capture.

ORDER STRATEGY

Your spawn point lies on the south side of the map. Fireball Mortar is right next to you, so hop off the slope to the northeast and grab your first points. Control of the Gyrocopter Hanger not only gives the most points, but it also enables the possessor to use bombs against captured enemy locations. With that firepower, you want to concentrate your forces there and gain the points and firepower advantage. Avoid lingering on the bridges—knockback is deadly here—and don't fight in the open fields in front of each side's spawning ground. Open ground equals death with so many enemies running around.

DESTRUCTION STRATEGY

Your spawn point lies on the north side of the map. Blasting Cart is right next to you, so hop off the slope to the southwest and grab your first points. Control of the Gyrocopter Hanger not only gives the most points, but it also enables the possessor to use bombs against captured enemy locations. With that firepower, you want to concentrate your forces there and gain the points and firepower advantage. Avoid lingering on the bridges—knockback is deadly here—and don't fight in the open fields in front of each side's spawning ground. Open ground equals death with so many enemies running around.

LOCATION: THUNDER MOUNTAIN (TIER 4)

ELIGIBLE RANKS: APPROXIMATELY 30–40

SCENARIO TYPE: KING OF THE HILL

SIZE: 18 ON 18

TIME LIMIT: 20 MINUTES

VICTORY CONDITIONS: 500 POINTS

SCORING: 2 POINTS PER PLAYER KILL; GYROCOPTER HANGER: 25 POINTS EVERY 10 SECONDS; FIREBALL MORTAR: 10 POINTS PRE CAPTURE, 5 POINTS EVERY 10 SECONDS; GUNGNIR'S FIST: 10 POINTS PER CAPTURE, 5 POINTS EVERY 10 SECONDS; BLASTING CART: 10 POINTS PER CAPTURE, 5 POINTS EVERY 10 SECONDS; FIRING RANGE: 10 POINTS PER CAPTURE, 5 POINTS EVERY 10 SECONDS, 1 POINT PER BOMBER SHOT DOWN

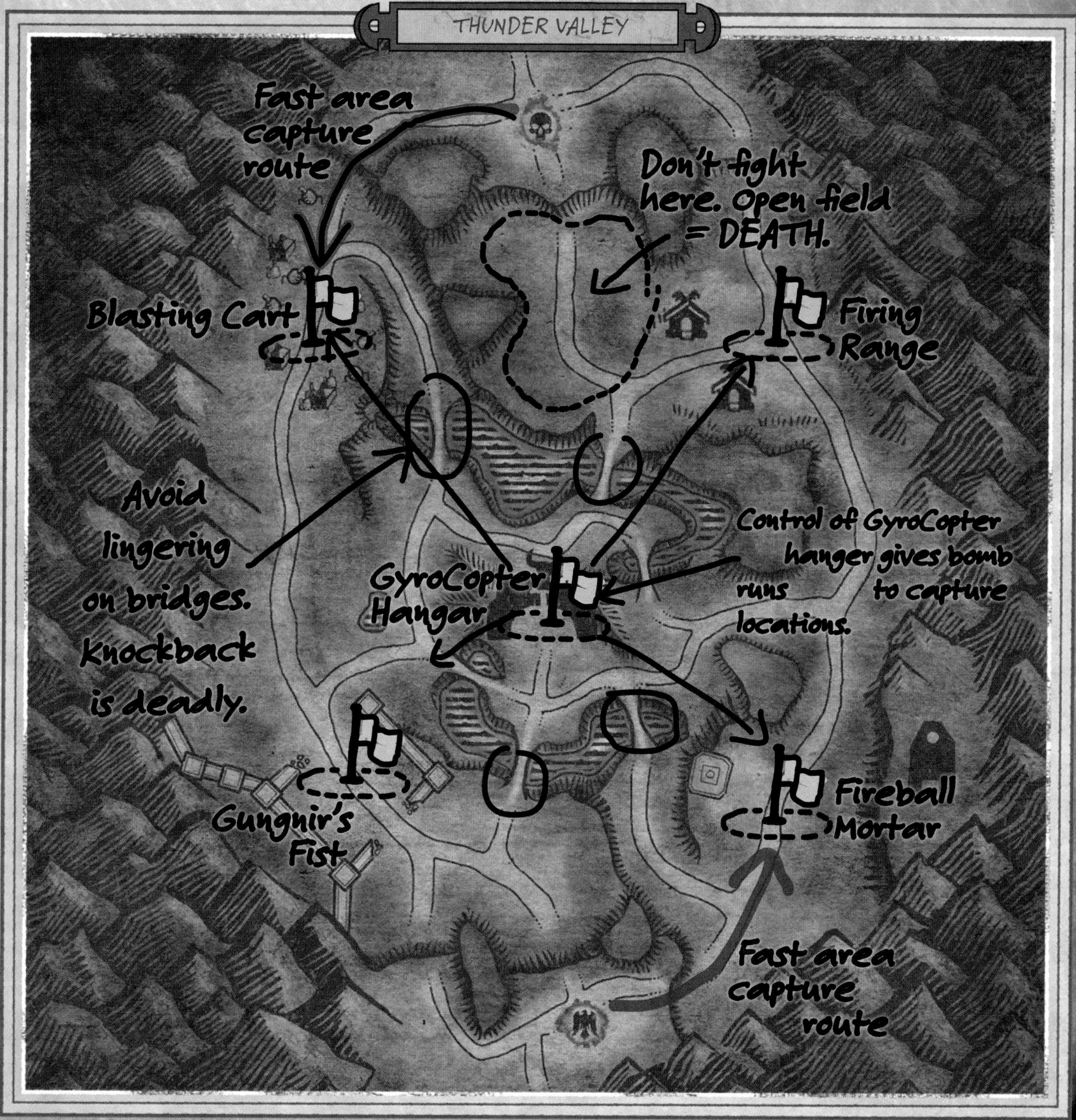

THUNDER VALLEY

Fast area capture route

Don't fight here. Open field = DEATH.

Blasting Cart

Firing Range

Avoid lingering on bridges. Knockback is deadly.

Control of GyroCopter hanger gives bomb runs to capture locations.

GyroCopter Hangar

Gungnir's Fist

Fireball Mortar

Fast area capture route

TOR ANROC

Overview

The Dragon Mage Eridial was one of the most promising young mages ever to study in the White Tower. When he left to seek out the dragon that would be his mount, he took with him what he thought was great knowledge in the art of imbuing items. With his mount tamed and his drive to increase his skill gnawing at him, he created the Amulet of Dragon's Breath. This incredibly potent magical item was created to harness the essence of the dragon and unleash it at the user's request. Eridial's skill was not as great as he assumed, however, and when he brandished the Amulet, his Dragon, Thiralies, was torn and his essence was forever trapped in the Amulet. Distraught over the death and destruction he caused, Eridial fled deep into the heart of Tor Anroc, the home of his dragon mount, never to be seen again.

Order Strategy

It's all about controlling the one War Ball and using it for maximum damage. Rush out toward the center, being careful not to fall off the sides into the lava. The thinner paths around the center are risky knockback areas, so watch where you step. The high ground where the War Ball spawns is easiest to defend, especially if you have melee to repel charges, ranged attackers to pick guys off from afar, and a few healers to keep everyone intact.

Destruction Strategy

It's all about controlling the one War Ball and using it for maximum damage. Rush out toward the center, being careful not to fall off the sides into the lava. The thinner paths around the center are risky knockback areas, so watch where you step. The high ground where the War Ball spawns is easiest to defend, especially if you have melee to repel charges, ranged attackers to pick guys off from afar, and a few healers to keep everyone intact.

RvR Tip

The whole point of a scenario is to reach 500 points, so it's pointless to chase other groups just for points. Remind the group of this if you see players running around in a frenzy. Some players tend to get selfish and kill everything in sight.

LOCATION: HIGH ELVES VS. DARK ELVES (TIER 3)

ELIGIBLE RANKS: APPROXIMATELY 20–30

SCENARIO TYPE: WAR BALL

SIZE: 12 ON 12

TIME LIMIT: 15 MINUTES

VICTORY CONDITIONS: 500 POINTS

SCORING: 10 POINTS PER PLAYER KILL, 12 POINTS PER PLAYER KILL WHILE HOLDING THE WAR BALL, 3 POINTS EVERY 5 SECONDS WHILE HOLDING THE WAR BALL

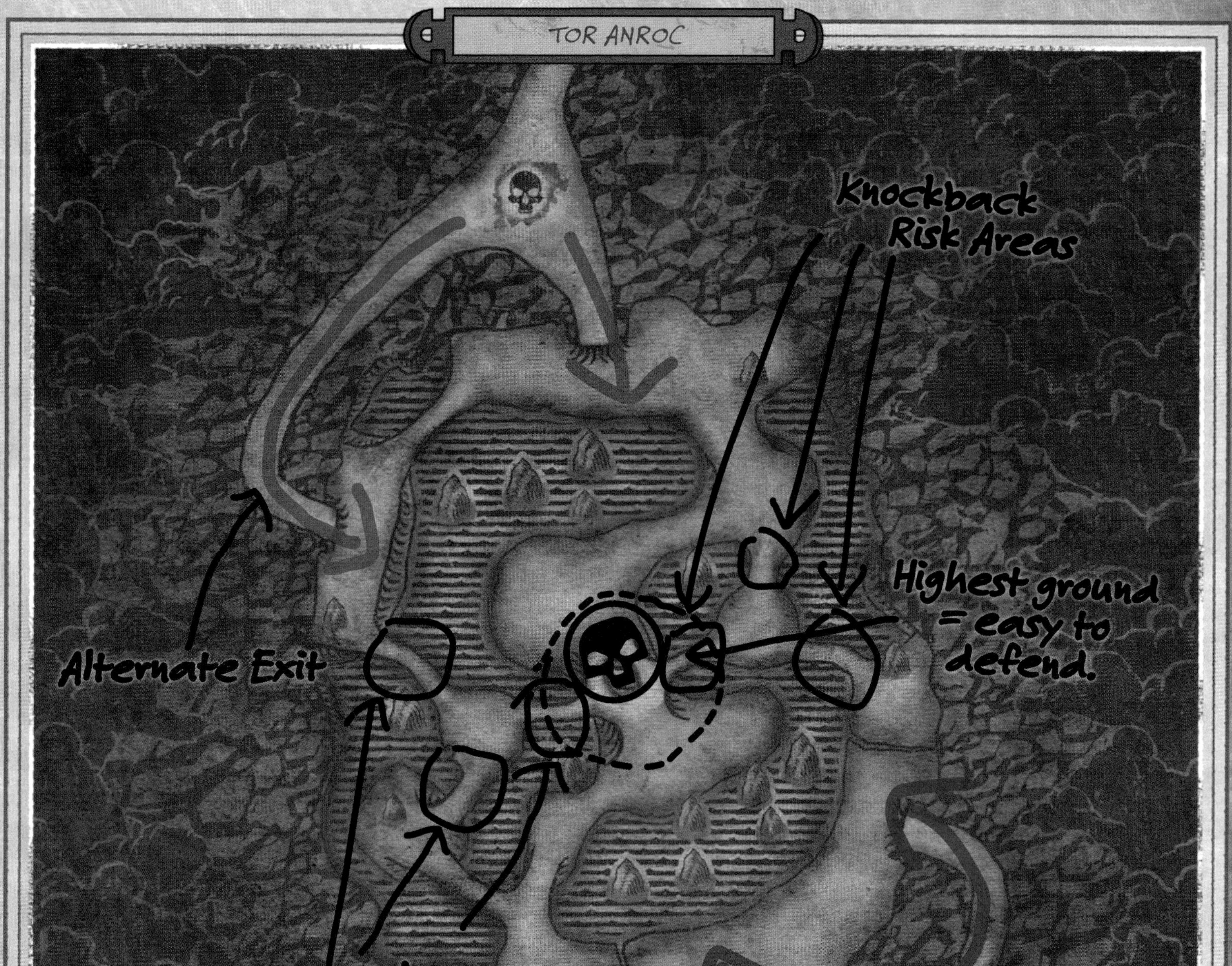

TOR ANROC

Knockback
Risk Areas

Highest ground
= easy to
defend.

Alternate Exit

Knockback
Risk Areas

Alternate
Exit

💀 = War Ball

BASTION STAIR

DUNGEON DETAILS

Erected by the malicious will of the Lord of Skulls, the Bastion Stair towers over a twisted and torn landscape, walls stained red with the blood of countless sacrifices. Stairs never meant for human feet climb toward burning skies where the vague outline of the Bastion itself can barely be seen, and beyond, the faint flickering light of the Rift of Rage. For it is the rift itself that draws both Order and Destruction to this place, a source of Chaos power with which the servants of Tzeentch could remake the world in the twisted image of their dark god... if the defenders of the Empire cannot find some way to close the portal first.

TRAIL OF CARNAGE (RANKS 33-34)

This segment of the Bastion Stair is occupied by the Bloodherd tribe of Beastmen, a Khornite clan kept under some sort of control by the Blood Trolls and Bloodbeast watching over them in the Nine Skulls Trench. Three nearby holding pens contain mortal captives of the Bloodherd, awaiting sacrifice (or rescue).

Accessible from the Nine Skulls Trench room is the Tainted Herdstone, which the Blood Trolls have blocked off from the rest of the Bloodherd, to prevent a Beastman frenzy from erupting. Here the Doombull, Thar'Ignan, waits for foolish mortals to enter and be destroyed.

PATH OF FURY (RANKS 35-36)

This segment of the Bastion Stair is occupied primarily by mortal Khornites, human warriors of the Blood God, set against each other in constant training for war and sportive killing. Daemons come here to spar with each other, and with the best of the mortals. The reigning Mortal Champion of Khorne, Lord Slaurith, once the commander of the Empire expedition to conquer the Bastion Stair, looks over the Arena of Fury as dozens of gladiators test their mettle in seemingly endless hostilities.

This area also was where the bulk of the Altdorf Grey Lancers Regiment was battled, cornered, and annihilated by Khornite adversaries. Dozens of these dead elite soldiers are strewn about in the Path of Fury, constant reminders of the danger of the Bastion Stair.

STEPS OF RUIN (RANKS 37-39)

The Steps of Ruin proceed to the highest reachable location within the Bastion Stair, the Portal of Rage. Before one can get there, however, they must first overcome the many challenges and obstacles of the Fortress of Brass, a portion of the Bastion Stair where the deadly Brass Legion of daemons maintains a firm grip on the approaches to the Realm of Khorne.

PORTAL OF RAGE (FINAL BOSS, RANK 40+)

The Portal of Rage is Khorne's own access portal to the Chaos dimension. The Blood God forbids any but Khornites to approach this place. None are meant to interfere with the portal in any way, yet both the Empire and the Raven Host of Tchar'zanek are interested in doing just that. By securing a Holy Relic of the Empire and placing it upon the Portal Altar, the magic winds emanating from the Portal can be greatly reduced (for the benefit of the cause of Order). By securing a vile artifact of Chaos and placing it upon the Portal Altar, the magic winds can be increased (for the benefit of the Raven Host).

Regardless of which side tampers with the Portal Altar, and for what purpose, a Bloodthirster named Spineripper will pop out of the Portal of Rage portal and attempt to eviscerate and destroy *anyone* who doesn't belong here (be they followers of Sigmar, Tzeentch, or allies thereof). Subduing the Bloodthirster will be very difficult, unless adventurers have managed to learn the True Name of the Bloodthirster and can assemble his name in Chaos Runes within a niche somewhere in the chamber.

LOCATION: CHAOS WASTES

RANKS: 33-40

TYPE: REALM-INSTANCED

GRADE: 4

KEY LOOT: BLOODLORD ARMOR AND WEAPONS

FIVE SEALED GATES SEPARATE WOULD-BE CONQUERORS FROM THEIR ULTIMATE PRIZE: GATES THAT CAN BE OPENED ONLY BY INVOKING THE POWER OF KHORNE.

BOSSES

Azuk'Thul

Ability Name	Description
Cleave	This is a frontal arc damage ability.
Stomp	This is a PBAE damage ability
Spine Shot	This is a random target ability for ranged damage.
Terror	No one can rez within 5000 units of this monster when it is in combat.

Borzhar Rageborn

Ability Name	Description
Enraged Blow	A single-target, high-damage hit.
Banner of Bloodlust	As long as the Banner of Bloodlust is up, Borzhar will charge at a new target and should stay locked on the target for a medium duration before charging at a new target. Players can destroy the banner which will prevent him from using this charge anymore.
Banner of the Bloodherd	As long as the Banner of the Bloodherd is up, Bloodherd Gors will rally to Borzhar's side. To stop the reinforcement, players must destroy the Banner of the Bloodherd.

Gahlvoth Darkrage

Ability Name	Description
Energy Flux	Every 15 seconds Gahlvoth Darkrage will summon a lightning font on a random player. This font will last for 60 seconds and deal a great amount of damage to anyone standing in it.
Thundering Blow	This is a single target melee hit.

Zekaraz the Bloodcaller

Ability Name	Description
Taunt Immunity	Clawfang cannot be taunted.
Ardent Breath	Channeled breath of flame that applies damage over time.
Auxiliary Empathy	At all times during the fight, Doomspike's health must remain close to that of Clawfang's. If they stray too far apart their damage is increased by 100%.

DAEMON- AND BEASTMEN-
SLAYING TOME TACTICS WILL
AID YOU INSIDE.

Bastion Stair

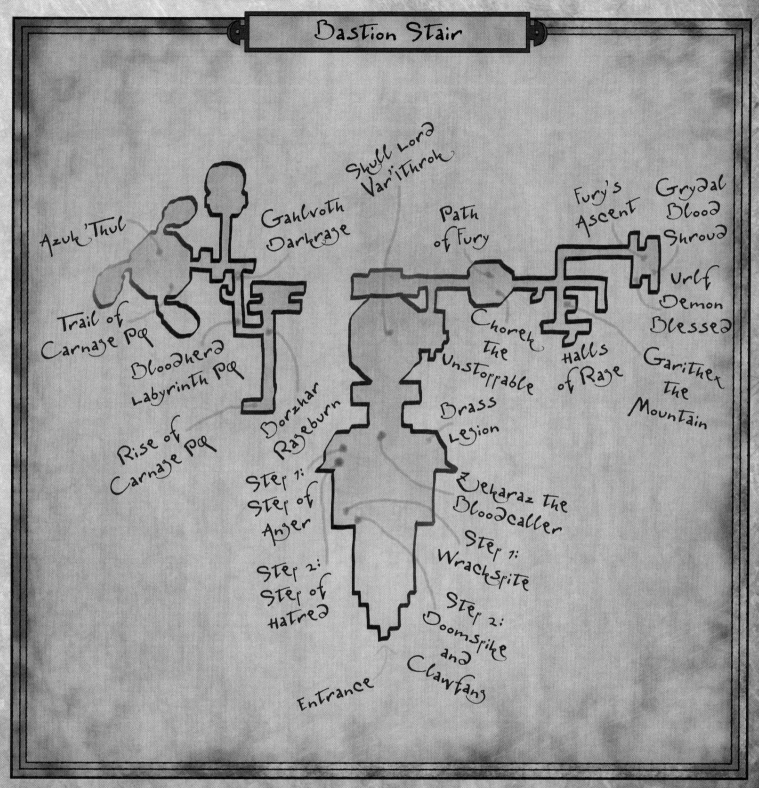

Azuk 'Thul

Gahlvoth Darkrage

Skull Lord Var'ithrok

Path of Fury

Fury's Ascent

Grydal Blood Shroud

Urlf Demon Blessed

Trail of Carnage PQ

Bloodherd Labyrinth PQ

Rise of Carnage PQ

Dorzhar Rageburn

Chorek the Unstoppable

Halls of Rage

Garithen the Mountain

Brass Legion

Step 1: Step of Anger

Zekaraz the Bloodcaller

Step 1: Wrackspite

Step 2: Step of Hatred

Step 2: Doomspike and Clawfang

Entrance

THE DUNGEON IS BROKEN UP INTO
THREE WINGS, EACH ENDING IN A
PUBLIC QUEST AND ONE OR TWO
SIX-PLAYER, INSTANCED BOSS FIGHTS.

Brass Bloodhowler

Ability Name	Description
Rampant Slash	Single target damage
Disabling Strike	Single target disable

Brass Bloodletter

Ability Name	Description
Rampant Slash	Single target damage
Bloodlust	Short duration offensive buff

Brass Skullhowler

Ability Name	Description
Obliterate	Massive single target damage

Chorek the Unstoppable

Ability Name	Description
Blood Mark	Short duration increased damage buff
Deteriorate Armor	Stacking armor debuff
Sweeping Arc	Frontal cone damage

Frenzied Skulltaker

Ability Name	Description
Stinging Blow	Single target damage

Juggernaut

Ability Name	Description
Taunt Immunity	Juggernaut cannot be taunted and will switch targets every 8 seconds.

Lord Slaurith

Ability Name	Description
Bloodpulse	This places a pulsing damage aura at the location of an enemy target.
Bloodscent Aura	Cast at the same location as Bloodpulse after the aura has ended, it places a debuff on a player in the radius for 15 seconds causing Lord Slaurith to mercilessly attack that player.
Bleeding Shout	Instance-wide damage over time cast when Slaurith does not have the scent of blood.
Dead Silence	PBAE silence.

Skull Lord Var'Ithrok

Ability Name	Description
Bloodwrath	A red mist will grow over an area of the room, causing anybody in the effected area to be hit with lasting damage.
Infectious Rage	Khorne's rage will infect a player for a short duration, causing them to damage friendly players every time they do damage to the Skull Lord.
Skull Cleave	Var'Ithrok will swing his Giant Rune Axe sweeping it in an arc below his waste. All players caught in this arc will be knocked back.
War Sunder	An overhand smash with his axe causes massive frontal damage and a short duration knockdown.

Skull Lord Var'Ithrok

Ability Name	Description
Destroy Mind	A 10 second complete disable that effects 1 player in the group.
Volatile Injection	A 30 second debuff at the end of which causes a Volatile Burst.
Volatile Burst	PBAE damage that severely hurts nearby allies.

Skulltaker Berserker

Ability Name	Description
Delete this table	

Skulltaker Bloodgiant

Ability Name	Description
Giant Swipe	A massive swipe of the arm causes frontal damage and a knockback.
Thundering Shock	PBAE short duration stun.
Crippling Below	PBAE debuff that reduces attack speed.

Skulltaker Champion

Ability Name	Description
Obliterate	Massive single target damage.

Skulltaker Eviscerator

Ability Name	Description
Slice	Single target damage.
Pummel	Single target damage and stun.

Thar'Ignan

Ability Name	Description
Bloodgreed	Anytime a player or mob dies in the instance, Thar'Ignan will heal himself.
Cleave in Two	This will hit a player for half of their health.
Blood Roots	This is a root that targets players who are between 150 units and 600 units away. This will also place a damage over time on them.
Blood Stomp	PBAE damage.
Thar"Ignan Hurl	Every once in awhile Thar'Ignan will throw players down to his Bloodsnouts.
Terror	No one can rez within 5000 units of this monster when it is in combat.

BILEROT BURROWS

BOSSES

LOCATION: INEVITABLE CITY

RANKS: 40+

TYPE: 6-PLAYER, INSTANCED

GRADE: 5

KEY LOOT: SENTINEL ARMOR AND WEAPONS

DUNGEON DETAILS

Winding passageways are covered in slime, with teeth protruding from the floors and walls. Humanoid fanatics, who apparently love the smell of sewers, are down here in Bilerot Burrows, as are fleshy plaguebeasts. The oozing green and brown slime is everywhere, and in some cases, is partnered with a green and brown gas cloud.

Bilerot Burrow starts on a linear track along maggot-infested burrows, and then segways into three different branches. The first is comprised mainly of Nurgle-aligned mortals, the second full of Nurgle-aligned daemons and the final is the resting place of the Bile Lord, a Great Unclean One.

MAGGOT BURROWS

The first area of the Bilerot Burrows is run by the Maggotfiend. You can see his influence in the area, since there will be literally hundreds of maggots around the place.

NURGLE MORTAL BURROWS

The second area of Bilerot is full of Nurgle-Infected warriors.

NURGLE DAEMON BURROWS

The third area of the dungeon is full of Nurgle-themed daemons.

THE BILE DEN

This is the Great Unclean One area. It only becomes accessible once the Wing 1, 2, and 3 bosses have been killed.

PLAYERS WILL NEED A FEW PIECES OF LESSER WARD ARMOR. EACH PIECE ABSORBS A PERCENTAGE OF ALL INCOMING DAMAGE RECEIVED IN BILEROT.

Bartholomeus the Sickly

Abilities	Description
Death's Head	This boss will randomly throw Death's Heads at people. These are skulls filled with pus and will explode on impact. Anyone who is hit by this will spawn Nurglings at their feet.
Sneeze	This boss will randomly sneeze during the fight doing cone knockback and damage.
Nurgling Enrage	When Nurglings die near him, he will enrage increasing his dps for a short time.

The Bile Lord

Abilities	Description
Defile	The Bile Lord will randomly select a target and taint the ground beneath them with Defile. This will deal damage to the targeted player and will spawn a damage font at their location. Players will want to move away from the Diseased Ground.
Unclean One Spew	This is a frontal cone damage vomit.
Phases	Dynamics
80% Health	When the Bile Lord reaches 80% hp, he will call for 10 Nurglings to come help him.
60% Health	When the Bile Lord reaches 60% hp, he will call for 10 Nurglings to come help him.
40% Health	When the Bile Lord reaches 40% hp, he will call all the Bilerot Humans on the ledges above to come help him. These will all run to a door on the upper ledge and will slowly begin to spawn into the fight. Upon spawning they will run to assist the Bile Lord. They will not stop spawning until the Bile Lord reaches 20%
20% Health	At 20% the Bile Lord will stun everyone in the room and go up to each of them one by one and Devour them.
Bile Lord's Innards	Stomach Bile will rain down on players inside the stomach slowly draining them of their life. They will have to damage the Bile Lord's Innards until his stomach is upset enough to spit them back out.
Regurgitate	When the Unclean One's stomach gets upset, he will regurgitate all players in his belly. All the mauraders and nurglings will be dead and the Bile Lord should set his health fairly low. Now the players must finish him off.

Maggotfiend Urhil

Abilities	Description
Maggotfiend Spew	This is just like the Bilerot Pustongue's spew, except it lasts much longer and spawns more than one maggot.
Phases	Dynamics
Phase 1	The Maggotfiend will constantly keep spewing forth maggots. You will want to focus on the maggots first, and then when time is left over deal damage to the Maggotfiend for a bit.

Ssyridian Morbidae

Abilities	Description
Bilerot Sickness	During the fight, this monster will randomly throw a ball of sickness at someone who is on its hate list. If the player is hit, they will become sick. While sick, a player will regenerate significantly less Action Points and they will have an ability added to their hotkey bank called "Induce Vomiting". If they use this ability, it will get rid of the sickness, but they will vomit doing frontal cone damage to themselves and all friendly targets. The player will also spawn maggots while vomiting, simulating that the player just vomited maggots.

Bilerot Burrows

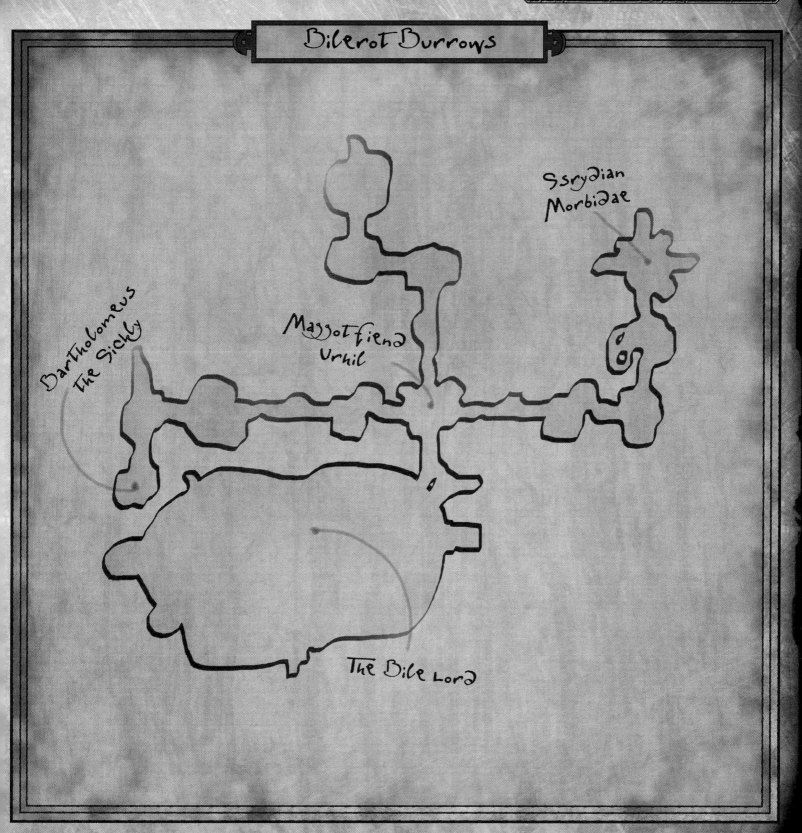

Ssrydian Morbidae

Bartholomeus The Sickly

Maggotfiend Urhil

The Bile Lord

PLAYERS CAN ACCESS THE BILEROT
BURROWS ONLY WHEN THE
INEVITABLE CITY HAS A HIGH CITY
RANK—INVADED OR PEACEFUL STATES

BOSSES (CONTINUED)

Ssyridian Morbidae

Abilities	Description
Rotting Zymosis	Every so often the boss will do a PBAE called Rotting Zymosis. This is a stacking debuff and each time a player is hit their ability to heal and deal damage will go down and the damage they take will go up.
Phases	Dynamics
Bilerot Plaguebeasts	3 Plaguebeasts reside in the halls near Ssrydian and if not killed they will come to his aid when he enters combat.
Bilerot Fanatic / Witherer / Plaguechosen	There are 2 sets of Bilerot Humans bent over in worship of Ssrydian. These mobs will not show as agro, since they are focused on their prayers. They will however agro if players get too close. (200 radius) They will also agro if Ssrydian becomes agro.

MONSTERS

Name	Description
Bilerot Chosen	Becomes enraged at the death of Nurglings Kill these guys before killing any Nurglings.
Bilerot Foulbearer	This Plaguebearer has an aura that significantly lessens AP regen. The story behind this will be that it's the odor they emit. laguebearers will attempt to explode when it gets close to death. Anyone who is hit by the explosion will have a significant DoT.
Bilerot Maurader 1	Becomes enraged at the death of Nurglings Kill these guys before killing any Nurglings.
Bilerot Maurader 2	Becomes enraged at the death of Nurglings Kill these guys before killing any Nurglings.
Bilerot Moldbearer	This Plaguebearer has an aura that significantly lessens the amount you are healed for by healing spells. The story behind this will be that it's the odor they emit. Plaguebearers will attempt to explode when it gets close to death. Anyone who is hit by the explosion will have a significant DoT.
Bilerot Plaguebeast	This is a big lumbering beast. Its body is full of fleshy tumors that will explode when the beast is taking damage. Depending on the type of tumor will determine what effect will be cast on the players near the Plaguebeast. The best tactic would be to tank with one player and deal ranged damage from the rest of the group.
Bilerot Pustongue	This mob is mostly a nuker, but will occasionally do a cone vomit spew that will spawn maggots and deal damage. Ideally you want to kill these as soon as possible before they have a chance to create additional maggots.
Bilerot Slimehound	Slimehounds are coated in slime. Ideally you will kill these with magic, because each hit you land with a melee weapon will lower that weapons ability to do damage with each stroke.
Bilerot Sickness	While adventuring through this wing of the Bilerot Burrows, random members of the player party will become sick with Bilerot Sickness. While a player is infected with Bilerot Sickness they will regen 20 less AP a tick. In order to rid themselves of Bilerot Sickness they will need to use the ability granted to them called 'Gag Self'. This will do a frontal cone damage to all friendly players and will remove the debuff "Bllerot Sickness and will have a small chance to spawn Bilerot Bilefeeders.
Nurgling	These lil guys have a chance to explode on damage. This will deal significant damage in a radius around them. If any humanoid nurgle monster is nearby, it will become enraged at the death of the nurgling. The more Nurglings that die nearby, the more enraged it will get. Best tactic would be to save these guys till last.
Wretched Bilefeeder	Bilefeeders are very annoying. They suck the Action points right out of you. VERY HIGH priority, if you don't kill these fast you wont have power the whole fight.
Wretched Bilespawn	Bilespawn maggots will spit acidic bile onto your armor. Each time you're hit, your armor will lose a little more defense value. Alone, these aren't a problem, but you want to focus on them if there are several up, otherwise your armor will go down fast.

BLOODWROUGHT ENCLAVE

BOSSES

LOCATION: INEVITABLE CITY

RANKS: 40+

TYPE: 6-PLAYER, INSTANCED

GRADE: 5

KEY LOOT: SENTINEL ARMOR AND WEAPONS

DUNGEON DETAILS

The Bloodwrought tribe, known for their ungodly murder sprees, once hunted holy men and eventually expanded their reach to anyone who crossed their path. Tales say the tribe has been locked underneath the Inevitable City in an eternal war with each other, and woe be to the mortal who unlocks their prison.

The Bloodwrought Enclave has a short hallway past the entrance that branches out to three wings. To the left is the beastman section, straight ahead is the daemons and to the right are Khorne warriors leading portal pads that will transport players to an ice cave with undead, a poorly lit cave with gorgers, and a large room with a bloodbeast.

PLAYERS WILL NEED A FEW PIECES OF LESSER WARD ARMOR. EACH PIECE ABSORBS A PERCENTAGE OF ALL INCOMING DAMAGE RECEIVED IN BLOODWROUGHT.

Barakus the Godslayer

Abilities	Descriptions
Bloodlust	Short term enrage - increase damage dealt
Whirlwind	PBAOE melee Damage
Charge	Randomly selects a ranged target and locks on to that target. Brutemaul will run at that player at high speed knocking down all players in his path and doing damage to them. Once brutemaul reaches his target he will deliver a high damage melee blow and knockback.
Enfeeble	Periodically throughout the fight Brutemaul will do a shout and screenshake and debuff everyone in the group. Players will be highly vulnerable to damage and must move away from Brutemaul as quickly as possible.

Phases	Dynamics
Phase 1	Players will need to use the Bloodwrought Key that they obtained from Korthuk the Raging to open the gate into Brutemauls room. In the front of the room there will be 8 Rageclaw Bloodletters. These are core mobs and should be easy to deal with.
Phase 2	Players will directly engage Barakus the Godslayer. He will use all of his abilities. During the fight, players can use the three items that they obtained from the three portal bosses/events. · Empty Heart- Single Use Dmg/Attk Speed Debuff. · Blood Claw- Single Use Dmg Increase, Toughness/HP Debuff. · Obsidian Orb- Single Use Blindness.

Culius Embervine

Abilities	Descriptions
Random AOE Nuke	Randomly targets a player on his hate list and casts an AOE nuke on them. The player and all other players around them will take damage
Root + DoT	Randomly Targets a player on his hate list and casts a Root on that player. While the player is rooted he will take periodic damage.
Cone Nuke	Long range cone/breath nuke
Random AOE Morale Debuff	Randomly targets a player on his hate list and casts an AOE nuke on them. The player and all other players around them will have their morale reduced.

Phases	Dynamics
Phase 1	Players will engage and fight Culius Embervine alone where he will use all of his abilities.
Phase 2	Culius will disappear and spawn 5 core Soulwrought Knights. They will use pbaoe melee attacks. These must be killed as quickly as possible. After 30 seconds Culius will re-appear and attack, any adds that are still up must be delt with quickly.
Drop	Culius should drop an Empty Heart to be used on the final boss fight.

Gorger Event

Abilities	Descriptions
Brute Force	Standard Melee Strike
Bellowing Roar	Healing Debuff

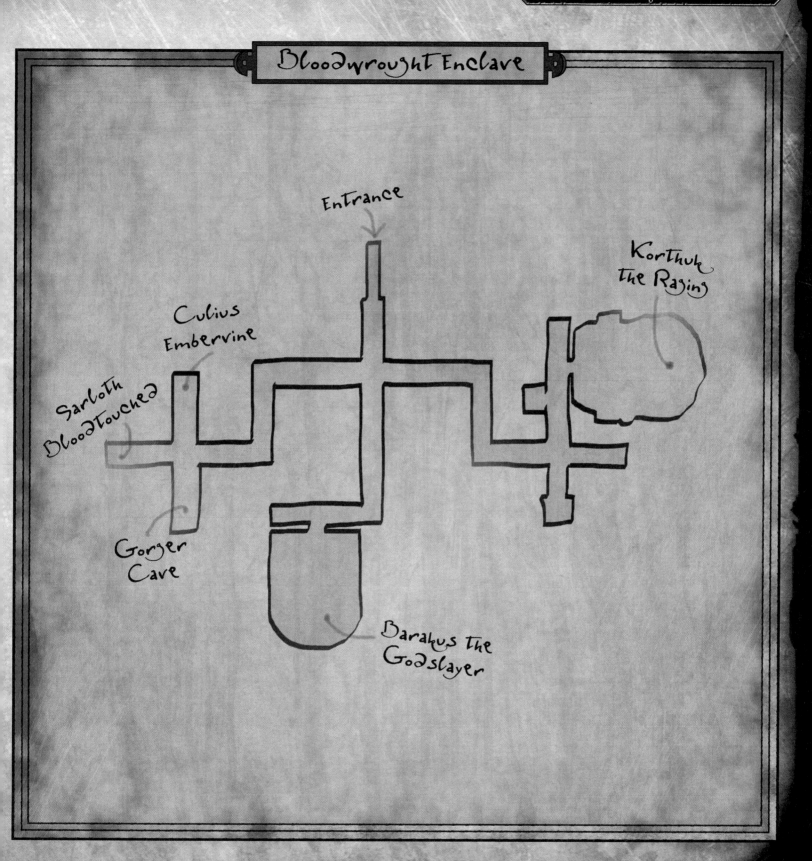

Bloodwrought Enclave

Entrance

Korthuk the Raging

Culius Embervine

Sarloth Bloodtouched

Gorger Cave

Barakus the Godslayer

PLAYERS CAN ACCESS THE BLOOD-
WROUGHT ENCLAVE ONLY WHEN THE
INEVITABLE CITY HAS A HIGH CITY
RANK—INVADED OR PEACEFUL STATES.

BOSSES (CONTINUED)

Gorger Event

Abilities	Descriptions
Phases	Dynamics
Phase 1	Upon killing a certain gorger in the cave players will trigger the gorger event. Players will be assaulted by waves of gorgers until all waves have been defeated.
Drop	Players who successfully survive and kill the last Gorger should receive an Obsidian Orb which may be used in the final boss fight.

Korthuk the Raging

Abilities	Descriptions
Bloody Cleave	Standard Melee Cleave
Bloody Roar	AE Silence, 2 second duration
Phases	Dynamics
Ragedrunk Centigor	Standard Bearer. Has a passive Damage Add ability. The damage add has a range of 1350 units. If the Musician or Korthuk are in range they will do extra damage when they attack.
Ragedrunk Musician	Casts two spells. Group heal and a Morale Damage spell. These can be outranged
Bugman's XXXXXX	Barrel spawned around the area - grants the use of a firebreath for 15 seconds by any mob that drinks it
Tilean Ale	Barrel spawned around the area - debuffs the mobs attack speed and damage.
Altdorf Stout	Barrel spawned around the area - grants a short duration enrage, increasing damage.
Phase 1	Korthuk and his two adds are spawned in the middle of the room with barrels scattered about. Players can attack and destroy the Barrels at anytime.
	The players will need to engage Korthuk and this two adds at the same time. Every 15 seconds one of the centaurs will run to a barrel and get a buff.
Drop	Korthuk will drop the Bloodwrought Key upon death.

Sarloth Bloodtouched

Abilities	Descriptions
Cleave	Standard Melee Cleave
Stomp	Sarloth will stomp the ground and everyone in the room will be knocked down and take massive damage.
Spite Shot	Sarloth will target a random ranged player on his hate list and fire a spine at them for high damage
Bloodfrenzy	Sarloth will place the Bloodfrenzy buff on a random player on his hate list. That player will take high damage over time but will also be given a damage and healing increase. If the player dies while the bloodfrenzy is active they will spawn a bloodbeast.
Phases	Dynamics
Phase 1	Sarloth is a very difficult tank and spank encounter. He does massive damage to everyone in the group. The key to the fight is making sure that the player with the bloodfrenzy buff is spam healed so they do not die, losing just 1 player can me failure.
Drop	Sarloth should drop a Blood Claw upon death that may be used in the final boss fight.

MONSTERS

Name	Description
Bloodmaddened Gorger	Melee mob. Uses the following abilities: Brute Force - standard melee, Bellowing Roar - Healing Debuff.
Bloodwrought Aspirant	Melee mob with Aggro switch. Has the following abilities: Cleave - Standard melee cleave, Axe Throw - Throws an axe at a random ranged target for high damage, Aggro switch - Stun + damage + knockback + wipe threat.
Bloodwrought Champion	Melee mob. Has the following abilities: Cleave - Standard Melee cleave, Enrage - Will enrage for a very short duration and do extreme damage, must be CC'd, Channeled whirlwind - PBAOE melee damage that players can run away from, Axe Throw - Throws an axe at a random ranged target for high damage.
Ragetusk Charger	Core+ mob. Melee. Cleave. Will attack any players with the mark placed by the Savage Ragehorn.
Savage Bloodletter	Melee mob. Has the following abilities: Cleave - Standard melee cleave, Bleed - Stacks with bleeds applied by other mobs. Each bleed multiplies the other bleeds damage. 2 Bleeds will multiple the damage of both bleeds by 2. 3 bleeds will multiple all three bleeds by 3. It is very risky to tank more than 1 or 2 mobs at a time.
Savage Howler	Melee hound. Has the following abilities: Melee strike, Cone Shout - AP Regen debuff, Bleed - Stacks with bleeds applied by other mobs. Each bleed multiplies the other bleeds damage. 2 Bleeds will multiple the damage of both bleeds by 2. 3 bleeds will multiple all three bleeds by 3. It is very risky to tank more than 1 or 2 mobs at a time.
Savage Ragecaller	Melee mob. Will agro switch. Has the following abilities:PBAOE bleed melee attack, PBAOE shout debuff - debuffs morale and AP regen.
Savage Ragehorn	Melee mob. Has the following abilities: Frontal Arc melee strike / cleave, Melee strike, Call Target - Places a marker on 1 player. Any chargers in the area will agro on that player and attack.
Soulwrought Mage	Caster mob. Has the following abilities: Random Cast AoE damage - high damage, Root - short duration, Frontal cone nuke - Long range cone nuke.
Soulwrought Warrior	Melee mob. Has the following abilities: Cleave, The mob will occasionally cast a PBAOE root and then disappear and appear on another target.

GUNBAD

LOCATION: THE BADLANDS

RANKS: 23–30

TYPE: REALM INSTANCED

GRADE: 3

KEY LOOT: REDEYE ARMOR AND WEAPONS

DUNGEON DETAILS

Once a Morkain place of power, for a thousand years Gunbad has been home to a strange breed of greenskin. The mushroom-crazed forces of the Night Goblins—furtive maniacs clad in black and flecked with spit—gibber and scurry in the darkness. Alone in the gloom, their unhinged minds have fashioned all manner of madness, from teetering Goblin cities to pulsating squigs of nightmarish proportions. Now change has come to the timeless depths. The greenskins seek to break the unruly Night Goblins to their brutish will. Meanwhile, the Dwarfs have a more desperate mission. Gunbad is the sole source of Brightstone—a key component of the mighty Doomstriker Weapons. They must claim this precious ore and destroy another potential Goblin enemy. Still, the prospect of spattering Goblin brains while underground has cheered more than one Oathbearer, despite the grim tales of the Night Goblin's insane strength.

ALCHEMISTS' WING

Thick with glowing spores, the corridor air takes on the damp taste of mildew. Fungi of every shape and size line the walls and floor where greedy greenskin hands have not yet reached. Numerous Goblins share the task of harvesting, sorting and carting the precious mushrooms down to where Fibrig the Brewer prepares his special draughts. The cream of the crop is then handed over to the Masta Mixa for use in his experiments.

SQUIG NURSERY

An undescribable smell greets those adventurous enough to make their way down the slime encrusted corridor leading to the Squig Nursery. Even the most hardened of adventurer has found themselves losing not only their stomach contents but stomachs themselves in quite short order.

No one is really certain how squigs come into being (and no one has been willing to hang around long enough to find out thus far), but here in the slime festooned chamber of the squig nursery, Glomph the Squig Herder makes it his business to poke, prod and bludgeon his sporeling charges into vicious bounding mounts for the Redeye tribe.

REDEYE BARRACKS

The Redeye tribe takes up much of the heart of Gunbad. Clumsily erected watchtowers lean out over the abyss, commanding awe inspiring views of their fellow greenskins and a yawning inky blackness. Occasionally a smaller Goblin is "overcome" by curiosity and punted into the darkness by his patrol.

The milling chaos can be misleading however, upon the recognition of a common enemy the entire tribe boils forth from behind their wooden palisades; a storm of angry ants armed with crude pointed weapons and having absolutely no compunction against using teeth. A perfectly acceptable tactic is to gnaw off the feet of an enemy as it saves more for later.

MONSTER DOWN BELOW

Shudders trace their way up the winding corridors of Mount Gunbad, feigning seismic events. It is only when the bellows begin that one begins to understand: something lurks at the roots of Mount Gunbad. A creature so fierce and powerful that its frustrations shake the mountain itself. Something 'ard to feed.

Arathremia

Ability Name	Description
Deceived Souls	At 80% (and every 20% threshold) she releases 6 Deceived Souls to aid her fight.
Soul Turn	At 30% and 10% if the souls are still alive, they turn on her in her weakened state.
Soul Death	At 25% and 5% she will kill the souls attacking her.
Arathremia's Slumber	Places a random target into a sleeping state for up to 6 seconds.

Ard ta Feed

Ability Name	Description
Gate Close	When players engage Ard ta Feed the gate will close behind them.
Corrosive Vomit	A cone damaging attack with damage over time.
Slimy Vomit	A cone damaging attack with a movement snare.
'ard Stomp	Knockback which snares players for 15 seconds and throws player back a large distance.
Spit Bomb	Switches to second head and begins using spit attack.
Cavern Quake	The cavern shakes, stallagtites fall and damage players every 20 seconds.
Enrage	The mourkain pillar lights up and he gains an Enrage for 20 seconds.

Elder Kizzig

Ability Name	Description
Forceful Stab	Cost: 100 AP, Cooldown: 5 Seconds, Activation Time: Instant, Deals heavy damage to his main target
Whirl an' Twirl	Cost: 100 AP, Cooldown: 10 Seconds, Activation Time: Instant, Deals moderate damage to all nearby targets.
Snotling Affinity	Cost: 0 AP, Cooldown: N/A, Activation Time: Instant, Duration: 20 Seconds, Deals 75% more damage in the event that Chipfang da Lit'l dies.

Foul Mouf da 'Ungry

Ability Name	Description
Chomp	Cost: 100 AP, Cooldown: 5 Seconds, Activation Time: Instant, Deals heavy damage to its main target.
Grotesque Belch	Cost: 100 AP, Cooldown: 30 Seconds, Deals heavy damage to all opponents within 100 feet.
Foul Wound	Cost: 0 AP, Cooldown: 30 – 60 Seconds, Activation Time: 3 Seconds, Duration: 8 Seconds, Places an Ailment on all nearby opponents that lasts for 8 seconds. If left untreated, the wound causes Pestilent Crawlers to burst forth and attack the warband.

Garrolath da Poxbearer

Ability Name	Description
Gore	Cost: 100 AP, Cooldown: 5 Seconds, Activation Time: Instant, Deals heavy damage to its main target.
Headbutt	Cost: 100 AP, Cooldown: 15 Seconds, Activation Time: Instant, Deals heavy damage to its main target and knocks him or her back a moderate distance.

Gunbad Tunnels

Entrance

'Ard Ta Feed

Squig Crazy

Mangle the Wrangla

Masta Wrangla Glix

Griblik da Stinka

Garrolath da Poxbearer

A Taint from Below

Elder Kizzig

Wight Lord Solithex

Redeye Stompin' Grounds

Herald of Solithex

Squig Nursery

Kizzig's Gobbo Place

Foul Mouf da 'Ungry

Mad Mixas

Masta Mixa

Redeye Big Oaf

Arathremia

Glomp da Squig Masta

Velkyrrix & Blaz da Trainin' Masta

Redeye Nightmare

Shadowweb Spawning Grounds

BOSSES (CONTINUED)

Glomp da Squig Masta

Ability Name	Description
Expert Shot	Glomp da Squig Masta is an expert in ranged attacks in and out of melee range. He will attack players even if they hide behind collision
Massive Arrow Attack	He will occasionally disengage from the main target, face a new target and fire a conical arrow attack that is represented by a massive green bolt. Once this is done he will re-engage his prior target.
Teleport	Once Glomp Da Squig Masta reaches 80% health he will teleport himself up to one of the three platforms and become invulnerable.
Skewerin' Squigs	Approximately five seconds after teleportation and Glomp da Squig Masta will then release the Skewerin' Squigs to attack the players.
Acidic Muck	Every 10 seconds while on a platform, Glomp da Squig Masta will fire a slow-moving, green arrow. Upon impact on the player target, the arrow will burst into a pool of acidic muck, causing damage to any player standing atop it. This pool of muck will remain for the full duration of the fight. Basically the longer the players take to kill the Squigs off, the less ground they have to safely maneuver around.
Stinkspewin' Squig	Approximately five seconds after teleportation and Glomp da Squig Masta will then release the Stinkspewin' Squigs to attack the players.
Spikestabbin' Squig	Approximately five seconds after teleportation and Glomp da Squig Masta will then release the Spikestabbin' Squigs to attack the players
Warchargin' Squig	Glomp da Squig Masta then appears to be a Warchargin' Squig as he gains new abilities. His specialized ability is "Smash 'Em 'Ard!" which he channels a PBAE damaging ability, causing the ground to shack and dust to rise up.

Griblik da Stinka

Ability Name	Description
Chomp	Cost: 100 AP, Cooldown: 5 Seconds, Activation Time: Instant, Deals heavy damage to its main target.
Vile Vomit	Cost: 100 AP, Cooldown: 5 Seconds, Activation Time: Instant, Duration: 10 Seconds, Deals heavy damage to its main target and moderate damage over time to all nearby, frontal opponents.

Herald of Solithex

Ability Name	Description
Sweeping Strike	Cost: 100 AP, Cooldown: 5 Seconds, Activation Time: Instant, Deals heavy damage to all nearby, frontal opponents.
Mourkain Rift	Cost: 0 AP, Cooldown: 30 Seconds, Activation Time: Instant, Duration: 120 Seconds, Places a rift on the ground at a random target's location which deals moderate damage to all nearby opponents.
Frozen Touch	Cost: 100 AP, Cooldown: 10 Seconds, Activation Time: Instant, Duration: 5 Seconds, Deals moderate damage to all nearby, front opponents and reduces all healing effects cast upon afflicted targets by 25%.

Masta Mixa

Ability Name	Description
Whirlin' Brain Bursta	AOE Damage, Only occurs when he is wielding his staff
Jar of Pummeling	AOE Damage, Occurs over a randomly-selected player, Effect lasts for approximately 60 seconds, Fists of Gork pummel the location where the damage is being dealt, Unkillable, but avoidable by simply repositioning oneself
Gitzappa da Stick	Single Target Disable, Occurs on a randomly-selected player, Effect lasts for approximately 60 seconds (unless the staff is killed)

Masta Wrangla Glix

Ability Name	Description
Troll Assault	During the fight he will spawn young Trolls that will assault the players for a random time period between 30 – 60 seconds. They are Core-cons.
Adult Trolls	If a young Troll is not killed within that timer, then it will burst into a full adult Troll – triggering Wrangla Masta Glix to say the following:

Redeye Big Oaf

Ability Name	Description
Wide Swing	Cost: 100 AP, Cooldown: 5 Seconds, Activation Time: Instant, Deals heavy damage to all nearby, frontal opponents.
Leave Me Alone	Cost: 100 AP, Cooldown: 30 Seconds, Activation Time: Instant, Smashes the ground causing moderate damage and knocks up all nearby opponents.

Velkyrrix & Blaz da Trainin' Masta

Ability Name	Description
Venom Cloud	Cost: 100 AP, Cooldown: 30 Seconds, Activation Time: Instant, Deals heavy damage to all players within 100 feet
Stabbity	Cost: 100 AP, Cooldown: 5 Seconds, Activation Time: Instant, Deals heavy damage to his main target.

Wight Lord Solithex

Ability Name	Description
Spawn of the Deceiver	At every 10% threshold he will stun players, teleport to area center and call down 6 Spawn of the Deceiver to aid his fight.
Consume Soul	Cost: 0 AP, Cooldown: 30 Seconds, Duration: 10 Seconds, Activation: Instance, Chooses his second most-hated opponent, disables and places him or her within a dome of cursed energies which causes significant amounts of damage. Party members may destroy the dome from outside to halt this effect.
Vampiric Shadows	Cost: 0 AP, Cooldown: 60 Seconds, Duration: 10 Seconds (Channeled), Activation: 3 Seconds, A channeled ability over the next 10 seconds which causes the caster of this ability will deal point-blank damage to all nearby opponents and heal the caster for all damage done in this manner. The caster may not take any action while under these effects.
Guise of Deception	Cost: 0 AP, Cooldown: 30 Seconds, Duration: 6 Seconds, Activation: Instant, Places a Curse on a random opponent which, after 6 seconds, causes the afflicted to burst with wicked energies. The afflicted, and all nearby allies, take significant damage and are launched into the air.
Mourkain Rift	Cost: 0 AP, Cooldown: 60 Seconds, Duration: 120 Seconds, Activation: Instant, Places a rift on the ground at a random target's location which deals moderate damage to all nearby opponents.
Whispering Shadows	Cost: 0 AP, Cooldown: 60 Seconds, Duration: N/A, Activation: 1 Second, Increases the casters movement speed by 100% and causes the caster to attack a target at random after dealing any melee damage.
Massive Cleave	Cost: 0 AP, Cooldown: 5 Seconds, Duration: N/A, Activation: Instant, Deals heavy damage to the caster's main target.
Bone Shredder	Cost: 0 AP, Cooldown: 5 Seconds, Duration: N/A, Activation: Instant, Deals moderate damage to all targets nearby the caster.

MONSTERS

Monster/NPC	Level	Class	Type	Area
Alchemist Grogmaka	APQ Boss	NG-Alchemist	HERO	Squig Nursery Slime Walls APQ
Ard ta Feed	Encounter Boss	Squig	HERO	Ard ta Feed
Bash Squig	Common	Squig	SPEC	Mushrooms And Potions
Beaten Prisoner	Common	Prisoner	CORE	Alchemy Lab
Big Gubber	Encounter Boss	Squig	HERO	Mushrooms And Potions
Bilebreath	Encounter Boss	Troll	HERO	Squig Nursery
Blaz Squigtender	APQ Boss	NG-Boss	HERO	Blaz's Mushroom Stikkas
Blaz's Captain	Common	NG-Warrior	HERO	Blaz's Mushroom Stikkas
Blaz's Driller	Common	NG-Warrior	SPEC	Blaz's Mushroom Stikkas
Blaz's Elite	Common	NG-Warrior	SPEC	Blaz's Mushroom Stikkas
Blaz's Scout	Common	NG-Squig Herder	SPEC	Blaz's Mushroom Stikkas
Blaz's Stabba	Common	NG-Warrior	SPEC	Blaz's Mushroom Stikkas
Blaz's Stikka	Common	NG-Warrior	SPEC	Blaz's Mushroom Stikkas
Blitza Bloodarrer	Common	NG-Squig Herder	SPEC	Might of the Red Eye
Blitza Bloodnetter	Common	NG-Squig Herder	SPEC	Might of the Red Eye
Blitza Bloodspear	Common	NG-Warrior	SPEC	Might of the Red Eye
Blitza Doomhood	Common	NG-Shaman	SPEC	Might of the Red Eye
Blitza Madcapper	Common	NG-Shaman	SPEC	Might of the Red Eye
Blitza Mushroom Addict	Common	NG-Shaman	SPEC	Blaz's Mushroom Stikkas
Blitza Mushroom Spitta	Common	NG-Shaman	SPEC	Blaz's Mushroom Stikkas
Blitza Troll Clubber	Common	NG-Warrior	SPEC	Might of the Red Eye
Booma	Encounter Boss	NG-Shaman	HERO	Squig Nursery
Brudig Stouthelm	NK		NK	
Bugwort	Encounter Boss	NG-Warrior	HERO	Squig Nursery
Buzz Squig	Common	Squig	SPEC	Alchemy Lab
Buzz Squig	Common	Squig	SPEC	Mushrooms And Potions
Cave Squig	Common	Squig	SPEC	Might of the Red Eye
Collecta Grisnik	Encounter Boss	NG-Warrior	HERO	Mushrooms And Potions
Colorful Squig	Common	Squig	SPEC	Alchemy Lab
Crazed Alchemist	Common	NG-Alchemist	SPEC	Mushrooms And Potions
Crazed Burnrot Picker	Common	NG-Alchemist	SPEC	Alchemy Lab
Crazed Cave Hunter	Common	NG-Squig Herder	SPEC	Mushrooms And Potions
Crazed Cave Lurker	Common	NG-Squig Herder	SPEC	Mushrooms And Potions
Crazed Chemist	Common	NG-Alchemist	SPEC	Alchemy Lab
Crazed Collector	Common	NG-Alchemist	SPEC	Mushrooms And Potions
Crazed Goorot Picker	Common	NG-Alchemist	SPEC	Alchemy Lab
Crazed Mushroomer	Common	NG-Warrior	SPEC	Mushrooms And Potions
Crazed Mushroomist	Common	NG-Shaman	SPEC	Alchemy Lab
Crazed Pusrot Picker	Common	NG-Alchemist	SPEC	Alchemy Lab
Cruel Rot	Common	Squig	SPEC	Alchemy Lab
Da Nanny	Common	Squig	CORE+	Squig Nursery Slime Walls APQ
Didbin Darkhood	Encounter Boss	NG-Shaman	HERO	Might of the Red Eye
Doppleganger	Common	NG-Warrior	CORE	Gritzle the Wotsit
Drugni Deepblade	Common	Ironbreaker	SPEC	Mining inThe Dark
Drugni Deepblade	NK		NK	
Dugit Blastahead	Encounter Boss	NG-Squig Herder	HERO	Squig Nursery
Farbit da Gnawer	Encounter Boss	NG-Warrior	HERO	Squig Nursery
Fibrig da Brewer	Encounter Boss	NG-Alchemist	HERO	Mushrooms And Potions
Firwik Gudeye	Encounter Boss	NG-Squig Herder	HERO	Might of the Red Eye

MONSTERS (CONTINUED)

Monster/NPC	Level	Class	Type	Area
Fleshy Squig	Common	Squig	SPEC	Alchemy Lab
Foul Acid Squig	Common	Squig	CORE+	Squig Nursery Slime Walls APQ
Foul Blaster Squig	Common	Squig	SPEC	Squig Nursery
Foul Chomp Squig	Common	Squig	SPEC	Squig Nursery
Foul Cold Squig	Common	Squig	CORE+	Squig Nursery Slime Walls APQ
Foul Fire Squig	Common	Squig	CORE+	Squig Nursery Slime Walls APQ
Foul Handler	Common	NG-Warrior	SPEC	Squig Nursery
Foul Herder	Common	NG-Squig Herder	SPEC	Squig Nursery
Foul Horned Sporeling	Common	Squig	CORE	Squig Nursery Slime Walls APQ
Foul Horned Squig	Common	Squig	CORE+	Squig Nursery Slime Walls APQ
Foul Large Squig	Common	Squig	SPEC	Glomp the Squig Hearder
Foul Large Squig	Common	Squig	SPEC	Glomp the Squig Hearder
Foul Monstrous Squig	Common	Squig	HERO	Glomp the Squig Hearder
Foul Monstrous Squig	Common	Squig	HERO	Glomp the Squig Hearder
Foul Overseer	Common	NG-Squig Herder	SPEC	Squig Nursery
Foul Spawner Squig	Common	Squig	SPEC	Squig Nursery
Foul Spiky Sporeling	Common	Squig	CORE	Squig Nursery Slime Walls APQ
Foul Spiky Squig	Common	Squig	CORE+	Squig Nursery Slime Walls APQ
Foul Sporeling	Common	Squig	CORE	Squig Nursery Slime Walls APQ
Foul Sporeling	Common	Squig	CORE	Glomp the Squig Hearder
Foul Sporeling	Common	Squig	CORE	Glomp the Squig Hearder
Foul Squig Gnasher	Common	NG-Squig Rider	SPEC	Squig Nursery
Foul Squig Herder	Common	NG-Squig Herder	CORE+	Squig Nursery Slime Walls APQ
Foul Warped Sporeling	Common	Squig	CORE	Squig Nursery Slime Walls APQ
Foul Warped Squig	Common	Squig	CORE+	Squig Nursery Slime Walls APQ
Frenzied Spectator	Common	NG-Warrior	CORE+	Warboss Powat
Garak the Sludgespawn	Hidden APQ Boss	Mutant	HERO	Alchemy Lab
Glomp	Encounter Boss	NG-Squig Herder	HERO	Glomp the Squig Hearder
Glomp	Encounter Boss	NG-Squig Herder	HERO	Glomp the Squig Hearder
Gooeater Mudnirk	Encounter Boss	NG-Shaman	HERO	Mushrooms And Potions
Goontz the Maniacal	APQ Boss	NG-Alchemist	HERO	Alchemy Lab
Gritzle the Wotsit	Encounter Boss	NG-Warrior	HERO	Gritzle the Wotsit
Grobbag	Common	NG-Warrior	SPEC	Forward Gits
Grobbag	NK		NK	
Grotuz	Common	Bloody Sun Warrior	SPEC	Forward Gits
Grotuz	NK		NK	
Herdmaster Kilgrut	Encounter Boss	NG-Squig Herder	HERO	Might of the Red Eye
Hugbik Eyebiter	Encounter Boss	NG-Warrior	HERO	Mushrooms And Potions
Intoxicated Prisoner	Common	Prisoner	SPEC	Alchemy Lab
Kurga Squig-Maka	Encounter Boss	NG-Alchemist	HERO	Squig Nursery
Largnoz Brainhurta	Encounter Boss	NG-Shaman	HERO	Might of the Red Eye
Mad Chanta	Common	NG-Shaman	SPEC	Alchemy Lab
Mad Mixa	Common	NG-Alchemist	SPEC	Alchemy Lab
Masta Mixa	Encounter Boss	NG-Alchemist	HERO	Masta Mixa
Morgit da Waaagher	Encounter Boss	NG-Shaman	HERO	Might of the Red Eye
Mugnog	NK		NK	
Mutated Squig	Common	Squig	HERO	Masta Mixa
Pen Boss Squank	APQ Sub boss	NG-Squig Herder	SPEC	Alchemy Lab
Pen Warden	Common	NG-Squig Herder	SPEC	Alchemy Lab

Monster/NPC	Level	Class	Type	Area
Redeye Potion Git	Common	NG-Alchemist	SPEC	Mushrooms And Potions
Shaman Verdboom	Common	NG-Shaman	HERO	Squig Nursery Slime Walls APQ
Snotrock the Lurker	Encounter	NG-Squig Herder	HERO	Mushrooms And Potions
Splitsik Toofsplitter	Encounter Boss	NG-Warrior	HERO	Might of the Red Eye
Squighopper Boingy	Common	NG-Squig Hopper	HERO	Squig Nursery Slime Walls APQ
Stone-Eater Troll	Common	Troll	SPEC	Might of the Red Eye
Stunted Mutant	Common	Mutant	SPEC	Alchemy Lab
Toofmaw	Encounter Boss	Squig	HERO	Squig Nursery
Ukor Skafson	Common	Hammerer	SPEC	Mining inThe Dark
Ukor Skafson	NK		NK	
Warboss Powat	Encounter Boss	NG-Warrior	HERO	Warboss Powat
Warghaz da Trainer	Encounter Boss	NG-Warrior	HERO	Might of the Red Eye
Warped Squig	Common	Squig	HERO	Masta Mixa

THE LOST VALE

LOCATION: THE LOST VALE

RANKS: 40+

TYPE: 6-PLAYER, INSTANCED

GRADE: 6

KEY LOOT: DARKPROMISE ARMOR AND WEAPONS

DUNGEON DETAILS

If you claim yourself a practiced Bright Wizard, believe yourself Tzeentch's favored Chosen, or pray that you are a balanced Archmage, the Lost Vale awaits you. Take arms alongside five of your strongest allies when venturing into this six-player instance, for the challenges therein are like none other found in the Old World. Your prowess with the sword, bow, and arcane will be pushed to its limits against creatures and daemons both rare and terrible. Only the most skilled and innovative of players working together will manage their way through the many threats and solve the many mysteries this majestic island holds. Those successful few will learn the Everqueen's fate, and reap the greatest rewards.

THORNVALE WILDS

The Thornvale Wilds are the area outside the Everqueen's Palace. The area used to be inhabited by some of the rarest creatures Ulthuan had to offer, all of which were subservient to the Everqueen and her court. Including the Whitefire Spiders, from which their queen's silk was woven the most prized garments in Ulthuan. With the taint of Chaos infecting the Evercourt, the creatures have turned to evil. They have been corrupted beyond repair, their souls caught in the rapture that is the Dark Prince of Chaos.

After emerging from the Chaos Portal with Sechar, the beastmen of the Writhing Herd quickly flocked to the sundered waystones centering the wilds. Led by the Majestic White Doombull Orghal, the herd finds themselves locked in a stalemate against the Whitefire spiders, over the greatest of these corrupted stones.

BLACKWILLOW FOREST

Blackwillow Forest was once a tranquil oasis full of the most peaceful and beautiful wildlife in all of Ulthuan. That was until the Gorge Maw Tribe's arrival. The enormous Ogres had truly found gluttonous paradise. The earth shook as the clan joyously trampled through the forest in a berserk feeding frenzy. The careless rampage was halted when finally the ancient spirits of the forest rose up against them.

Initially, the forest spirits fought the corruption seeping into their forest but once Sarthain the Worldbearer, the oldest living Treeman in the known world, began to fault the Elves for this trespassing the Forest Spirits quickly fell in line. Now, the corrupted Forest Spirits tend to their eternal forest and guard it against all comers.

THE EVERQUEEN'S PALACE GARDENS

The once-peaceful palace is now the source of the corruption in the Gaen Vale. The Chaos Portal through which Darkpromise Warband emerged pierces the heart of these gardens. The Everqueen's most trusted protectors, the Handmaidens, have been overcome by Slaurn's tribe. Slaanesh Daemons now stalk the halls and gardens seeking those who have not turned to worship of the Dark Prince.

The Everqueen herself has been brought to her knees. Her beauty is used in unspeakable acts for a dark ritual feared to bring forth the ultimate manifestation of decadence and pain, a Keeper of Secrets.

Ahzranok

Abilities	Description
Stone Skin	Immune to all magic every 25 seconds for 10 seconds. This is meant to force players to switch dps to the eggs during this instead of arbitrarily, otherwise not enough total dps will be done by appropriately blanced and geared group to finish Ahzranok before Lurquass' arrival.

Phases	Dynamics
Ahzranok's Eggs	20 Eggs lay about the area. They all hatch at expiration of 2 minute timer. Players can attack and destroy them before then (5k hit points). Doing so will cause Ahzranok to drop all hate, and then add 2x tank taunt worth of hate to that player. Broadcast when changing hate: "Ahzranok cries in agony at the destruction of one of her eggs. She focuses her wrath on |n."
	If the eggs manage to hatch a Stone Lizard emerges. It is a 10% pull mask core with no abilities.
Lurquass' Approach	A 3 minute timer starts on aggro of Ahzranok. At expiration of the timer Lurquass spawns in the water and swims toward the center of the boss fight area aggroing as normal. A broadcast is played every 30 seconds indicating progress of the approach · A large wave on the horizon approaches. · Lurquass nears. · Lurquass has arrived!

Butcher Gutbeater

Abilities	Description
Cleave	Standard high damage cleave
Gut Spew	Cone DD that leaves affected area on ground for 20 seconds. Pulsing damage received by anyone in affected area.
Gut Bounce	Periodically will pick a random target, charge them, knock them back far and then resume aggro on original target. / The room has several collapsed walls, and is near a steep ledge. All players will need to be consciences of their facing.

Phases	Dynamics
Tooth Gnoblar	Gutbeater will always have one Tooth Gnoblar by his side. He is attached to his gnoblar. Any time it is slain he will enrage – his dps will grow by 10%, and another Tooth Gnoblar will spawn. However, every 10 seconds a Tooth Gnoblar is in combat its own ferocity grows by 10%. Players will need to pace killing off the Tooth Gnoblars, with burning Gutbeater down.
Gut Spew/Gut Bounce	The damaging pool left behind by Gut Spew forces the tank to have to reposition the Butcher every so often which compromises everyone elses vector to him in relation to avoiding being knocked off the ledge when Gut Bounce fires off. Groups will have to coordinate this repositioning.

THE ENTRANCE TO THE LOST VALE IS VIA A BOAT FOUND NEAR EACH WARCAMP IN AVELORN.

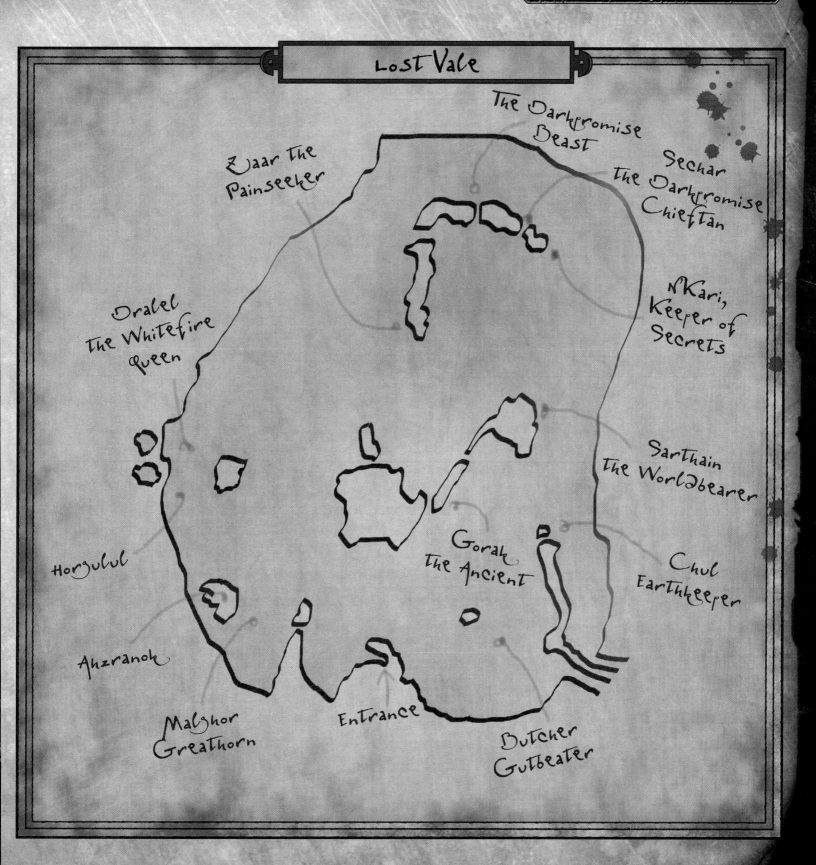

Lost Vale

The Darkpromise Beast

Sechar The Darkpromise Chieftan

Zaar The Painseeker

N'Kari, Keeper of Secrets

Oralel The Whitefire Queen

Sarthain The Worldbearer

Horgulul

Chul Earthkeeper

Gorak The Ancient

Ahzranok

Malghor Greathorn

Entrance

Butcher Gutbeater

PLAYERS NEED TO DO THE EPIC QUEST PURE OF HEART OR BLOOD OF THE VALE THEIR FIRST TIME THROUGH THIS DUNGEON. THESE 40-RANK QUESTS START WITH PHOENIX KING FINUBAR IN ALTDORF OR HELLEBRON IN THE INEVITABLE CITY.

Chul Earthkeeper

Abilities	Description
Chul's Swipe	Wide Arc Melee Cleave
Chul's Howl	Long Range Cone Silence
Chul's Knockback	Every 20 seconds Chul will knock his target away, clear hate, choose another target at random, and charge after that target.
Phases	Dynamics
Chul's Knockback	Every 20 seconds Chul will knock his target away, clear hate, choose another target at random, and charge after that target.
	Tanks will need to ration their taunts because of Chul's frequent aggro shuffle. Group might want to gradually shift toward knockedback player while that player runs back toward group to avoid synergy down time.
	All casters including healers will need to be on their toes to avoid Chul's facing to avoid silence, else heals and dps will be in short supply before enrage timer.

Dralel the Whitefire Queen

Abilities	Description
Web Bolt	Every 15 seconds Dralel will pick a random target and launch them back with a web bolt. Players must use their Torch of Lileath to remove the webbing.
Phases	Dynamics
Initial Aggro	When Dralel is initially aggroed she will fire webs from herself at all players. This web will knock everyone back and root them in place. This root will last up to 30 seconds.
Torch of Lileath	If a player has the Torch of Lileath, they can use it to remove the webbing from their body so they can move immediately.
Whitefire Parasites	At the same time Dralel is initially aggroed she will call for her babies. These will continue to spawn through the entire fight. Each one of these that gets within a radius of her will begin to cast a spell. If the spider casts the spell successfully it will die and send its essence to Dralel. Each essence will increase her damage by 5%.
80%	At 80% Dralel will do another AE web knockback and call forth a wave of Parasites.
60%	At 60% Dralel will do another AE web knockback and call forth a wave of Parasites.
40%	At 40% Dralel will do another AE web knockback and call forth a wave of Parasites.
20%	At 20% Dralel will do another AE web knockback and call forth a wave of Parasites.

Gorak the Ancient

Abilities	Description
Cleave	Moderate Range Melee Cone
Lash	High Damage melee attack
Phases	Dynamics
Summoning Lightening Blasts	Gorak will channel lightening energies through him knocking everyone back and then firing in succession at everyone. These blasts will target the area a player is in and then fire a couple seconds later. Players will have to keep moving to avoid the blast centered on them, and they will have to avoid crossing paths with fellow group members to ensure they don't run into a blast in someone else's wake.

Horgulul

Abilities	Description
Damage Blow	Attack increases with more damage taken.
Phases	Dynamics
Pain Buff	Horgulul loves pain and as he's damage he will gain a buff that also increases his damage. Every 5% of damage he takes will increment this buff until he reaches 25% of hp lost. At this point he will explode dealing damage to everyone and cancelling his buff.
Painlings	When Horgulul explodes, he will also release Painlings. These Painlings will multiply if not killed quickly enough. If a painling is glowing red, this means it is about to split. Focus on the red ones as soon as possible. Once all painlings are dead, focus on Horgulul once more.

Malghor Greathorn

Abilities	Description
Shove	This is a frontal cone damage ability that will knock back all players it damages.
Phases	Dynamics
Writhing Musk	Writhing Musk will be floating throughout the area. If a player comes into contact with Writhing Musk, the scent will infuse itself into their clothing and skin. Malghor will instantly detect this fresh scent and will head over to attack that player. Malghor will ignore any taunts and will always attack the player with the freshest scent of Writhing Musk. Each time a player comes into contact with Musk, the scent will be stronger caushing Malghor to want them that much more. Each time will cause Malghor to hit that player 5% harder (per buff).

N'Kari, Keeper of Secrets

Abilities	Description
Channelers	Channelers have single target and AOE nukes
Keeper's Cleave	Frontal cone nuke with 2000 unit radius, 30 arc, 100 linedist. Keeper must be faced away from the group
Devastation	Only happens during the Desires Phase. Does massive damage, must have Tank desire to survive
Circle of Pain	A font that is placed on top of a random ranged player that does periodic damage to the player
Circle of Pleasure	A font that is placed on top of a random ranged player that will snare and reduce the AP regen of the player
Keeper's Knock Up	Targets a random ranged player and fires a bolt at them that knocks them up in the air. When the player lands on the ground they do damage to themselves and those around them
Keeper's AOE Lifetap	As detailed below, does damage to players and heals the keeper for the result
Phases	Dynamics
Channelers Phase	During the channelers phase the keeper of secrets is not up. There will be 3 or 4 channelers up depending on if the PQ was completed. They will all agro at once. When killed each channeler will drop a tablet. These are used for the AOE lifetap phase. Only one player can hold a tablet and you cannot leave the area with the tablet.
Regular Phase	During this phase the keeper will use her cleave, circle of pain and pleasure, and knock up abilities. She must be faced away from the group and the group must spread out to avoid aoe damage

PLAYERS WILL NEED A FEW PIECES OF GREATER WARD ARMOR. EACH PIECE ABSORBS A PERCENTAGE OF ALL INCOMING DAMAGE RECEIVED IN THE LOST VALE.

N'Kari, Keeper of Secrets (Continued)

Abilities	Description
Desires Phase	After 45 seconds into the fight the keeper will summon 4 desires. 1 Tank, 1 healer and 2 dps desires. They are npcs that run around the room and cast a buff on a player when a player gets within range.
	Desire of the Defender - This is the tank buff. Grants the player 10k extra hitpoints, ap regen buff, damage
	Desire of Salvation - Grants an ap regen bonus, 100% healing bonus
	Desire of Vengance - Grants an ap regen bonus, 100% damage bonus
	During this phase the keeper will spawn 2 champion adds which must be dealt with. They have standard melee abilities and have low hitpoints. The two dps with the bonus must kill these as quickly as possible. The tank with the defender bonus must continue to tank the keeper. The keeper will begin using the devastate ability. The healer with the bonus must heal.
	After this phase comes to a close, everyone that had a bonus will receive a debuff that will not allow the player to receive the same buff twice in a row. As such 2 tanks are needed, 2 healers, and 2 dps (or healer hybrid) are needed.

Sarthain the Worldbearer

Abilities	Description
Cleave	Cone Melee
Nature's Wrath	High Damage PBAE
Regrowth	Regenerate's Health
Nature's Grasp	PBAE Root to all players in area
Nature's Bite	Damage reflection
Phases	Dynamics
Darkpromise Corruptors	Every so often three Darkpromise Corruptors will spawn on the outskirts of the grove one at a time in 15 second intervals.
	The first one will give Sarthain Nature's Bite.
	The second one will invoke Nature's Wrath.
	The Third will gradually escalate Sarthain's overall dps.
	The Darkpromise Corruptors are not vulnerable to attack until all three have spawned. A broadcast will indicate as much.
	Once all three are up Sarthain can no longer call upon Forest Allies for help (see below).
	However, once players attack the first Darkpromise Corruptor a timer will begin. At its expiration Sarthain will have cooled down from his inflated, corrupted wrath and attempt to mend his wounds. He will root everyone with Nature's Grasp and then will invoke Regrowth if no one is in melee range.
	Successful players will need to quickly dps down the corruptors and then return to melee range before the Nature's Grasp timer expires.
Forest Allies	Any time 0 players are within Sarthain's reach, he will call various creatures of the vale to his aid (Vale Bear, Wolf and Hawk). The exception to this is when all three Darkpromise Corruptors are up. If played well these adds should never spawn.

Sechar the Darkpromise Chieftain

Abilities	Description
Punishing Swing	Cleave
Powerful Strike	Melee
Phases	Dynamics

Sechar the Darkpromise Chieftain (Continued)

Abilities	Description
Pleasure and Pain	Sechar has two phases that repeat throughout the entire fight, Pleasure and Pain. Every 30 seconds he will switch phases.
	Pleasure: During the pleasure phase the boss will place a buff on himself that does constant damage to all players. However during this phase all players will receive a pleasure buff that heals themselves and all players around them. The radius is very small so players must bunch up as close as possible to the boss while avoiding the cleave.
	Pain: During the pain phase the boss will heal himself slowly. Players will receive a damage buff so they can overcome the damage. However, during this phase all of the attacks the player makes will damage their group-mates around them, as such it will be necessary for all players to spread out as far as possible to avoid damage.

Darkpromise Beast

Abilities	Description
Burst of Acid	A player is targeted at random and is hit with a bolt of acid, the acid will explode and do damage to all those around the player targeted, the group must stay spread out
Grasping Vines	Randomly casts a 5 second root
Phases	Dynamics
Infectious Poison	The main difficulty of the fight is the Prayer of Poison ability. It will be cast on a random player in the group. It will do damage to the player over 20 seconds. After 20 seconds it will jump to the nearest player and infect them with the poison. The player that originally had the poison will be left with a debuff that will increase the damage of the poison dramatically. Therefore a new player must get the poison each time. This will require players to move around so that a fresh player is closest to the one with the poison to avoid double debuffs. After all players have had the debuff it must be passed to another player at which point players will start dying. This is the soft enrage

Zaar the Painseeker

Abilities	Description
Cleave	Zaar has a hard hitting cleave that strikes any target in his frontal arc, he must be faced away from the raid
Phases	Dynamics
Punishment Cages x4	Inside the room there are 4 cages. During the fight at set intervals, Zaar will choose one player at random that is not the tank and place them inside the cage. While the player is inside the cage they will be completely stunned and unable to take any action, they will also be taking periodic damage. All other players must focus damage on the cage the player is in so that the player can be set free. Once the cage is destroyed the player is set free and the fight continues. This will happen 4 times.
Enrage	After all 4 cages have been destroyed Zaar will instantly enrage and grow larger and do more damage. This is not a wiping enrage but just more damage that the players will have to deal with.

MONSTERS

Name	Description
Ancient Branchwraith	Pulsing Pbae – split so don't stack
Ancient Branchwraith	Pulsing Pbae – split so don't stack
Bliss-Fury	Does a small knockback with agro switch, lower damage
Cannibalistic Gorger	Ravaging Blow bleed DoT. Uppercut.
Darkpromise Daemonette	Standard Melee mob
Darkpromise Fallen	Has a bleed, Debuff armor, and standard melee attack. Must juggle tanks as much as possible to avoid the armor debuff
Darkpromise Follower	Standard melee mob with cleaves
Darkpromise Hierophant	Casts a single target channeled nuke. Casts AOE channeled nuke that ramps up damage. Must be killed first
Darkpromise Masochist	Places an armor debuff on the player. Must be off-tanked, cannot be tanked with other mobs
Darkpromise Painbringer	Painbringers place a stacking debuff on the player that increases damage received. They must be tanked individually and killed quickly to prevent too many stacks from killing the tank
Darkpromise Pain-screamer	Casts a cone/line AE nuke. After every cast switches hate to a new target. Group must stayed spread out to avoid multiple hits
Darkpromise Sadist	Has a large high damage cleave, must be faced away from the group
Darkpromise Terror-hound	Casts an AOE stat debuff, should be tanked away from the group
Darkpromise Worshiper	Casts fonts on random players in the group every 10 seconds. These either debuff the player, buff the worshiper or do damage to the players.
Death Sprite	Non aggro. Ranged DD. Cautionary pull.
Death Sprite	Non aggro. Ranged DD. Cautionary pull.
Death Sprite	Non aggro. Ranged DD. Cautionary pull.
Ethereal Sprite	Ethereal Sprites are immune to all damage. They will swarm spawn around and attack any player who does not have Branch of Sarthain in inventory (acquired by completing epic quest).
Gorge-Fury	Cleave
Gorge-Maw Bull	Cleave. Heavy Strike / hard hitter with a cleave. Key is for tank to keep these guys turned away from the rest of the group.
Gorge-maw Gnoblar	Armor Plucking (stacking armor debuff). / should be off tanked and/or kited. Do not want same player receiving debuff receiving damage from rest of the pull. When accompanying a pull in excess of 100% should be kited or ccd.
Gorge-Maw Hunter	Cleave. Heavy strike. Commands Gorge-Maw Sabretusks to attack random target in group every 20 seconds at which time the sabretusk will enrage for 10 seconds and gain 50k hate on that player. / players will need to save their ccs for this while tank regains threat (more than a single taunt)
Gorge-Maw Irongut	Cleave. Heavy Strike / Another hard hitter with a cleave. Key is for tank to keep these guys turned away.
Gorge-Maw Maneater	Cleave. Heavy strike. Enrages after 40 seconds. / players will want to focus dps on these guys first lest the pulls dps overwhelm
Gorge-Maw Rhinox	Heavy Strike. Crippling Stomp PBAE knockdown. Charge knockback. / players will want to be careful where they pull these from because they will get knocked back. Also, they will charge any player anytime they are outside of 400 units. So healers and ranged are going to need to be on their toes to find the 100 unit sweet spot between stomp knockdown and charge target range.

Name	Description
Gorge-Maw Sabretusk	Heavy Strike. Bloody Claw – melee bleed dot. Enrages when commanded (see above).
Gorge-Maw Scout	On entering combat they will make a run for it to alert other pulls. They must be quickly ccd and killed.
Gorge-Maw Tyrant	Heavy Cleave. Pummel. / This guy is a heavy hitter and is usually surrounded by armor plucking gnoblars. Separating the two is key to success. A tank taking hits from this guy with armor pierced from the gnoblar will die.
Hate-Fury	Standard Melee Strike
Mindfall Scorpion	Debuffs casting speed, keep away from healers
Pain Sprite	Non aggro. Ranged Aoe caster. Cautionary pull.
Pain Sprite	Non aggro. Ranged Aoe caster. Cautionary pull.
Pain Sprite	Non aggro. Ranged Aoe caster. Cautionary pull.
Pain-Fury	Pain-Furies will cast a channeled PBAE during the fight, but will be immobile when they do this. Also when they get low on hp their skin will begun to bubble. If they are not killed quick enough, they will explode doing significant damage around them.
Painvine Burster	Casts a ranged nuke that does damage and then causes the target to bleed, can be range tanked
Painvine Feeler	Stuns the target and then does rapid damage that cannot be defended against
Painvine Needler	Melee
Pleasure Sprite	Non aggro. Ranged AE Corp Resist Debuffer. Cautionary pull.
Pleasure Sprite	Non aggro. Ranged AE Corp Resist Debuffer. Cautionary pull.
Pleasure Sprite	Non aggro. Ranged AE Corp Resist Debuffer. Cautionary pull.
Pleasure-Fury	Immune to taunt.
Prismatic Scorpion	High Damage resist, usually last target
Rageclaw Scorpion	Enrages at 50%, ideally first target
Sap Sprite	Non aggro. Ranged Snare. Cautionary pull.
Sap Sprite	Non aggro. Ranged Snare. Cautionary pull.
Sap Sprite	Non aggro. Ranged Snare. Cautionary pull.
Sorrowtongue Lizard	Bite. ST Paralyzing Bite. / Players will not want to burst dps and/or heals when tank is paralyzed from bite.
Stonehewer Gorger	Smash PBAOE. Uppercut. / Wary of the close quarters cave with the pbaoe.
Vale Branchwraith	Dd AE silence (disables casting). Dd ae dot. Enrages after 40 seconds. / Casters keep distance.
Vale Branchwraith	Dd AE silence (disables casting). Dd ae dot. Enrages after 40 seconds. / Casters keep distance.
Vale Graybark	PBAE Knockdown. Spawns Wrath Spites 1 every 5 seconds.
Vale Graybark	PBAE Knockdown. Spawns Wrath Spites 1 every 5 seconds.
Vale Guardian	Cleave, heavy strike. / Tank will need to point away from group, lest full pull dps become too high.
Vale Guardian	Cleave, heavy strike. / Tank will need to point away from group, lest full pull dps become too high.
Vale Mossfiend	AE Corporeal Debuffer. / Off tank will need to keep this away from main tank receiving corp damage lest full pull dps become too much to manage (most monster ability damage in wing is corporeal based).
Vale Mosskeeper	AE DoT. Ranged Snare. Ranged DD. / Ideal for off tank away from melee dps

Name	Description
Vale Seedkeeper	Heals allies. / DPS will want to focus fire and keep them interrupted otherwise group will not be able to burn through
Vale Spite	Corp based Knockdown, heavy strike. / For main tank.
Vale Thornbark	Always rooted. High Damage Channeled Ranged AE. / DPS stay spread out and focus on Thornbark while tanks pick up and endure thornling adds. Healers avoid adds and ae radii.
Vale Thornbark	Always rooted. High Damage Channeled Ranged AE. / DPS stay spread out and focus on Thornbark while tanks pick up and endure thornling adds. Healers avoid adds and ae radii.
Vale Thornfiend	Ranged DD. DoT that spreads on expiration. / Players will need to stay spread out, lest full pull dps becomes too high.
Vale Thornling	10% Snare attacks to thwart dps players movement toward Thornbark. Crippling Blow
Vale Thornling	10% Snare attacks to thwart dps players movement toward Thornbark. Criplling Blow
Vale Wanderer	Dd snare. Heavy strike. Drop hate every 10 seconds. / Healers obstacle. Ideal to focus dps on them first.
Viletongue Lizard	Bite. Random Targeted Spit DD AE DoT. / Players will want to stay spread out to ensure minimum dot application. Healers will have to be on their toes with cures.
Whitefire Broodling	These spiders come in 4 varieties – each type will be a smaller version of one of the 4 listed above. (Pleasurevenom, Painvenom, Webspinner, Sentinel)
Whitefire Broodmother	Broodmothers will lay eggs during the fight. If these eggs are not destroyed fast enough they will explode and hatchlings will pour out.
Whitefire Egg	This is an area dynamic. There are eggs spread throughout the area that must be destroyed via range. If players get too near the egg will explode and hatchlings will pour out. Eggs also have a very low chance to explode on damage, so even shooting them from ranged may cause hatchlings to spawn.
Whitefire Painvenom	This spider will attempt to inject painvenom into its victim. Any player that has painvenom in their veins will take damage over time.
Whitefire Painvenom	This spider will attempt to inject painvenom into its victim. Any player that has painvenom in their veins will take damage over time.
Whitefire Pleasurevenom	This spider will attempt to inject pleasurevenom into its victim. Any player that has pleasurevenom in their veins will have a small build time added to their abilities.
Whitefire Pleasurevenom	This spider will attempt to inject pleasurevenom into its victim. Any player that has pleasurevenom in their veins will have a small build time added to their abilities.
Whitefire Sentinel	This spider will enrage at 65% hp.
Whitefire Sentinel	This spider will enrage at 65% hp.
Whitefire Webspinner	This spider will root its target using webbing.
Whitefire Webspinner	This spider will root its target using webbing.
Wrath Spite	Fodder bomb – will explode after 10 seconds for massive damage. / Several tactics to deal with this. One could be a tank single target taunting graybark while ranged dps continues to pull, kite and keep distance from Wrath Spites until they explode. Another tactic might be stacking ae dps to drop them quick enough.
Wrath Spite	Fodder bomb – will explode after 10 seconds for massive damage. / Several tactics to deal with this. One could be a tank single target taunting graybark while ranged dps continues to pull, kite and keep distance from Wrath Spites until they explode. Another tactic might be stacking ae dps to drop them quick enough.

Name	Description
Writhing Ambusher	These mobs start off stealthed and should be hard to see. During combat, every 10 or so seconds the mob will evaluate all the players on its hate list and choose the one with the least percent of HP, so these mobs tend to stick to the players with the lowest current hp (percent wise).
Writhing Berserker	This mob is very magical resistant, immune to snares and roots. This mob will also do a frontal cleave to damage anything in front of it.
Writhing Crusher	This mob uses a high damage ability that slightly ignore armor.
Writhing Herdguard	This mob uses a frontal cleave to damage anything in front of it.
Writhing Herdkeeper	This mob will use an ability that orders any Writhing Tuskgor in a certain radius around the Herdkeeper to use a special ability. This increases the damage output of the Writhing Tuskgors. Ideally, if you are a player you will pull the Herdkeeper away from Tuskgors.
Writhing Herdseer	This mob is a healer and will cast PBAE heals throughout the fight.
Writhing Longtusk	If the Writhing Longtusk receives a command from a Herdkeeper, it will let loose a high damage snare attack.
Writhing Paingor	This mob uses interrupting attacks that will cancel any cast that the player is attempting to do.
Writhing Painseer	This mob summons a font buff that will damage any player in the radius of the front.
Writhing Pleasureseer	This mob summons a font buff that will increase the cast time of any player in the radius of the font.
Writhing Rager	This mob will enrage once it hits 80% hp.
Writhing Shaman	This mob is a single target high damage long range nuker.
Writhing Stonehoof	This mob is very magical resistant, immune to snares and roots. This mob will do a killing blow to any player with less than 40% hp.
Writhing Tuskhide	If the Writhing Longtusk receives a command from a Herdkeeper, it will let loose a high damage attack that partially ignores armor.

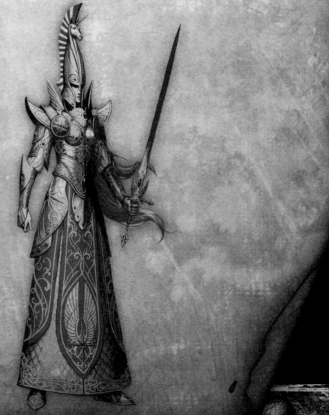

THE SACELLUM

DUNGEON DETAILS

Caged and readied beasts, as well champions, stay in the Sacellum while waiting to be called out to the Arena. Enraged servants also make their home here, as do the more volatile and destructive forces the Sacellum has to offer. The layout consists mostly hallways with side rooms holding the named combatants, with three different layouts for the degree of difficulty (there are low-, mid-, and high-level entrances).

WING 1

The Ragehorn tribe of Khorne beastmen has followed their leader Vul the Bloodchosen to fight in the Sacellum in order to honor their God of Blood.

WING 2

The Mawgut ogres have brought some of their wilder cousins and creatures to the Sacellum to fight for prizes...and food

WING 3

A menagerie of beasts from across the world, kept by defeated and broken servants of the Sacellum.

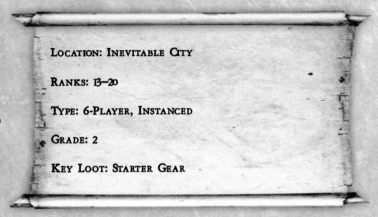

LOCATION: INEVITABLE CITY

RANKS: 13–20

TYPE: 6-PLAYER, INSTANCED

GRADE: 2

KEY LOOT: STARTER GEAR

EACH OF THE THREE SACELLUM WINGS HAS ITS OWN INDIVIDUAL ENTRANCE FOUND ON THE INSIDE WALLS OF THE SACELLUM ARENA IN THE INEVITABLE CITY.

BOSSES

Ghalmar Ragehorn

Abilities	Description
Challenging Roar	AE Knockback plus root.
Malghar's Challenge	Single target dummy mark after Challenging Roar, Malghar will focus on this player with…
Bestial Flurry	Malghar will use this channeled melee attack on his challenge target.
Wild Strike	Frontal Cleave, does not use during Challenging Roar
Phases	Dynamics
	They key to this fight is to make sure the challenge target stays alive through out the Bestial Flurry.
Regurgitate	When the Unclean One's stomach gets upset, he will regurgitate all players in his belly. All the mauraders and nurglings will be dead and the Bile Lord should set his health fairly low. Now the players must finish him off.

Goremane

Abilities	Description
Lacerating Talons	Random target melee range strike.
Tail Spikes	Random target ranged attack.
Furious Roar	Stun on tank + hate wipe, needs to be picked up by second tank.
Phases	Dynamics
	The whole group will be taking damage, while the 2 tanks must be ready to respond to Furious Roar being used.

Hoarfrost

Abilities	Description
Freezing Aura	The Yhettee will drop a freezing aura and his current location and it will remain there for 30 seconds, it will damage and slow the attacks of any player standing in it.
Grasp of Frost	Single target root on the tank, needs to be cured so tank is not stuck in the freezing aura.
Phases	Dynamics
	The boss needs to be moved around the room so that the tank and others are not standing in the freezing aura.

Lorth and Slorth Thunderbelly

Abilities	Description
Leadbelcher Blast	A high damage longe range line attach.
Swinging Cannon	A short duration stun plus knockdown on the tank.
Phases	Dynamics
	The 2 leadbelchers must be kept facing away from the group, and players must not get caught in the crossfire of the cannon blasts.

Sebcraw the Discarded

Abilities	Description
Gorging Bite	A channeled focused melee attack on the tank.
Smash	Channeled stomp attack, Sebcraw roots himself and begins to pound the ground, players need to move away from him when this occurs.
Phases	Dynamics
	Keeping the tank alive through the Gorging Bite and avoiding the Smash are the challenges to this encounter.

THERE ARE SEVERAL MONSTERS OF VARIOUS LEVELS
FIGHTING EACH OTHER THROUGHOUT THE SACELLUM,
BUT THEY ARE HARMLESS IF YOU DO NOT ATTACK.

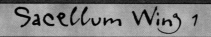

Sacellum Wing 1

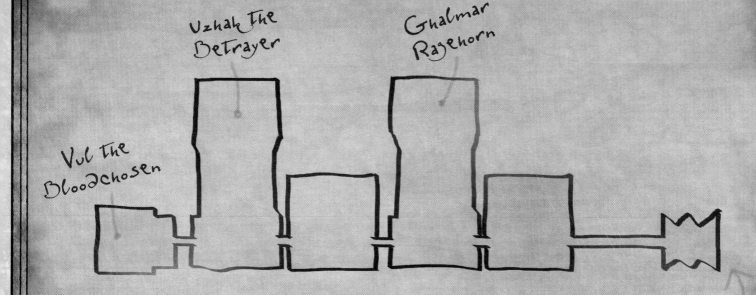

Vul The
Bloodchosen

Uzhak The
Betrayer

Ghalmar
Ragehorn

Entrance

THE IDEAL GROUP MAKE UP IS TWO PLAYERS OF
EACH OF THE THREE CORE CLASS ARCHETYPES:
TANK, HEALER, AND DPS.

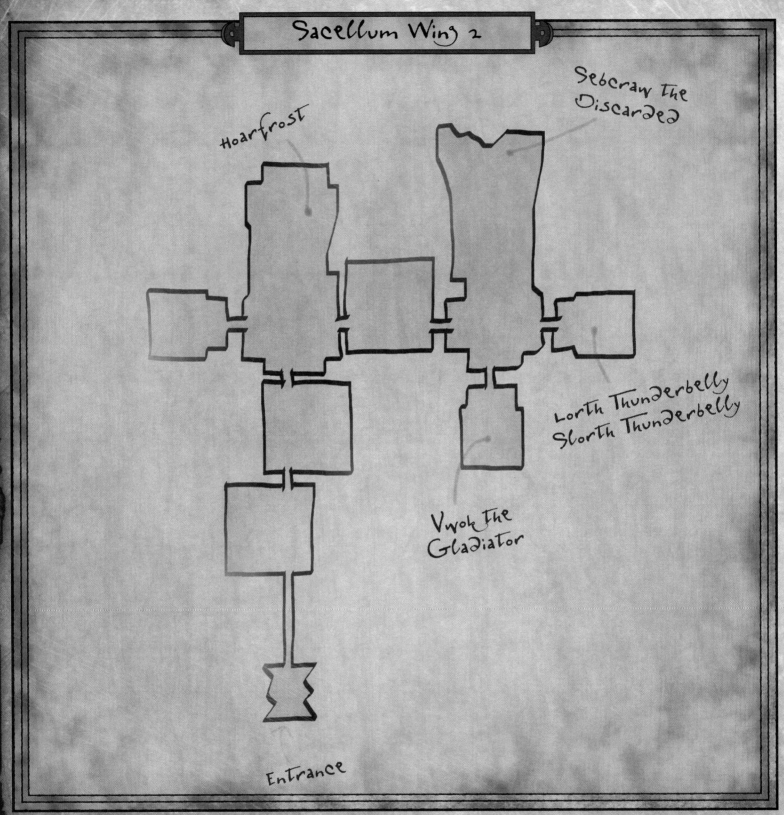

Sacellum Wing 2

Sebcraw the
Discarded

Hoarfrost

Lorth Thunderbelly
Slorth Thunderbelly

Vvok the
Gladiator

Entrance

YOU CAN ENTER THE DUNGEON AT RANK
9...IF YOU DARE.

Sacellum Wing 3

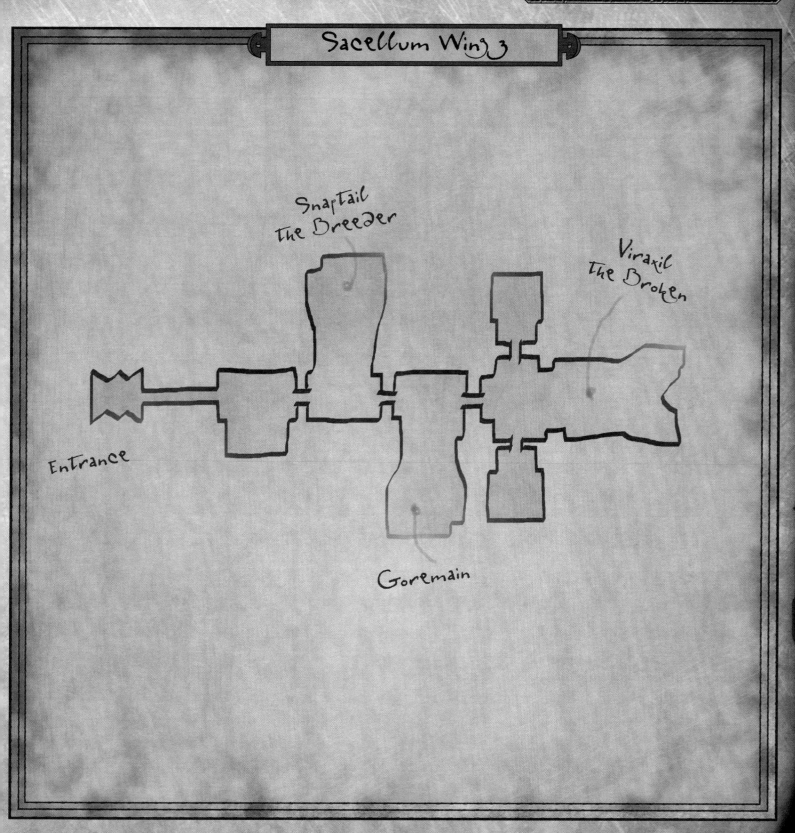

Snaptail
The Breeder

Viraxil
The Broken

Entrance

Goremain

Don't worry about your equipment too much. So long as you have a good core party, you can survive in here even in poor quality gear.

BOSSES (CONTINUED)

MONSTERS

Snaptail the Breeder

Abilities	Description
Anguished Screech	AE silence, long range, each time this ability is used an egg will hatch.
Wyvern Sting	360% knockback + DoT
Phases	**Dynamics**
	Each time Anguished Screech is used one of the eggs around the room will spawn 2 core con Wyvern Brood-lings that must be dealt with.

Uzhak the Betrayer

Abilities	Description
Centigor Charge	Uzhak will randomly charge targets through out the fight, this will stun and do a small knockback on them for 7 seconds
Phases	**Dynamics**
	Players must react to having various members of their party, including healers, out of commission for a brief period of time.

Viraxil the Broken

Abilities	Description
Hydra Smash	Melee range cleave attack
Torrent of Flame	Random target projectile that will leave a fire font, must be moved out of.
Cone of Flame	Very high damage cone breath attack, Viraxil will announce he is doing this attack and root himself, players must then move away from him.
Phases	**Dynamics**
	The group must remain mobile to avoid the torrents of flame, and be ready to react to the use of Cone of Flame.

Vul the Bloodchosen

Abilities	Description
Gushing Axes	AE Axe throw at players at range
Skulltaker	Melee range 360 degree strike
Bloodrage	Increased damage outout by 20%
Phases	**Dynamics**
	Players must react to the entire group taking damage. At 10% he will gain Bloodrage, increasing his damage by 20%, players should save their cooldowns and morales for this time.

IF YOU CHOOSE THE FORCES OF
DESTRUCTION, THE SACELLUM SHOULD BE
YOUR FIRST DUNGEON.

Name	Description
Bloodblessed Beast	High DPS – lower HP
Bloodblessed Gor	Mark of Khorne – Slows spell casting in an area around the Gor
Broken Warhound	Immune to Taunt
Enslaved Screecher	Final pull before boss. As players approach the Wyverns room, 7 harpies will spawn from the side rooms, and after 45 seconds, 6 more will spawn. So it is a larger than average pull split up into 2 sub groups.
Mawgot Gnoblar	Throw Things – Curable random target DoT
Mawgut Bull	Bull Charge on aggro – damage and knockback
Ragehorn Gor	Frontal arc cleave.
Ragehorn Netter	Does a targeted AE root upon aggro.
Ragehorn Ungor	Weak DD + Stun, switch aggro
Sacellum Thrallkeeper	360 degree melee strike, each pair gates a boss.
Sacellum Willbreaker	360 degree melee strike, gates boss encounters/
Sacellum Willtamer	360 degree melee strike, gates first 2 bosses.
Subjugated Beastbreaker	Melee cleave.
Subjugated Spellweaver	Single target magic DD

THE SEWERS

BOSSES

LOCATION: ALTDORF

RANKS: 13–20

TYPE: 6-PLAYER, INSTANCED

GRADE: 3

KEY LOOT: STARTER GEAR

The Sewers beneath Altdorf are set up in three different sections, for low-, mid-, and high-ranked adventurers. The rotten flesh of zombies adds to the odorous passageways below, where clanrats skitter and man-eaters dwell. Corpses line the waterways, and fallen wizards talk to themselves, when not casting spells to thwart those foolish enough to enter these environs. Rat ogres, packmasters, recluses, and other various vermin call this place home. Should players venture into the high-level area, they shall meet Goradian, a scientist gone mad, mumbling and performing tests on those who stumble upon him...

This dungeon is composed of three small instances that make up the Aldorf Sewers. Wing 1 is composed of entirely Skaven mobs culminating in the boss fight with Kokrit Man-Eater. Wing 2 is a mix of Skaven and zombie mobs with two boss fights: Bulbous One, and Prot Chitterfang. Wing 3 is half skaven and half corrupted humans with two boss fights: Master Moulder Vitchek and Goradian the Creator.

Bulbous One

Abilities	Description
Plague Aura	This Aura has a large radius, all players will take damage every 3 seconds while engaged in combat with the Bulbous One.
Plague Weakness	The Bulbous One will place a debuff on the tank every 4 seconds. This debuff increases the damage that the Aura does.
Cleave	Standard cone melee strike
Phases	Dynamics
Phase 1	When attacked the Bulbous One will start his aura. All players in the group will be affected by this aura and start taking damage. The tank will begin to get hit with the debuff. The damage the tank takes will increase constantly until it is too much for the healers to handle. The two tanks must take turns tanking the boss so that the debuffs don't get to high and fade off the other tank.

Goradian the Creator

Abilities	Description
Way of Goradian	Randomly casted damage over time.
Vision of Goradian	Randomly casted AoE nuke
Phases	Dynamics
Phase 1	Goradian will use his abilities
Phase 2	At 80% health Goradian will run to a nearby table and spawn 6 Goradian's Nurgling. These will start small and then scale up and attack the players.
Phase 3	At 60% health Goradian will run to a nearby table and spawn 6 Goradian's Spider. These will start small and then scale up and attack the players.

Goradian the Creator (Continued)

Abilities	Description
Phase 4	At 40% health Goradian will run to a nearby table and spawn 6 Goradian's Maggot. These will start small and then scale up and attack the players.
Phase 5	At 20% health Goradian will run to a nearby table and nothing will happen. He will be angry.

Kokrit Man-Eater

Abilities	Description
Lumbering Blow	Cone melee strike, Kokrit should be faced away from the group to avoid damage.
Ogre Spit	Kokrit randomly targets 1 person in the group and spits on them. This gives that player a long duration dot that should be dispelled.
Ground Pound	Kokrit will occasionally stop attacking and begin slamming the ground with his fists. This does AOE damage. It is possible to run out of the damage.
Phases	Dynamics
Phase 1	This is a fairly simple fight. Kokrit will use all of his abilities. Players will need to make sure that they purge the spit quickly so that it doesn't get on multiple people and outpace the healers. Ranged can stand at max range to avoid the pounds.

Master Moulder Vitchek

Abilities	Description
Ogre's Feel Better	Heals the Rat Ogre's
Vitchek's Order	Randomly places a marker on a player and that player is then attacked by Ogre's
Vitchek's Obedience	Increases the damage of Ogre's within range
Phases	Dynamics
Vitchek's Brute's	These are rat Ogre's and use the Ground pound ability, a PBAOE pulsing damage that can be out ranged.
Master Moulder Vitchek	He will constantly heal the Ogre's and command them to attack specific targets. He must be kept away as much as possible from the ogre's to keep them from being healed and from getting the damage buff. However, as the Ogre's will randomly attack players this will be challenging.

Prot Fangchitter

Abilities	Description
Cloud of Deadly Poison	This is a damage font. It has a short cooldown and a long duration. A cloud of poison is placed where the person being attacked is standing. Anyone standing in the cloud will take damage.
Broad Sweep	Standard Melee Cone attack
Phases	Dynamics
Prot Fangchitter	Prot Fangchitter will have the Font and the Cone Melee. He will need to be tanked.
Vermer Fangchitter	Prot's Minion will only have the font, he will do much less damage than Prot. He will switch agro every time he uses the Deadly Poison font.
Phase 1	This fight will be entirely movement based and controlling the minion. Prot and his Minion will both be laying down a lot of fonts. The tank will have to move him around a lot to avoid taking a lot of damage. The minion will be switching agro and dropping fonts on the rest of the group, so the rest of the group will need to move around.

If you choose the forces of Order, the Sewers should be your first dungeon.

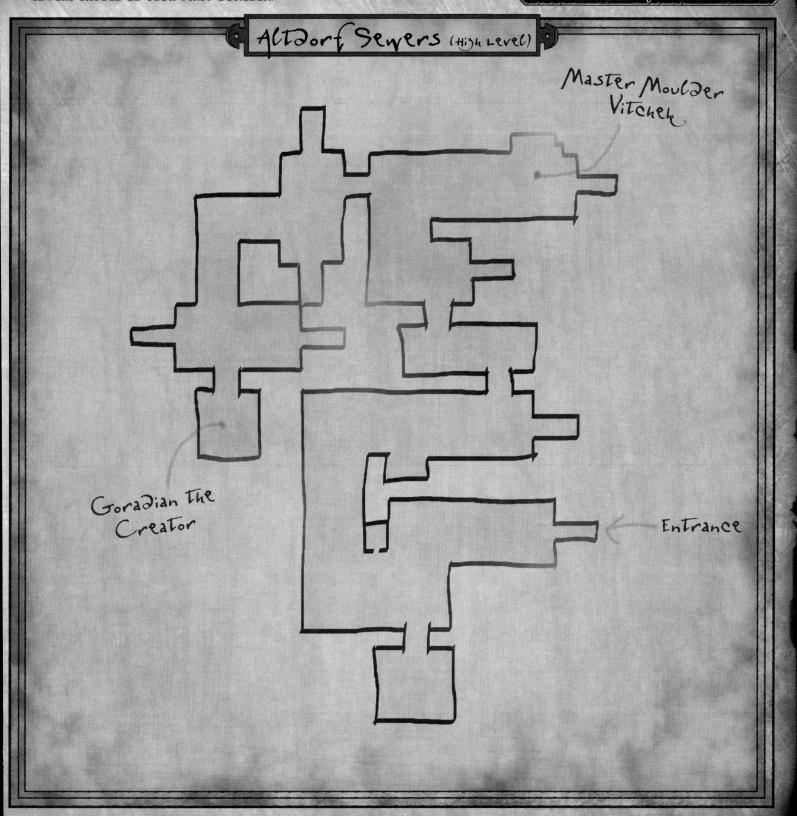

Altdorf Sewers (High Level)

Master Moulder Vitchek

Goradian the Creator

Entrance

MONSTERS

Name	Pull Role / Description
Corrupted Wizard	Caster mob. Has two nukes. Randomly casts a damage over time on members of the group and casts an AoE nuke on random members. Summons up to 4 Twisted Spectre's.
Plague Zombie	Core mobs. Plague zombies will randomly select between two abilities. They will either have a melee strike or a debuff that reduces your outgoing damage. When killed zombies have a chance to explode and do damage to any players near them.
Twisted Spectre	Summoned by Corrupted Wizards. Has a cone nuke. Should be picked up by the offtank and faced away from the group.
Vermin Swarm	10 rats lower level guard the exit, should be simple to AOE these mobs. Standard rats.

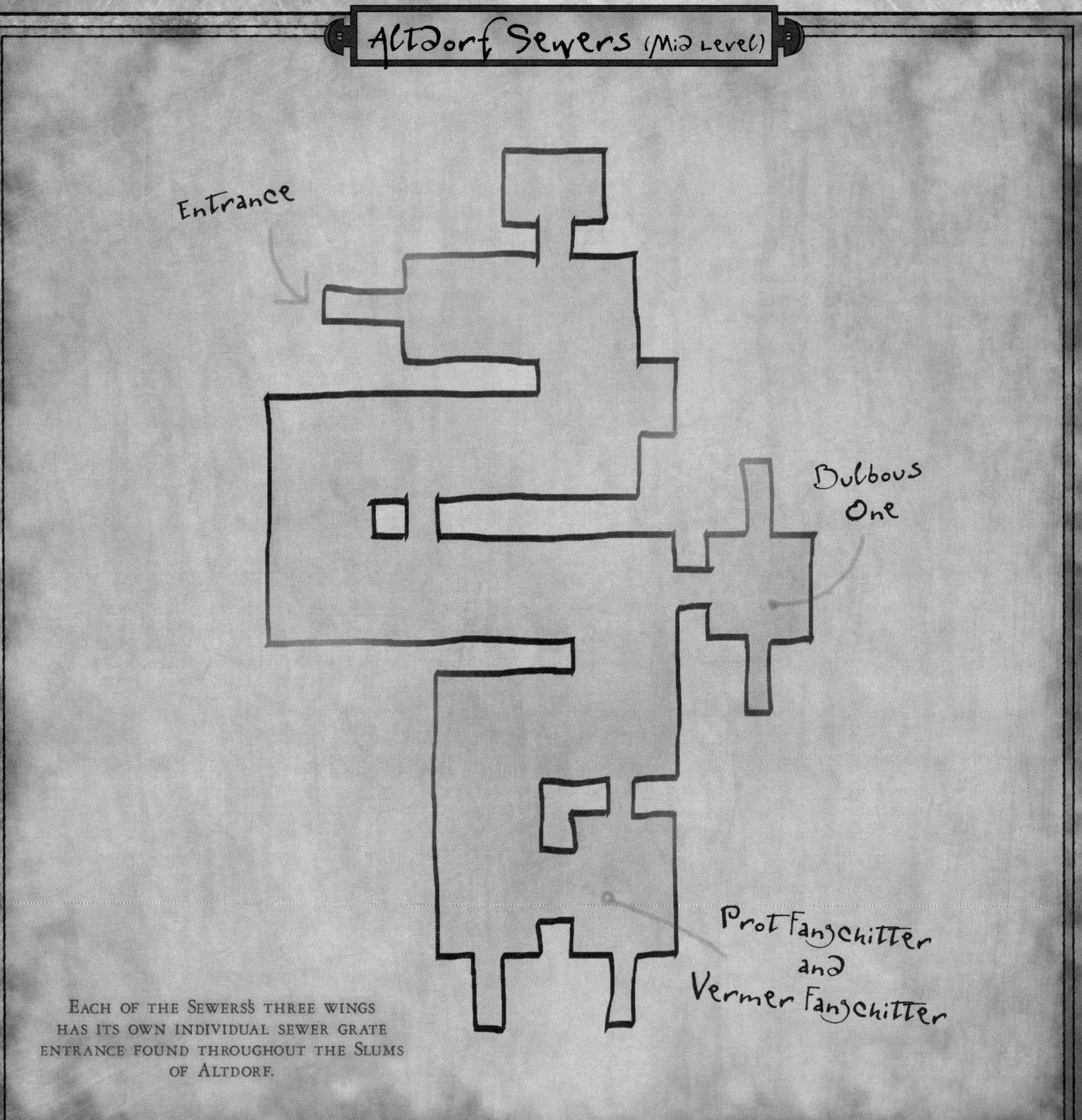

Altdorf Sewers (Mid Level)

Entrance

Bulbous One

Prot Fangchitter
and
Vermer Fangchitter

Each of the Sewers's three wings has its own individual sewer grate entrance found throughout the Slums of Altdorf.

MONSTERS (CONTINUED)

Name	Pull Role / Description
Warprat Gutter Runner	Melee mob. Has a cone melee attack and should be faced away from the group. Gutter runners place a damage over time on the tank that will double in damage if two dots are placed on them. Therefore 2 mobs shouldn't be tanked by 1 character
Warprot Assassin	Stealther mob. Will attack a random player when aggro'd. Has a melee strike that is used from stealth, melee strike and a bleed. Every so often the assassin will do a small knockback and switch targets, the tank will need to taunt to recover the mob.
Warprot Brute	Rat Ogre melee mob. Has a melee cone attack and should be faced away from the group. Also uses a Ground Pound PBAOE attack that players can run away from. They also have a 10 second enrage that is only used when instructed by the Warprot Packmaster.
Warprot Clanrat	Standard Skaven Melee mob. Has a melee strike and a long duration curable bleed.

Altdorf Sewers (Low Level)

The ideal group make up is two players of each of the three core class archetypes: tank, DPS, and healer.

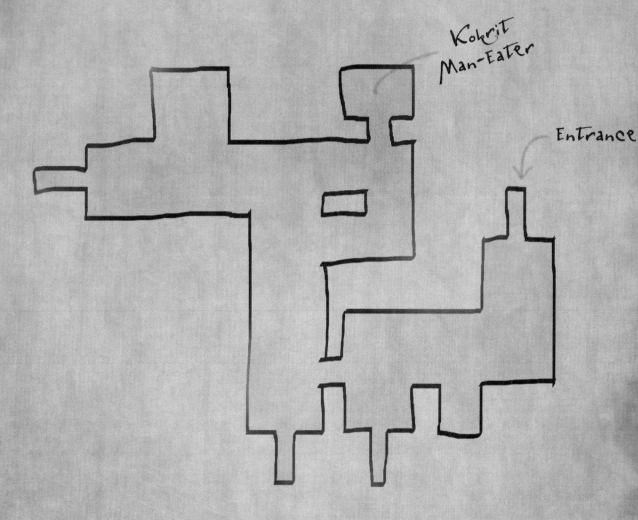

Kohrit Man-Eater

Entrance

Don't worry about your equipment, even if it's falling apart. So long as you have a good core party, you can survive in the Sewers.

MONSTERS (CONTINUED)

Name	Pull Role / Description
Warprot Packmaster	Skaven Melee mob. Has a standard melee strike and a Buff Aura. The Buff Aura only affects Warprot Brute's and increases their damage. Packmasters should be pulled away from Brutes.
Warprot Plague Monk	Melee/Caster. Monks place a bleed on their melee target. They also will cast a dot on a random member of the group.
Warprot Priest	Priests are casters. Priests have a randomly targeted nuke and a font. The font will be placed on a random player and last for a short duration, any players near the font will take damage.
Warprot Stormvermin	Melee Skaven mob. Has a melee cone attack, and an AP regeneration cone debuff. This mob should be faced away from the group at all times.

SIGMAR'S CRYPTS

LOCATION: ALTDORF

RANKS: 40+

TYPE: 6-PLAYER, INSTANCED

GRADE: 5

KEY LOOT: SENTINEL ARMOR AND WEAPONS

DUNGEON DETAILS

Legends say two lectors, twins Maxwell and Markus Matzenbach, let corruption crawl into their hearts and abused their positions of power. Tempted by death magic, the twins were reborn unto darkness as the fallen lectors Zakarai and Verrimus. The Order of the Cleansing Flame requires fearless adventurers to purge the Temple of Sigmar's underbelly of its foul denizens before the citizens of Altdorf learn even the most sacred of places is vulnerable in this dark age.

BOSSES

Arch Lectors Zakarai and Verrimus

Abilities	Description
Cleave	Melee Cleave
Melt Armor	Used on primary Target, reduces armor to 0.
Bunker of Faith	Long cooldown, reduces incoming damage by 80%
PBAOE Disarm	Disarms everyone in a 2000 radius for 3 seconds
Random DD	Random high damage nuke
Random AOE DD	Random high damage AOE nuke
PBAOE Root	Roots everyone within 2000 units.
Phases	Dynamics
Phase 1	Zakarai and Verrimus lay on stone tablets at the back of the room. They will not be attackable until all of the trash mobs in the room are killed.
	Zakarai will start with Cleave, Melt Armor and Bunker of Faith.
	Verrimus will start with Disarm, Random DD, Random AOE DD, PBAOE Root.
	Zakarai must be tanked by 2 tanks due to the melt armor debuff. As such Verrimus will not have a tank and he will be constantly hitting the raid with magic spells.
Phase 2	Zakarai and Verrimus will constantly check each other's life. If at any time one is 10% lower than the other they will stop combat and cast a spell on each other. The one with lower health will be healed up to the others current health. At this time they will also switch abilities.
Phase 3	Once one of the two dies the other one will say a line of dialogue committing his soul to a greater daemon in exchange for power. He will enrage and kill the player that killed the brother. After that he will convulse and a void will appear and pull the doomed brother into it.

Crypt Web Queen

Abilities	Description
Ambush	Drops down from the ceiling on players when they pass by.
Bite	Melee attack
Root Cone	DOT - Frontal cone that roots and dots all targets in front of the queen.
Random Target Root	DOT - Random ranged target will be rooted and take damage.

Necromancer Malcidious

Abilities	Description
Bleed	High damage bleed placed on top threat melee target
Random Dot	Same high damage bleed as above only placed on a ranged target
Spirit Drain Debuff	Used in conjunction with the "Spirits", reduces AP regen by 15% and movement speed by 20%.
Phases	Dynamics
Phase 1	Necromancer Malcidious is non agro to start.
Phase 2	Necromancer Malcidious will enter combat with the players and use his two dots on the group. Every 30 seconds he will summon the "|n's Spirit" from a random player in the group. That player will receive a debuff on them reducing their AP and movement speed permanently. Players must kill this mob in 25 seconds or the buff will not be removed. If the mob is killed within 25 seconds then the buff is clensed. After 25 seconds the Spirit will degen.
Phase 3	At 50% health Necromancer Malcidious will run to the alter and cast a spell. This will summon two Deathbringers. These mobs are no-kill but can be rooted and snared. They will randomly select a player to agro every 10 seconds and path towards them. If they reach a player they will do tremendous damage. It is very very important that no one get the spirit drain debuff or else they will have difficulty getting away from the Deathbringers.

The Reaper

Abilities	Description
Swing	Standard Melee Swing
Random AE DOT	Random targeted AOE DoT. Players must stay spread out to avoid multiple players getting hit.
Damage Font	Font of damage placed on a random player in the group. Players must stay spread out so that multiple players are not hit by the font. Players must move out of the font or take damage.
Phases	Dynamics
Phase 1	Players fight The Reaper, he will use all of his abilities.
Phase 2	At 40% health The Reaper will start to spawn adds. He will spawn 1 champion con add every 15 seconds. These have reduced hit points, however if players do not deal with them quickly enough they will build up and overwhelm the player.

Sigmar's Crypts

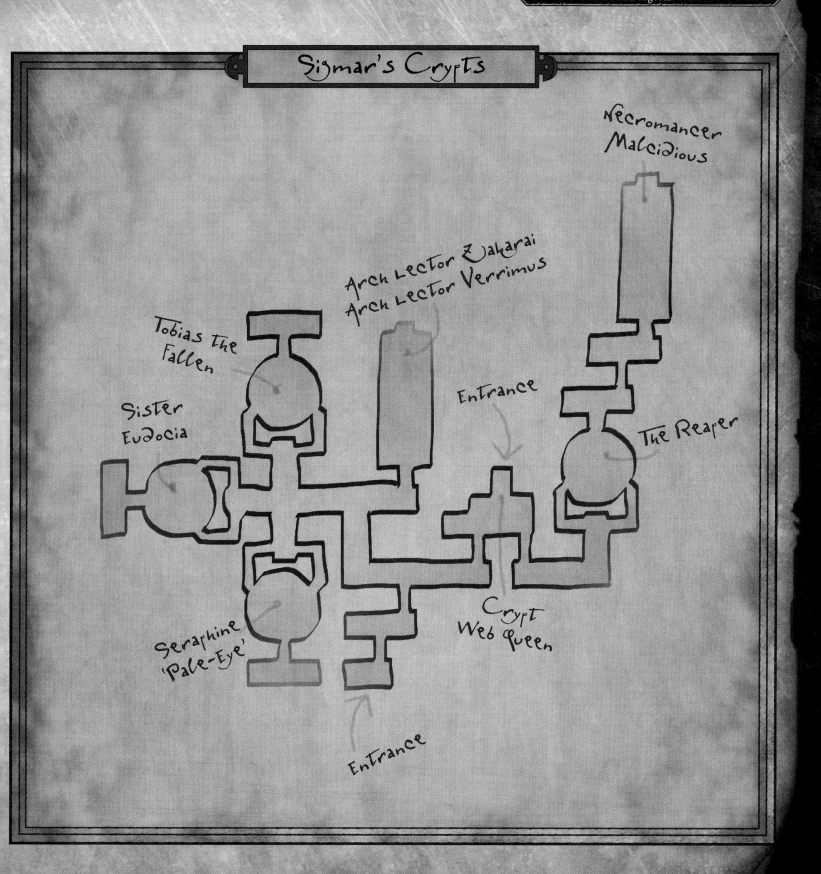

Necromancer
Malcidious

Arch Lector Zakarai
Arch Lector Verrimus

Tobias the
Fallen

Sister
Eudocia

Entrance

The Reaper

Seraphine
'Pale-Eye'

Crypt
Web Queen

Entrance

PLAYERS CAN ACCESS SIGMAR'S CRYPTS ONLY WHEN ALTDORF
HAS A HIGH CITY RANK—INVADED OR PEACEFUL STATES.

BOSSES (CONTINUED)

Seraphine 'Pale-Eye'

Abilities	Description
Random Shot	Shoots at a random player on her hate list
Frontal Cone Shot	Frontal cone shot hitting all players in front of her
Grenade Toss	Throws a grenade at a random player in the group exploding for AOE damage.
Disarm	Disarms her current target
Phases	Dynamics
Phase 1	Players will fight Seraphine while she uses all of her abilities.
Phase 2	At 10% Health she will break combat and become non-aggro. Players will be able to speak to her at that point. She will tell the players that she can pick the lock leading to the final boss room. If the two other mini-bosses have been defeated she will open the gate. If not, she will inform the players of such.

Sister Eudocia

Abilities	Description
Frontal Cone Nuke	Does damage to all targets in front of her.
Random Nuke	Does Random Damage to one person in the group.
AE Silence	Silences the entire group for several seconds.
Phases	Dynamics
Phase 1	Players will Sister Eudocia while she uses all of her abilities.
Phase 2	After 20 seconds Sister Eudocia will start to spawn bats from the back of the room. The bats will continue to spawn constantly until the players are completely overwhelmed.

Tobias the Fallen

Abilities	Description
Passive AP Drain	Once engaged in combat Tobias will constantly drain players AP. Players will have to deal with reduced AP for the entire fight.
Knockback Snare	Periodically in the fight Tobias will knockback every player in the group and then begin to cast a heal on himself. The heal has a long build time and can be interrupted.
Knockback Aggro switch	Every 15-20 seconds Tobias will knockback his primary target and clear hate on that target.
Heal	Long build up, only used after the knockback snare.
Phases	Dynamics
Phase 1	Players will fight Tobias as he uses all of his abilities. His heals must be interrupted.

MONSTERS

Name	Description
Crypt Web Crawler	Spider mob. Has a stun + dot that will completely immobilize the tank and do high damage. Also has a ranged DOT cast on a random target. Tanks will need big heals when stunned.
Deathwrought Bat	Comes in groups of two. Has a frontal cone screech and will charge at random players.
Deathwrought Crypt Keeper	Caster Mob. Uses a random AOE damage over time cast on a random ranged target. Also has a passive morale debuff and a single target nuke.
Deathwrought Devotee	Caster mob, comes in groups of 4 with 2 other Devotee's and 1 Fanatic. Has many ranged abilities. It will randomly cast a nuke and a dot on the group as well as cast a lifetap on its current target. These do not need to be tanked specifically but they should be controlled to keep them off healers.
Deathwrought Fanatic	Melee mob. Uses a cleave. At 40% health they will enrage and begin to use a knockdown ability.
Deathwrought Screamer	Caster mob, comes in groups of 3 with Death-wrought Spirits. Same abilities as above however it has a cone nuke instead of a random disable. This mob should be tanked to avoid the cone hitting more people.
Deathwrought Spirit	Caster mob, comes in groups of 3 with Death-wrought Screamers. Has a random targeted AOE, a random targeted single target nuke and a random targeted disable. These mobs spread out the damage to many different players and don't necessarily need to be tanked.
Tomb Robber	Human Melee / Ranged mob. Has a melee cleave, a frontal cone shot and a random gun shot. Should be tanked facing away from the group.
Undead Priest	Melee caster hybrid, comes in groups of 2 warriors and 1 priest. Priests have a cleave, a cone damage over time melee attack and a random targeted root + damage over time.
Undead Templar	Melee Hybrid. Has a cleave that leaves a high damage over time on any that are affected by it. Will occasionally cast a large radius PBAOE silence.
Undead Warrior	Melee mob, comes in a groups of 2 warriors and 1 priest. Warriors have a cleave, a random axe throw at a ranged target and an agro switch to random targets. Tanks must save taunts to taunt the warriors off.

PLAYERS WILL NEED A FEW PIECES OF LESSER WARD ARMOR. EACH PIECE ABSORBS A PERCENTAGE OF ALL INCOMING DAMAGE RECEIVED IN THE CRYPTS.

WARPBLADE TUNNELS

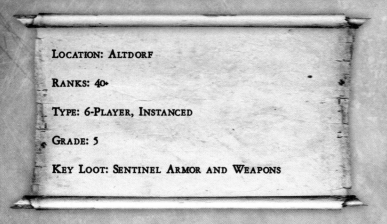

LOCATION: ALTDORF

RANKS: 40+

TYPE: 6-PLAYER, INSTANCED

GRADE: 5

KEY LOOT: SENTINEL ARMOR AND WEAPONS

DUNGEON DETAILS

The Skaven clan of the Warpblade has burrowed from unknown depths to lie waiting beneath the city of Altdorf. Man-made structures or foundations of layered rock and wooden supports give way to the Warpblade Tunnels, which are more organic-looking, with twists and turns. The tunnels are long, with clanrats and rat ogres acting as the physical muscle, while moulders practice their sorceries. Pipes, broken ladders, and unusable bridges furnish the walls, which are supported with wooden beams and archways throughout. The apparent leader of this magical clan of rat people, Grey Seer Quol'tik, lies at the end of the winding passageways.

BOSSES

Bruak

Abilities	Description
Crushing Blow	This is a single target melee hit.
Slam	This is a frontal cone knockback and damage
Frightening Roar	This will drain all players AP within 250 radius.

Grey Seer Quol'tik

Abilities	Description
Warp Energy	This is a direct damage bolt spell
Defile Ground	This will cause the land a random player is on to become diseased. It will pulse PBAE damage for the next 45 seconds before it fades away.
Phases	Dynamics
90%	Once the grey seer crosses the 90% threshold for hit points he will begin to spawn Warped Growths.
Warped Growth	If a warped growth sits idle without a player interacting with it for too long, it will sprout into a Warped Tentacle.
Warped Tentacle	Warped Tentacles will randomly shoot globs of spit at people throughout the room.

Master Moulder Skrot

Abilities	Description
Warp Healing	This is a PBAE heal.

Skiv Redwarp

Abilities	Description
Skiv Blade Dance	This is a channeled PBAE that will do increasing damage each swing. Get out of his PBAe range when he does this.
Skiv Shadow Smoke	This will do a PBAE knockback and teleport Skiv to a random location in the room where he will be stealthed. He will then pick a random target and attempt to Shadow Strike them.

Skiv Redwarp

Abilities	Description
Throwing Star	Every 5 seconds Skiv will use throwing stars that do AE damage and interrupt casting.
Shadow Strike	This is a very high damage from stealth.
Phases	Dynamics
Attack from the Shadows	Ideally players wont see Skiv until he attacks from the Shadows. He will do a significant chunk of damage in his first attack.
Blade Dance	Every now and then Skiv will swing his blades around. When he does this get out of his way, do not stay in the AE.
Shadow Smoke	Every 20-30 seconds Skiv will throw down smoke bombs and clear his agro list, re-stealth, and teleport to a random part of the room to resume his attacks. (See attack from the Shadows)

Warlock Peenk

Abilities	Description
Warp Energy	This is a single target ranged nuke.
Warp Fusion	This infuses one player with Warp Energy. This energy will cause any nearby Warp Bomb to explode.
Warp Bombs	Warlock Peenk's room is full of Warp Bombs. These will only explode if someone has the debuff "Warp Fusion" on them. If they explode they will do PBAE 2000 damage and knock all players near it back.
Dropping Warp Bombs	Every 20 seconds in combat, Peenk will drop a new Warp Bomb. If these are triggered they will do 2000 damage and a knockback.

ENTRANCE TO THE LOWER TUNNELS CAN BE FOUND IN THE CELLARS OF BOTH THE BLOWHOLE AND REIKLAND ARMS TAVERNS OF ALTDORF.

MONSTERS

Name	Description
Warpblade Assassin	This mob will start stealthed and have a big attack that will pop stealth. Every 5 seconds after that it will use throwing stars that do AE damage and interrupt casting.
Warpblade Brute	These hulking beast has a high damage hit, and a frontal cone knockback. He will also roar every 15-25 seconds causing anyone within 250 units of him to lose 200 AP. He will enrage at 40%. Probably best to have one tank on this guy and have healers at range. Back to the wall!
Warpblade Clanrat	The weapons of this mob will have a 5% chance to proc Warpblade Taint. Warpblade Taint can do a variety of things to the player from DD, DoT, to AP Drain.
Warpblade Moulder	This is the healer of the Skaven Tunnels and it will cast AE heals. Probably wanna kill these first.
Warpblade Rat Ogre	These hulking beast has a high damage hit, and a frontal cone knockback. He will also roar every 15-25 seconds causing anyone within 250 units of him to lose 200 AP. Probably best to have one tank on this guy and have healers at range. Back to the wall!
Warpblade Stormvermin	The weapons of this mob will have a 5% chance to proc Warpblade Taint. Warpblade Taint can do a variety of things to the player from DD, DoT, to AP Drain. This mob will also Enrage at 40%
Warpblade Warlock	At range this mob will continually nuke. It will also cast chain lightning on random targets every 15-20 seconds.

Entrance to the Upper Tunnels can be found in the cellars of both the Screaming Cat and Mastiff's End taverns of Altdorf.

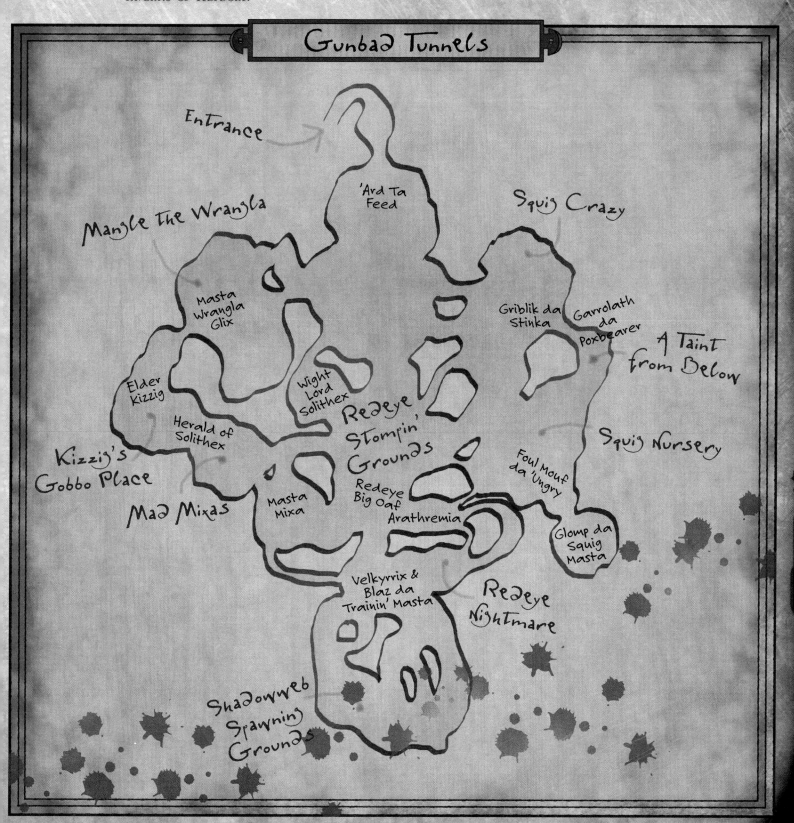

Gunbad Tunnels

Entrance

'Ard Ta Feed

Squig Crazy

Mangle The Wrangla

Masta Wrangla Glix

Griblik da Stinka

Garrolath da Poxbearer

A Taint from Below

Elder Kizzig

Wight Lord Solithex

Redeye Stompin' Grounds

Squig Nursery

Herald of Solithex

Foul Mouf da 'Ungry

Kizzig's Gobbo Place

Redeye Big Oaf

Mad Mixas

Masta Mixa

Arathremia

Glomp da Squig Masta

Velkyrrix & Blaz da Trainin' Masta

Redeye Nightmare

Shadowweb Spawning Grounds

Players can access the Warpblade Tunnels only when Altdorf has a high City Rank—invaded or peaceful states.

LAIRS

Weary from a day's travels and the skirmishes of the war-torn battlefield you've just left behind, you decide you deserve a nap. Your pack slips off your cramped shoulders with a clunk as the canteen hits a rock. Still, your one change of clothes and loaf of stale bread will make a formidable pillow. There's no rain in sight, and the smell of nearby wild honeydew should mask the blood on your shirt nicely. All is well. You plop down, rest your head on the backpack, and close your eyes.

Renatta Betz

What was that? You open your eyes and stare up the slope at the hole you thought you saw before the notion of a nap whispered pleasantries to your eyelids. Yep, it's still there. A secret cave entrance bores down into the earth, either an invitation to long-lost riches or a deadly descent into a decrepit dungeon. You've just discovered a hidden lair in the world. Will you take the challenge to see what's inside?

There are 24 hidden lairs across the world of *WAR*, eight in each zone pairing. Some require feats of dexterity to uncover, others may be puzzles to solve, still others may take superior combat skills to dispatch the lair boss and gain its treasures. You may be able to solo some of the lair bosses, if you're advanced enough in rank, but it's recommended for most lairs that you team up with a small party of two or three other players to vanquish the threat. More difficult lairs will require a full warband.

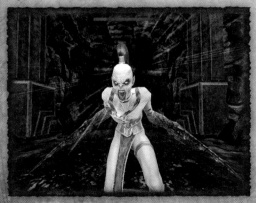

The following pages will give you the inside track to discovering lairs. The first section details all the Dwarf/greenskin lairs, the second section reveals secrets on the Empire/Chaos lairs, and the final section showcases the High Elf/Dark Elf lair. These are just a few of the many lairs out there to explore. Within each race section, the lairs are listed in alphabetical order. You'll find the lair's exact location in the zone, its relative rank, encounter type

(dexterity, puzzle, or hack and slash), as well as strategy tips on how to enter the lair and defeat the lair boss.

Now go out there and discover some lairs for yourself! The loot is worth the peril, so long as you don't think you can foolishly best ancient foes without the proper preparation.

LAIR OF THE BANDIT QUEEN

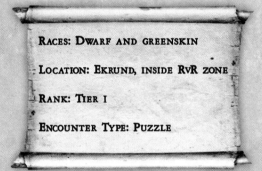

RACES: DWARF AND GREENSKIN

LOCATION: EKRUND, INSIDE RvR ZONE

RANK: TIER I

ENCOUNTER TYPE: PUZZLE

For a glass of ale and a leg of venison I can tell you a tale of a bandit queen by the name of Renatta Betz. She gathered around her a mighty force of brigands and cutthroats who were easily swayed by promises of treasure, and pushed deep into the Dragonback Mountains. They sought the mining fortress of Ekrund, knowing full well that it had fallen to the greenskins in years past. She believed this would be their best option, for it is well known throughout the Empire: a Dwarf and his gold are not easily parted.

Renatta's Highwaymen, as they were known throughout the Empire, moved silently and avoided all the trails as they made for Ekrund. When they arrived, they found the doors open and the glowstones mostly working. Within a couple days of searching, they happened upon a Dwarf cache of gold and gems in the dusty halls of the timeworn Dwarf hold. Yet, her luck was bound to run out, for a greenskin warband stumbled upon Renatta's force as they celebrated their find.

With her men dying all around her, Renatta gathered her bodyguards, along with a Dwarf king's ransom in gold and gems, and made for the heights of the Dragonback Mountains. She figured if she could get over the Dragonback she would be safe and set for life. Her attempt at escape, however, was quickly noticed by Goblin outriders who sounded the alarm. Goblin wolfriders hounded Renatta at every turn as she drove her band relentlessly up the mountain. Only after she had led her men inside a hidden cavern was she able to gain a moment's respite and give the beasts the slip.

Yes, you have heard this tale before as barroom chatter: the idle musings of drunks and charlatans attempting to persuade a gullible merchant into buying more ale on their behalf. So let me tell you the rest of the tale that is not so well known.

I have seen a round stone that bars entrance to this tomb of legend, and a woman's voice within that beckoned to me, offering a king's ransom of Dwarf gold to me simply to free her. All I had to do was find the key. As I searched, the voice told me a tale of gold, treasure, and ancient history.

Renatta found an ancient tomb high within the spine of the Dragonback Mountains and drove her small band in there to hide. Yet the gold lust was high in her blood and Renatta had her men ransack the tomb for more treasure. This is the type of greed a Dwarf can understand, but not at the expense of Ancestors.

A spirit, older than even the Dwarfs, was roused from its long slumber, and its malign power was unleashed upon the bandits. A stone slab sealed Renatta and her men within; this is why the wolfriders passed them by. The spirit was cruel in its revenge for disturbing its tomb; only after months of torture did the spirit let them die. Before the spirit returned to its slumber, though, Renatta told me it cursed her to guard its resting place for eternity. Renatta only wants to be released and will give up the hoard of gold and gems to anyone who will open her door.

Yet after searching for days around the mouth of the tomb, I could not find the key the voice spoke of. Finally, I was low on supplies when the rabid snotlings arrived, and I made my way to Altdorf in search of help in the recovery. Are you willing to help me recover this gold?

Yes, I know how to get back. We travel to Ekrund and go north of the Ekrund Defense Wall to a small trail that leads east up the mountain. At the top you will find the tomb entrance. Now for the unpleasant part. After searching the library in Altdorf, I think I know how to get the key. On the steps of this tomb is the remains of an ancient altar, we must sacrifice an opponent on these steps to recover the key hidden in the altar, but exactly how, we must puzzle out for ourselves.

Renatta awaits inside the lair, and her skin holds the gray pallor of the long dead. She hits with a Spirit Drain, so having your resists up helps mitigate this damage. Her skeletal fingers will slash through armor, and her Ethereal Strike will quickly drain the health of even the most robust tank. We must be strong.

Renatta Betz

LAIR OF THE FLESHRENDER

RACES: DWARF AND GREENSKIN

LOCATION: KADRIN VALLEY

RANK: TIER 4

ENCOUNTER TYPE: HACK AND SLASH

started to shout orders to his band. Had what they had discovered been deposited there by their enemies as a trap? Or had it lain dormant under tons of rock and stone since the mark of Chaos had been scattered throughout the world? It mattered not now. Kyreia was called forth.

Many speculate, but none can be sure, for the last that was heard of Karege's band was the sound of an epic battle that echoed throughout the valleys of Kadrin. Karege ordered his engineers to seal the tunnel while they held the ancient Chaos terror at bay, giving their lives to buy the engineers time. Desperately they worked with the priests to attempt to create machinery forged with powerful runes to seal the cavern shut.

Karege Stonebreaker knew the legend, but the gold lust had sealed their fate as the last blow of the hammer drove the drill into the rock. As the rock crashed down in front of them, Karege knew they had delved too deeply into the granite cliffs surrounding the great Slayer Keep. The terror of legend was real, and he had just unleashed a great horror upon their race. Several thoughts flashed through his mind as he

Kyreia had finished with the unfortunate miners, but now found herself sealed within the cavern with no egress. The powerful Dwarf runes prevented her escape into the material world, as well as her return to the nether. Her howls of anguish as she pounded on the seal were enough to make even a Slayer quake with fear.

It is within this vault of rock and stone that Kyreia Sek bides her time, waiting for some poor unfortunate fool to unleash her upon the world. In the Book of Grudges, there is a listing of all who fell with Karege, and the Dwarfs will have an accounting when that day comes.

If you are foolish enough to face her, then I can tell you the secret to her prison. In Kadrin Valley, just west of Gromril Junction, is a wrecked train. Hidden in some pines to the south is a valve. Turn this valve, then follow the goat trail up the mountain to the west. Continue to turn the valves as you go; the third and final one lies in the trees to the right of the tunnel seal. You might have to wait a minute for the steam pressure to build in these old pipes before the valve will turn. You can now enter the tunnel when the seal lifts, and may Sigmar guard your soul.

Kyreia is a melee-type encounter with dual-mutated sword arms. Her embrace will leave you with no flesh as her razor sharp arms strip it from your body. Her Heavy Strike will hit a cloth wearer for approximately 1,500 health points. Her disabling swing will make it harder for tanks to hold aggro. To engage her, have everyone stand in the tunnel until the tank has built up some hate, then swarm her. The healers will be busy keeping the tank up, because she hits for approximately 800–1,000 health points every time she swings.

LAIR OF NERX GUTSLIME

RACES: DWARF AND GREENSKIN

LOCATION: MOUNT BLOODHORN

RANK: TIER 1 (RANK 10)

ENCOUNTER TYPE: DEXTERITY, HACK AND SLASH

Mount Bloodhorn is home to many evil things. They lurk in the dark crevasses and behind fallen trees. The greenskins and Dwarfs have been fighting here for many years and Chaos has a strong hold. There are tales of a faint wisp of smoke that can be seen drifting from the mouth of a small cavern high on the cliff face. Late at night, Oathsworn swear they hear queer chanting echoing down the mountainside.

There are tales told among the greenskins of a mad Shaman who now makes Mount Bloodhorn his home. The tale recounts that Nerx was experimenting with size-altering mushrooms, and apparently he "accidentally" fed a cauldron of the fungus to a squig within the depths of the night Goblin stronghold. Once thought to be the most powerful Shaman in all of Mount Gunbad, Nerx Gutslime was exiled by the surviving members of his clan.

So if you want to go see for yourself, travel to Felridge, on the east-southeast side of Mount Bloodhorn. You will see a statue of a Dwarf with a flaming hat just in front of his lair. On the left side of this statue is a grass ledge that goes up to a downed tree. Jump across the gap to the tree, then shimmy up the tree. The entrance is just to the left of the tree.

Nerx Gutslime is an evil, twisted, warpstone-snuffing Goblin Shaman who lives to cause others trouble. He loves to curse you. He uses Sensitive to lower your resists. Then he hits you with Circle of Life Loss (damage-over-time), Blast Wave (area effect), Corporeal Blast (big nuke), Corporeal Push (knockback), and Silence. When Nerx is not casting a curse of some type, he does melee damage with his gnarled rock-hard hands and sharpened fingernails.

The tank should control the fight so that Nerx's back is to the party. At least one healer and lots of damage-dealers would be recommended. With Nerx facing away from the party, the tank can absorb the Silence and Blast Wave, leaving the healer to concentrate on healing the tank. A heal-over-time and single-target heals will be necessary to overcome the damage this little guy will put out. Everyone else should drop this boss as fast as they can.

Nerx Gutslime

LAIR OF METOH

RACES: EMPIRE AND CHAOS

LOCATION: TROLL COUNTRY

RANK: TIER 2

ENCOUNTER TYPE: DEXTERITY, HACK AND SLASH

Metoh likes to collect skulls to hang on his fur. That might give you a clue to how nasty he likes to get. His attack damages between 1,200 and 1,700 points to an appropriately geared adventurer looking for a good tussle in his ice cave. When angry, Metoh will break out his special weapon: Ethereal Breath. This can critical up to 2,200 points of damage and will make short work of anyone caught in the noxious fumes.

When engaging Metoh, be mindful of the terrain. There are ice shards sticking up from the ground and small alcoves along the side. Don't get caught on any of these, or you may lose your maneuverability and end up a frozen dinner. At least one healer is a must if you want to keep up with Metoh's superior damage dealing. Of course, if you have great damage-dealers yourself, you may be able to outrace him to death's door.

The Lair of Metoh is slightly north of Iceflow Maw, in the northwest corner of Troll Country. Climb the steep ice crevasses on the side of the mountain to reach it. Watch your step as you climb, because sliding down the mountainside won't be a pleasant beginning to your lair hunting.

LAIR OF SILVEROAK

RACES: EMPIRE AND CHAOS

LOCATION: NORSCA

RANK: TIER 1 (RANK 40)

ENCOUNTER TYPE: DEXTERITY, HACK AND SLASH

Lair of Silveroak is located down the river near Sturmvall, directly southwest of Thorshafn. If you go down the river southwest from where the two rivers meet, you will arrive at a clearing with burnt logs and stumps toward the right side of the river bank. Here you will find the outskirts of the lair.

There's a lot of space in the lair clearing, with tons of obstacles such as trees, stumps, and boulders, so use the environment to hinder its attacks. The Silveroak is not quick, but packs a huge punch when it does hit you. It is easily stunned and disabled, so do that. With a tank bashing on Silveroak and a healer to keep the tank alive, this one should be a quick win with a prepared party. Silveroak does deal heavy damage, so the healer needs to pay attention and be alert. Having a damage-dealer would be a great big help to make this kill go even faster.

Toward the back of the clearing is a fallen tree with a cut-out opening leaning against a plateau. Walk inside and through this tree opening to reach the top of the plateau. Next walk toward the front of the plateau to a tree bridge. Walk across this tree bridge until you reach the middle, then turn right and you will see a row of tree stumps. This is where you jump off and try to land on the first tree stump nearest to you. There are seven stumps in total. Take your time and jump from one to the next until you reach the last one. There, another tree bridge leads up to the next plateau. Walk up this tree bridge to a clearing. This clearing is the Lair of Silveroak.

Silveroak has a curse called Life Loss that hits for 10 seconds doing approximately 375 points of damage per second and criticals for 575 damage. Corporeal Stun is a stun that lasts for 3 seconds. Its third special, Claw Strike, attacks for 1,600 damage. Its normal attack hits for 1,200 damage, with criticals at 1,900 damage.

LAIR OF TEZAKK GNAWBONE

RACES: EMPIRE AND CHAOS

LOCATION: CHAOS WASTES

RANK: TIER 4 (RANK 4)

ENCOUNTER TYPE: DEXTERITY, HACK AND SLASH

Lair of Tezakk Gnawbone is located in the RvR area of Chaos Wastes. The entrance lies directly north of Zimmeron's Hold, by the lake next to battlefield objective Chokethorn Bramble.

You must jump seven pieces of ruins to get to the lair entrance. Look at the screenshots to see how to jump from one ruin to the next. Make sure to take your time as you scale the ruins and make turns. Have a bit of a running start for each jump. Once you reach the sixth ruin, do an extra jump to the high wall before moving to the last ruin.

Once you reach the lair proper, Tezakk Gnawbone has a normal attack that hits for approximately 800 damage and criticals at 1,150. It also has a Whirling Dervish attack that hits for 850. Then there's the Ethereal Strike that damages for 1,430 points, so watch out for those. All attacks can be mitigated, but only by a little.

Tezakk Gnawbone is not very fast. Inside its lair are many obstacles that can be used to buy some time while you heal up, attack from long distance, or cast a spell. Use those openings so Tezakk Gnawbone has to go all the way around to chase you down. A tank can bash away at this creature with an aid of a healer. It would be nice to have an additional damage-dealer to make it a quick kill. Tezakk Gnawbone can easily be knocked down and stunned, so take advantage of the precious seconds this affords.

LAIR OF GORTHLAK

RACES: HIGH ELF AND DARK ELF

LOCATION: THE BLIGHTED ISLE

RANK: TIER 1

ENCOUNTER TYPE: DEXTERITY, HACK AND SLASH

The entrance to the Lair of Gorthlak is located across the river near the Thanalorn Forest public quest. A simple jump puzzle near a Tainted Crystal grants access.

Gorthlak has two abilities that he uses throughout the fight. The first ability, Life Loss, is a curse that deals approximately 300 damage every 2 seconds for 10 seconds, and the second is Corporeal Strike, a direct-damage ability with some oomph: 1,400 damage to cloth wearers. Both can be resisted and/or mitigated slightly with more armor and resistances. The fight is a standard tank and damage-dealer fight so long as the main tank stays alive and no one else pulls aggro.

LAIR OF KELBRAX

RACES: HIGH ELF AND DARK ELF

LOCATION: CHRACE

RANK: TIER 1

ENCOUNTER TYPE: DEXTERITY, HACK AND SLASH

The entrance to the Lair of Kelbrax is in Chrace above the menhir stones in the Cliffs of Ushuru. You must traverse a simple jump puzzle in front of the lair.

Kelbrax has two abilities in addition to his normal attack. The first, Bleed, cripples for approximately 320 damage every 2 seconds for 10 seconds, and the second, Knockback, throws an opponent backward. You don't have to worry about the first ability too much; however, address Knockback by having the main tank put his back to a wall. This prevents the tank from being thrown around the room and having to continually reposition Kelbrax. His normal attack is a little less than that of other rare mobs of his rank, so it should not be hard to tank with the appropriate gear. This fight is a simple tank and damage-dealer fight, with the slight adjustment made by the main tank to accommodate Knockback.

LAIR OF STINKFANG THE VOMITOUS

RACES: HIGH ELF AND DARK ELF

LOCATION: ELLYRION

RANK: TIER 2

ENCOUNTER TYPE: HACK AND SLASH

Stinkfang the Vomitous has two abilities that he will use throughout the fight. The first ability is Life Loss, which is a curse that deals 300 damage every 2 seconds for 10 seconds, and the second is Corporeal Strike, which is a direct-damage ability that causes approximately 1,400 damage to anyone wearing cloth. Both can be resisted and/or mitigated slightly with more armor and resistances. The fight is a standard tank and damage-dealer battle, and as long as the main tank stays alive and no one else pulls aggro, the encounter should go relatively smoothly.

The Lair of Stinkfang the Vomitous is located in Ellyrion near the public quest "Shady Tower" in Reaverspring north of the Tower of Milurien.